D0128050

WORLD WAR I

The American Soldier Experience

Jennifer D. Keene

UNIVERSITY OF NEBRASKA PRESS

LINCOLN AND LONDON

Manufactured in the United States of America

∞

First Nebraska paperback printing: 2011

Library of Congress Cataloging-in-Publication Data
Keene, Jennifer D., 1962–
World War I: the American soldier experience / Jennifer D. Keene.
    p. cm.
Originally published: Westport, Conn.: Greenwood Press, 2006.
Includes bibliographical references and index.
ISBN 978-0-8032-3487-1 (pbk.: alk. paper)
1. World War, 1914–1918—United States. 2. World War, 1914–1918—Social aspects—United States. 3. Soldiers—United States—Social conditions—20th century. I. Title.
D570.K39 2011
940.4'0973—dc22   2010043606

CONTENTS

PREFACE

Doughboys, Sammies, Yanks, Pershing's Crusaders—these were all popular nicknames for the American enlisted man during World War I. "Doughboys" was by far the most popular label attached to the fighting men of World War I, although its origins remain unclear. One story claims that in the late nineteenth century cavalrymen mocked dust-covered infantrymen stationed along the southwest border by calling them "dough-boys," while another tale suggests that the nickname came from the large dough-shaped buttons on infantry uniforms. The French called the American soldiers "Sammies" (referring to Uncle Sam), and many popular wartime songs included this nickname in their lyrics. "Pershing's Crusaders" made a brief appearance on stateside propaganda posters but was never embraced by the troops themselves. American soldiers liked "Yanks" better, a term that now described soldiers from all parts of the country rather than just those from the north as it had in the Civil War.

This book explores the daily lives of doughboys in World War I, tracing their journey from the training camps to France and then home again. While providing an overview of the causes of the war and the overall strategy pursued by generals, this book focuses most-ly on the trials and tribulations of fighting in World War I and serving in the nation's first mass, conscripted army. More than a compilation of facts and figures, this book transports students and general readers of history to the trenches to feel the terror of constant bom-bardments and smell the rotting corpses on No Man's Land. Readers will share the seething anger of black troops subjected to the constant sting of racial prejudice, despite their military contributions and sacrifices for the country; sense the discontent and bore-dom of soldiers laboring in support roles behind the lines; and experience the exhilaration of aerial combat and the nerve-breaking tension of the war at sea.

The book begins with a general introduction to the war, reviewing the tortuous path that America took to entering the war two and a half years after it began in Europe and the overall strategy pursued by the American commander in chief, John J. Pershing.

Chapter 2 examines how these larger events affected the daily lives of men and women as the nation prepared to raise a mass army through conscription and transformed civilians almost overnight into infantrymen, artillerymen, pilots, sailors, nurses, and officers. Throughout the war, the army tried to keep morale high, promote virtuous personal habits, and safeguard the religious beliefs of enlisted men; topics all explored in Chapter 3. Chapter 4 focuses on diversity within the ranks, examining the particular experiences of African American and foreign-born soldiers and female nurses and female war workers. The reality of fighting at sea, in the air, and along the Western Front forms the core of Chapter 5, which also considers the daily lives of soldiers serving in key support and service roles behind the lines. Chapter 6 explores the wounds of war, noting the terrible toll of death, battlefield injuries, and the 1918 influenza pandemic on American soldiers and the long journey home for the disabled. The final chapter considers the reactions of soldiers to the Armistice, the months spent waiting in France to return home, and the postwar lives of veterans.

Readers can exercise some discretion in how they use the book, reading it from cover to cover or going directly to topics of interest, where they will find all the necessary information in one place. The chronology will help readers keep track of the general flow of events, while the topically arranged bibliography at the end of the book contains the sources consulted to write this volume; plus recommended reading, movies, collections of posters, and music of the war; and a valuable list of Websites containing important primary documents and visual materials such as posters and photographs. A glossary offers some brief definitions of commonplace terms still in use today that had their origins in the World War I–era and more specialized terms used primarily during the conflict.

I would like to thank David and Jeanne Heidler, the editors for Greenwood's American Soldiers' Lives series, for the opportunity to write this book and their helpful comments during the process of preparing the manuscript. Anne Thompson, my development editor, and Lindsay Claire, my project manager also offered critical guidance, while Heather Staines, the acquisition editor at Greenwood, graciously agreed to an extended deadline so I could undertake this project. I must also acknowledge the help of the interlibrary loan department at Chapman University for tracking down occasionally obsolete materials and thank Chapman University for a Faculty Research Grant that helped me with my research and writing. I would also like to extend special thanks to Randolph Boyd who served as a research assistant for this project, turning up many fascinating details about weaponary and combat. In his chosen career as a librarian, he will surely render similarly invaluable help for countless numbers of researchers to come. Finally, I give special thanks to my husband Paul Wilkins and my four-year-old son Caleb, who have both walked the trenches along the Western Front with me. In their own distinct ways, Paul and Caleb remind me daily that the horrors of war are balanced by the joys of living a life filled with love and adventure.

TIMELINE

1914

April 9, 1914	Mexican authorities detain several American Marines in Tampico
April 21, 1914	American troops land in Vera Cruz, Mexico to exact apology for arrest at Tampico
April 22, 1914	Mexico breaks off diplomatic relations with the United States
June 28, 1914	Gavrilo Princip assassinates Archduke Franz Ferdinand in Sarajevo, Bosnia
July 5, 1914	Germany agrees to support Austria-Hungary in stand-off with Serbia
July 15, 1914	Mexican President Victoriano Huerta resigns
July 23, 1914	Austria-Hungary presents Serbia with ultimatum
July 25, 1914	Serbia mobilizes after accepting all but one Austro-Hungarian condition
July 28, 1914	Austria-Hungary declares war on Serbia
July 29, 1914	Austria-Hungary invades Serbia
July 30, 1914	Russia orders general mobilization of military forces
August 1, 1914	Germany declares war on Russia
August 2, 1914	German troops enter Luxembourg
August 3, 1914	German troops enter Belgium, Germany declares war on France
August 4, 1914	Great Britain declares war on Germany, President Woodrow Wilson announces U.S. neutrality

August 6, 1914	Austria-Hungary declares war on Russia
August 7, 1914	British troops begin landing in France
August 23, 1914	Japan declares war on Germany
August 24, 1914	German Army enters France
September 5–10, 1914	First Battle of the Marne-Paris saved from invading German Army
September 17–October 18, 1914	Race to the Sea, trench deadlock established along Western Front
November 1, 1914	Russia declares war on Ottoman Empire
November 3, 1914	Britain declares North Sea a war zone and mines it
November 23, 1914	American troops withdrawn from Vera Cruz
December 29, 1914	Wilson protests British search of U.S. ships for contraband

1915

January 30, 1915	Wilson sends advisor Colonel Edward House on first peace mission to Europe
February 4, 1915	Germany declares waters around Britain a war zone
February 10, 1915	American government vows to hold Germany strictly accountable for U-boat sinkings of U.S. ships
March 11, 1915	Britain announces blockade of German ports
March 30, 1915	Wilson protests British blockade
April 25, 1915	Battle of Gallipoli begins
May 7, 1915	German submarine sinks the *Lusitania* off the coast of Ireland
May 13, 1915	Wilson protests sinking of *Lusitania* to Germany
May 23, 1915	Italy declares war on Austria-Hungary
May 28, 1915	Germany responds that *Lusitania* was carrying munitions and sinking was justified
June 7, 1915	William Jennings Bryan resigns as Secretary of State in protest over Wilson's response to *Lusitania* crisis
June 9, 1915	Wilson protests German policy of unconditional submarine warfare
July 21, 1915	Wilson sends third note to Germany demanding they respect U.S. rights as neutrals

August 10, 1915	First training camp in Plattsburg opens
August 19, 1915	German submarine sinks British passenger ship, the *Arabic*, killing two Americans
August 26, 1915	Italy declares war on Germany
September 1, 1915	Germany issues Arabic pledge agreeing to warn passenger ships of U-boat attack
September 16, 1915	Haiti becomes an American protectorate
July 26, 1915	American troops land in Haiti
October 19, 1915	United States recognizes Venustiano Carranza as President of Mexico

1916

February 21–December 18, 1916	Battle of Verdun along the Western Front
February 22, 1916	Wilson sends advisor House on second peace mission to Europe
March 9, 1916	Francisco "Pancho" Villa attacks Columbus, New Mexico, with 1,500 troops and kills 17 Americans
March 15, 1916	Pershing enters Mexico with 6,000 troops in pursuit of Pancho Villa
March 24, 1916	German U-boat sinks *Sussex*, an unarmed French channel ship, injuring several Americans
April 18, 1916	Wilson warns Germany to end sinkings or United States will sever diplomatic relations
April 24–29, 1916	British government supresses Easter Uprising in Ireland
May 1916	American troops land in Santo Domingo, Dominion Republic
May 4, 1916	German government issues Sussex pledge, will refrain from attacks on merchant or passenger ships except in self-defense
June 3, 1916	National Defense Act increases size of Regular Army and National Guard
June 16, 1916	Mexican government announces it will consider any further American maneuvers as hostile
June 21, 1916	Mexican and American troops clash in Carrizal, Mexico
July 1–November 19, 1916	Battle of the Somme along the Western Front
July 18, 1916	British government blacklists eighty American firms for trading with Germany

July 28, 1916	United States and Mexico agree to mediation
August 29, 1916	Naval Act funds construction of new battleships and destroyers
November 7, 1916	Wilson re-elected president, defeating Charles Evans Hughes by 277–254 electoral votes
December 18, 1916	Wilson asks warring nations to state peace terms

1917

January–February 1917	Beginning of "turnip winter" following the failure of potato crop in Germany
January 16, 1917	Zimmermann telegram offers Mexico land in return for declaring war on the United States
January 22, 1917	Wilson delivers "peace without victory" speech
January 28, 1917	American troops leave Mexico without capturing Pancho Villa
February 1, 1917	Germany resumes unconditional submarine warfare
February 3, 1917	United States breaks off diplomatic relations with Germany
February 24, 1917	British intelligence gives decoded Zimmermann telegram to United States
March 1, 1917	Contents of Zimmermann telegram made public
March 12, 1917	Wilson orders merchant ships armed
March 8–12, 1917	Revolution in Russia; monachy overthrown and republic established
March 15, 1917	Tsar Nicholas II abdicates his throne in Russia
March 16, 1917	German U-boats sink three American merchant ships
April 2, 1917	Wilson asks Congress for declaration of war against Germany
April 6, 1917	United States declares war on Germany
April 14, 1917	Committee on Public Information created to control flow of wartime information
April 16–29, 1917	Chemin des Dames offensive, mutinies in French army
April 30, 1917	Allies begin convoy system to combat submarine warfare
May 4, 1917	American destroyers enter British waters patrolling for U-boats
May 10, 1917	Pershing appointed commander of American Expeditionary Forces
May 18, 1917	Wilson signs Selective Service Act authorizing wartime conscription

May 26, 1917	First American troops arrive in France
June 5, 1917	First national draft registration day draws 10 million men to 4,000 draft centers
June 5, 1917	Congress passes the Espionage Act, prohibiting verbal interference with raising an armed force
June 20, 1917	First Liberty Loan campaign begins
June 26, 1917	First American troops arrive in France
July 4, 1917	American troops parade through Paris
July 20, 1917	Secretary of War Newton Baker draws first lottery number to set order for drafting eligible American men
July 31, 1917	Battle of Passchendaele begins
August 23, 1917	Racial rioting in Houston involves African American soldiers of the 24th Infantry Regiment
September 1917	First conscripted troops enter the training camps
October 21, 1917	First American troops enter the line in Lunèville, France
October 24– November 10, 1917	Italians routed in battle of Caporetto
November 2, 1917	First Americans injured in combat along the Western Front
November 7, 1917	Bolsheviks overthrow Russian Provisional Government and assume power
December 3, 1917	Bolshevik Russian government signs armistice with Germany
December 7, 1917	United States declares war on Austria-Hungary
December 15, 1917	Armistice between Russia and Central Powers goes into effect
December 18, 1917	Eighteenth Amendment on prohibition sent to states for ratification

1918

January 8, 1918	Wilson gives Fourteen Points Speech
March 3, 1918	Treaty of Brest-Litovsk ends war between Russia and Germany
March 11, 1918	Reports made of flu outbreak at Fort Riley, Kansas
Spring 1918– Spring 1919	Influenza pandemic spreads worldwide
March 21– July 17, 1918	German spring offensives on the Western Front begin against British forces on the Somme

March 26, 1918   Marshal Ferdinand Foch made supreme commander of Allied Armies on the Western Front

May 25, 1918   German U-boats entered American waters

May 27, 1918   Germans launch offensive against French forces along the Aisne River

May 27–
June 5, 1918   Battle of Chateau-Thierry

May 28–31, 1918   First offensive American action in the battle of Cantigny

May 31, 1918   German advances threaten Paris

June 6–25, 1918   Battle of Belleau Wood

July 6, 1918   Wilson agrees to send troops to Siberia

July 18–
August 6, 1918   310,000 Americans fight in Allied Aisne-Marne counter-offensive

August 16, 1918   American troops arrive in Vladivostok, East Siberia

August 18–
October 12, 1918   Americans fight in Allied Oise-Aisne Offensive

August 19, 1918   British begin offensive in the Somme, pushing Germans back

September 3–6, 1918   Police raids in New York City round up thousands of men suspected of evading the draft

September 4, 1918   American troops arrive in Archangel, North Russia

September 12–16,
1918   St. Mihiel Offensive

September 26–
November 11, 1918   Meuse-Argonne Campaign

September 30, 1918   Armistice between Bulgaria and Allies

October 3–4, 1918   Germany proposes peace based on Fourteen Points

October 4, 1918   Sergeant Alvin York single-handedly kills at least 20 German soldiers and captures 132 prisoners

October 21, 1918   Germany ends unrestricted submarine warfare

October 27, 1918   Armistice between Austria-Hungary and Italy

October 29, 1918   Bulgaria surrenders to Allies

October 30, 1918   Ottoman Empire surrenders to Allies

November 4, 1918   Armistice between Austria-Hungary and Allies

November 9, 1918   Kaiser Wilhelm II abdicates and goes to Holland, Germany becomes a republic

November 11, 1918   Armistice between Allies and Germany

December 1, 1918   American troops enter western Germany in zone of occupation

1919

January 18, 1919   Peace negotiations begin in Paris

January 29, 1919   Eighteenth Amendment, enacting prohibition, ratified

March 15, 1919   American Legion founded in Paris

May 7, 1919   Versailles Treaty given to Germany to sign

June 3, 1919   American troops begin leaving North Russia

June 28, 1919   Germany signs the Versailles Treaty

August 5, 1919   American headquarters closed in North Russia

September 1, 1919   Last American combat division leaves France

November 19, 1919   Senate rejects the Versailles Treaty for first time

1920

January 3, 1920   Last American troops leave France

January 26, 1920   American troops begin leaving Siberia, Russia

March 19, 1920   Senate rejects Versailles Treaty

April 1, 1920   Last American troops withdrawn from Siberia, Russia

August 26, 1920   19th Amendment ratified, granting women the right to vote

1921

July 2, 1921   President Warren Harding signs Congressional joint resolution ending war with Germany

August 25, 1921   Peace treaty between United States and Germany signed

November 11, 1921   Unknown soldier buried at Arlington National Cemetery, Virginia

1923

January 24, 1923   Last American troops leave Germany

1924

March 18, 1924   Adjusted Compensation certificates issued to American veterans

1932

May 29–July 28,
1932   Bonus March in Washington, D.C.

1936

February 29, 1936   Congress overrides presidential veto to pay veterans their bonus

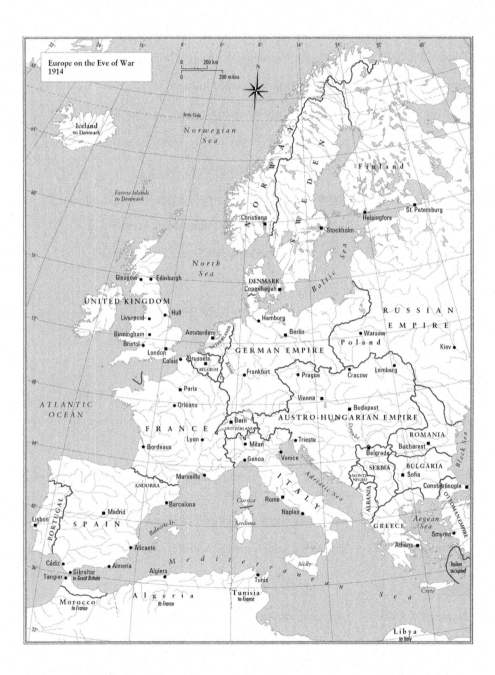

1 THE UNITED STATES IN THE FIRST WORLD WAR

In April 1917, after two and half years of attempted neutrality, the United States finally declared war on Germany and entered the First World War. When the war began in 1914, President Woodrow Wilson saw no immediate reason for the nation to join the fight. Eventually, however, the war spread from the battlefield to the seas and American vessels and passengers headed for Europe soon found themselves caught up in the naval and trade war unleashed by Germany and Britain. Believing that Germany represented a clear danger to the nation's economic and territorial security, Wilson reluctantly asked Congress to declare war.

The formal decision to enter the conflict had an immediate impact on millions of American men and women. The First World War was a total war that required both troops in the field and the support of a vast network of workers and volunteers at home to supply them. Nearly 15 percent of the American male population served in the military and over one million saw combat along the Western Front. The decisions made by American military and political leaders and the ebbs and flows in the fighting along the Western Front all influenced the daily lives of soldiers. American veterans took pride in the part they played in defeating Germany, but the failures of the peace process left many disillusioned about the overall meaning of their wartime sacrifices. A clear appreciation of the war's causes, the overall strategy pursued by the American army, and the flaws in the eventual peace treaty is therefore essential to truly understand the forces shaping ordinary soldiers' experiences during the war.

EUROPE'S PATH TO WAR

Did a simple wrong turn down a narrow street cause the First World War? On the morning of 28 June 1914, Gavrilo Princip, a Bosnian Serb, waited with five others in Sarajevo for a procession carrying the Archduke Franz Ferdinand and his wife to drive past. Princip and his comrades belonged to a terrorist group called the Black Hand. They had come to Bosnia, then part of the Austro-Hungarian Empire, with the express purpose of assassinating Franz Ferdinand. The Black Hand was based in neighboring Serbia, and the group hoped that one day Bosnia would become part of this independent nation. Slavic nationalists accused the Archduke of purposely timing his state visit to coincide with the anniversary of the 1389 Battle of Kosovo when Turkey defeated the Serbs, a humiliating memory for Slavic people. He had done so, the Black Hand believed, to underscore Bosnia's present status as an imperial province. Seething with anger, the group plotted its revenge.

The plan quickly went awry, however, when the bomb thrown at the car carrying the Archduke and his wife bounced off the side and exploded without harming the Archduke or his wife. The police quickly arrested the Black Hand member who threw the bomb, and it appeared that the group had bungled its one chance to assassinate Franz Ferdinand. Princip escaped, melting away in the crowd. The blast had, however, injured two Austrian officers and after the official festivities surrounding his visit concluded, Franz Ferdinand made the fateful decision to pay these men a personal visit. On the way to the hospital, his driver made a wrong turn down a narrow street and began slowing down to put the car in reverse. As fate would have it, standing at the end of the street was none other than Gavrilo Princip. Dejected, Princip had been walking the streets of Sarajevo ever since the morning debacle. As the car came towards him and slowed, Princip could barely believe his good fortune. Sensing that this was his chance to make history, Princip seized the opportunity. He stepped forward and fired. The Archduke and his wife bled to death as the car sped away. Princip was quickly arrested and died of tuberculosis in 1918 while serving a twenty-year prison sentence (at eighteen, he was too young to receive the death penalty).

The First World War began with these two killings and ended four years later after nearly fourteen million more deaths. Europe and the United States followed very different paths to war. By August, all the major European powers were mobilizing mass armies and marching into battle. Intoxicating doses of patriotism and romanticism about war prevented most Europeans from taking the time to pause and consider what a prolonged war would mean. Americans, however, took two and a half years to ponder whether the fighting in Europe threatened the national security and well-being of the United States. By the time America entered the war there were few remaining illusions about the horror of industrialized warfare. Unlike Europeans in 1914, Americans knew they were deciding for total war when they joined the Allied side in 1917.

Europe, however, did not have a crystal ball to predict how different a general European war might be from the regional and colonial conflicts that preceded it. No European nation intended to provoke a worldwide war, but several intended to use the murder as an opportunity to fulfill a limited set of long-held territorial ambitions. After a flurry of diplomatic exchanges and perhaps some brief fighting, Austria-Hungary and Russia each hoped to be in control of the Balkans, while Germany expected to be firmly established as the dominant power in Europe.

Supported by Germany, Austria-Hungary implemented a plan that used the assassination as a pretext for incorporating Serbia into its empire. As a first step, the Austro-Hungarian government sent a set of harsh ultimatums to Serbia with the full expectation that the Serbian government would reject them and provide Austria-Hungary with an excuse to occupy the country. The ultimatums demanded that Serbia outlaw anti-Austrian propaganda, denounce the involvement of the Serbian military in the assassinations, and pledge to avoid any further involvement in Bosnian affairs. Austria-Hungary also demanded that Serbia allow a joint Austro-Serbian commission to investigate the circumstances of the assassinations and let Austrian officials participate in deciding the guilt and sentences of any suspects. Austria-Hungary made these demands despite learning from its own investigation that the Serbian government and military had played no role in the assassination. Acknowledging that these ultimatums severely undercut Serbia's ability to govern its own nation independently, British Foreign Secretary Edward Grey read the note and called it "the most formidable document that was ever addressed from one state to another."[1]

To many world leaders, including those in Berlin, the crisis appeared over when Serbia accepted all of Austria-Hungary's demands except the one insisting that Austro-Hungarian judges participate in the Serbian trials of the terrorists. Even this condition Serbia did not reject outright. Serbia only asked that this request be submitted to the International Tribunal at The Hague for arbitration.

They were mistaken. Confident of German support, Austria-Hungary decided to use the assassination as a pretext for annexing Serbia. In the final moments before Austro-Hungary declared war on Serbia, Germany sent its ally some mixed messages. On 27 July 1914, before actually reading the Serbian response, Germany had urged Austro-Hungary to quickly invade and annex Serbia before other European nations had a chance to react. The following day, when the Kaiser actually read the reply, he wrote on the margins "a great moral victory for Vienna; but with it every reason for war is removed."[2] The Kaiser's suggestion that Austria-Hungary briefly occupy Belgrade to underscore its regional dominance and then begin negotiations with Serbia came too late. An hour after the Kaiser wrote these remarks, Austria-Hungary declared war on Serbia.

This regional conflict between Austria-Hungary and Serbia was immediately transformed into a full-fledged international crisis when Russia resolved to defend Serbia. This was not an altruistic gesture on Russia's part. Russia claimed to be coming to the assistance of a fellow Slavic nation, but in reality Russia harbored its own ambition to extend its influence into the Balkans. As Austrian naval artillery bombarded Belgrade, the Russian Tsar made a fateful decision when he ordered a partial mobilization of his army along the border separating Russia and Austria-Hungary. In ordering only a partial rather than full mobilization, Tsar Nicholas II was attempting to assure Germany that Russia was only threatening Austria-Hungary. Although the German Kaiser and the Russian Tsar were cousins, relations between the two countries were strained by 1914 because of the 1894 alliance between Russia and France in which each pledged to aid the other in the event of a German attack. This alliance with France, a traditional enemy of Germany, caused many German officers and politicians to doubt how long peace would prevail on the German-Russian border. As a result, Germany had long prepared for a two-front war against both France and Russia.

In 1905, the chief of the German General Staff, Alfred von Schlieffen, had developed an offensive plan designed to avoid the problems of fighting a two-front war against Russia and France. In the event of war, the Schlieffen Plan required going immediately on the offensive to take advantage of the time it would take Russia to mobilize its massive army. Germany was not alone in believing that the advantage would go to the first nation in the field. In 1911, France developed Plan 17, which reflected the same belief that the offensive was the key to victory. In the event of war with Germany, rather than waiting for Germany to attack, Plan 17 called on the French military to seize the initiative by launching a presumptive attack.

The details of the Schlieffen Plan were particularly important in 1914, in part because the German Army implemented a modified version of it in August, and in part because it discouraged Germany from exhausting all diplomatic initiatives before going to war. The plan called for Germany to attack and quickly defeat France while the eastern front with Russia was still relatively quiet. In launching its assault against France, the Schlieffen Plan called for the German army to bypass the heavily fortified French border between Germany and France and instead march through Belgium and Holland to attack France from the north. Meeting little opposition, the Germans would quickly reach Paris, encircle the city, and defeat France within six weeks. With its Western Front secured, Germany could then concentrate its army against a much larger Russian army. The success of this plan depended on the element of surprise and precise timing. Because a completed mobilization of the Russian Army would force Germany to defend its eastern border while attacking France, Russia's decision to mobilize its army in defense of Serbia created a grave dilemma for Germany.

In response to the partial mobilization of the Russian army, Germany ordered a partial mobilization of its own. Now the fear of losing the initiative began to dictate events. Informed by his General Staff that Germany's mobilization left Russia's Polish provinces vulnerable to attack, the Tsar responded by ordering a full mobilization of his army. Unable to secure a guarantee of neutrality from France in the event of a war between Germany and Russia, Germany demanded that Russia cease its preparations for war. Russia refused, although the Tsar continued to send appeals to the Kaiser to avoid taking any action that might provoke a war between Germany and Russia. On 1 August, Germany ordered a full mobilization of its army and declared war on Russia. That evening, German troops began implementing a modified version of the Schlieffen Plan. Within days, German troops had invaded Luxembourg, Belgium, and France. On 4 August, Britain declared war on Germany in fulfillment of its pledge to defend Belgium neutrality and out of concern that German expansion posed a direct threat to Britain. Europe was now at war.

In the summer of 1914, these European powers believed they were entering a short war of movement. They quickly realized their miscalculation. Exhausted by the enormous amount of ground that the Schlieffen Plan required them to cover and the difficulties of re-supplying a mass army on the move, German troops got within thirty-five miles of Paris but failed in their attempt to seize the capital quickly and knock France out of the war. The system of trenches that would dominate the Western Front began as shallow foxholes that men built quickly to protect themselves temporarily from enemy fire before changing position. After the Battle of the Marne in September, however, the Germans resolved to dig stronger defensive trenches to hold the line and retain German possession of large parts of Belgium and France. Frustrated in their attempts to breakthrough the Germans' hastily dug system of earthworks, the French and the British followed their lead and sought the protection of more substantial trenches to re-group before launching a decisive breakthrough that pushed Germany out of the occupied territories. Both sides expected their time in the trenches to last a couple of months at the most. Yet within a few weeks, the trench line had spread down the entire front and men would live and die in this complex system of earthworks that ran from the North Sea to Switzerland for nearly four years.

Within a matter of weeks, the war of movement ended and the trench deadlock of the Western front began. Another chilling development was the quick spread of the war to the world. Taking advantage of their position as leading colonial powers, Britain, France, and Germany immediately enlisted the help of their far-flung colonies to fight the war. By 1915, the Ottoman Empire and Italy had also joined the fight. The United States, however, hesitated. Unconvinced that the war was necessary or just, Wilson opted instead to pursue a neutral path.

AMERICA'S PATH TO WAR

In 1914, President Wilson believed all the warring nations had abandoned diplomacy too quickly and rushed into war. Initially, few Americans thought the war directly concerned them and the multitudes of first and second generation immigrants from both the Allied and Central powers within the United States ensured that Americans remained divided over who bore primary responsibility for starting the war. Hoping to bring the belligerents quickly to the peace table, Wilson proclaimed the United States neutral and urged Americans to stay neutral in thought as well as deed.

The United States Tries to Remain Neutral

Neutrality, however, proved a hard path to follow. Even before the nation officially joined the Allied side, Americans found it difficult to ignore the war. How to remain neutral without inflicting too much damage on its economy was the most immediate problem facing the United States. Because the bulk of American exports went to Europe, interpreting neutrality to mean the discontinuation of all trade with warring nations would certainly hurt the American economy. In 1914, Wilson banned private loans to belligerent nations as a way to limit Americans' financial involvement in the conflict. By 1915, however, European nations had expended their cash reserves. With the option before him of either allowing loans or risking a recession, Wilson chose to lift the ban. Trading goods and loaning money to both sides was another way to maintain neutrality. In reality, however, American material and financial aid went overwhelmingly to the Allied side.

Seeking all possible advantages, Britain and Germany also tried to counter America's neutral stance by using their navies to disrupt the trade of their enemy. The British established a naval blockade that included mining the North Sea, while Germany turned to its new weapon, the U-boat or submarine, to launch surprise attacks against Allied merchant and military vessels. Both tactics met with protest from the United States, but in the long-run Wilson proved more willing to accept and accommodate the British blockade. Because the Americans' traditional trading route to Europe through the English Channel remained open, the effective closure of the North Sea to international shipping did not disrupt normal American trading patterns. In theory, the British maintained the right to search for contraband in the ships headed to Germany, and then promised to provide them with directions to negotiate the mines in the North Sea. In reality, the inclusion of food and cotton as well as munitions and arms to the contraband list effectively limited American trade with Germany to less than one percent of what it had been before the war. The American government protested that the inclusion of food and cotton on the contraband list violated international law but then found a way to solve its differences with Britain peacefully. American ships stayed out of the North Sea, and the government accepted payments from Britain to maintain cotton prices at home.

By contrast, relations between the United States and Germany quickly soured when Germany declared a submarine blockade around Britain and warned all ships, belligerent or neutral, to stay out of the war zone. Wilson maintained that as citizens of a neutral nation, American passengers and ships had a right to travel unimpeded throughout the world. In Wilson's view, using ships to enforce a blockade protected the rights of neutrals because international law required that passengers be given time to vacate a ship carrying contraband before its cargo was sunk. This antiquated rule, however, negated the very element of surprise that made the U-boat a valuable weapon. Once spotted, armed merchant and passenger ships could easily attack and sink the fragile submarines. Firing their torpedoes sight unseen was the only way to use a submarine effectively.

Wilson denied that it was a double standard to hold Germany strictly accountable to the rules of international law, but accept illegal British blockade policies. The difference, he claimed, was that British violations did not directly threaten American lives. Secretary of State William Jennings Bryan vehemently disagreed, pointing out that the British blockade posed no threat to American lives because American ships did not enter the North Sea. If Americans and American ships stayed out of British waters, Bryan argued, German U-boats would not harm Americans or their property.

This impasse over the rights and responsibilities of neutral nations escalated dramatically in May 1915 when Germany sank the *Lusitania*, a British passenger ship carrying munitions, off the coast of Ireland. The attack killed 1,198 passengers, including 128 Americans. American newspapers highlighted the tragic deaths of women and children, stirring outrage within the United States. One news report described for readers the corpse of a mother clinging to her three-month-old baby, noting that "her face wears a half smile. Her baby's head rests against her breast. No one has tried to separate them."[3] This description became the inspiration for a famous poster by Fred Spear, one of the first drawn by an American regarding the war, which depicted a mother and her baby descending into the depths of the sea accompanied by one simple word, "Enlist." German Americans tried to counter mounting anger against Germany for this ruthless attack by pointing out that if the contraband carried by the *Lusitania* "had reached its destination it would undoubtedly have killed far more Germans than the total number of passengers lost on the *Lusitania*."[4]

In the wake of the sinking, Wilson hardened his stand on the rights of neutrals. He demanded that Germany pay reparations and accept the right of Americans to travel on any ship they wished. The Germans defended the attack, noting that they had published warnings in the American press telling passengers to stay off the ship. A passenger ship carrying munitions as well as civilians was a legitimate military target, Germany argued. The responsibility for these civilian deaths, the Germans asserted, lay with the British who knowingly and intentionally used passenger ships to carry war supplies to Europe. Wilson refused to concede this point and ordered the State Department to send a series of increasingly harsh and confrontation notes to Germany.

At this point, the domestic debate centered on how vigorously to pursue the economic opportunities created by a vibrant war trade. Few Americans in 1915 advocated direct intervention in the war. Convinced that Wilson's preoccupation with the rights of neutrals would inevitably bring the United States into the war, Bryan resigned in protest. Bryan represented a significant segment of American opinion in 1915. Leading female reformers and suffragists vocally supported strict neutrality and formed the Women's Peace Party to seek a diplomatic solution to the war. In the Midwest, German-American farmers refused to accept Wilson's one-sided application of international law and viewed Germany's actions and explanations with sympathy. Other rural folk in the Midwest and South worried about the influence of northeastern banks and businesses on the nation's foreign policy. They feared that these financial institutions intended to force the country into war against Germany to continue their profitable war trade with Great Britain and ensure repayment on the loans they had made to the Allies.

These critics correctly understood that financial ties between the United States and the Allied nations were growing stronger every day. In the months preceding the sinking of the *Lusitania*, American businesses had formalized their close trading ties with

Americans reacted with horror to the sinking of the *Lusitania*, and this poster of a mother and infant drowning as a result of the attack helped turn public opinion against Germany. (*Courtesy of the Library of Congress*)

Britain. In January 1915, the financial behemoth J.P. Morgan became the purchasing and contracting agent for the British government within the United States. Over the next two years, the House of Morgan worked closely with British military and financial officials to award more than 4,000 contracts worth over $3 billion to American businesses. In addition, American bankers extended commercial credit to the Allies that averaged nearly $10 million a day. By 1917, the British were overwhelmingly dependent on American credit and supplies to continue the war. Almost overnight, the United States transformed itself from a debtor to a creditor nation and made inroads into world and domestic markets traditionally dominated by British capital. The jobs and steady income provided by these war contracts spread the benefits of wartime trade throughout the American economy. These financial and economic ties helped to build strong support for the Allied cause in urban areas and raised suspicions in many rural ones.

With the United States and Germany still in dispute over the *Lusitania* disaster, two other controversial sinking of ships increased tensions between the United States and Germany. The *Arabic*, another British passenger ship, was hit in August 1915 by German torpedoes, and two Americans were among the dead. Seven months later, the Germans sunk the *Sussex*, an unarmed English Channel steamer. This U-boat attack killed 80 passengers and injured several Americans. In the wake of each additional incident that directly killed or injured Americans, Wilson issued Germany ultimatums to stop threatening American lives and property or face a break in diplomatic relations. Each time, Germany faced a choice between modifying its use of U-boats in the war zone or driving the Americans into the waiting arms of the Allies. Each time, Germany yielded. In the *Arabic* Pledge on 1 September 1915, Germany agreed to refrain from sinking passengers ships without warning and in the *Sussex* Pledge on 4 May 1916, Germany halted surprise attacks on merchant ships. At this point, Germany decided that the drawbacks of the United States joining the Allied side outweighed the benefits of continuing to indiscriminately sink boats in the war zone. To further repair its damaged relations with the United States, Germany also settled the *Lusitania* impasse by expressing regret for the loss of life and agreeing to pay an indemnity.

Wilson bought the nation some time, but little else. The longer the war went on, the more pressure Germany felt to resume unrestricted attacks on Allied shipping. During this period of relative calm, Wilson renewed his efforts to negotiate a settlement to the crisis. Wilson sent his trusted advisor Colonel Edward House to Europe in 1916, but House found little enthusiasm for anything but complete victory from any quarter. By this point, each nation had simply sacrificed too many men and expended too much capital to imagine ending the war without a clear-cut victory.

As Germany continued to build U-boats at a frenzied pace, British propagandists methodically worked within the United States to turn public opinion permanently against Germany. A massive advertising campaign highlighted German atrocities in Belgium and cast German submarine attacks as contrary to the laws of civilized warfare. After the *Lusitania* disaster, for instance, British agents distributed thousands of commemorative coins in the United States that they claimed the German government had manufactured to celebrate the sinking. One side of the coin depicted guns and airplanes going down with a ship, while the other side showed Death selling tickets to passengers with the caption "Business above all." In reality, a German citizen had privately created the coin before the sinking to satirize the Allied willingness to put munitions shipments on passenger ships.

The anger that British propagandists formented in the United States against Germany and the strong financial ties created by the lucrative war trade did not eliminate all tensions between Britain and the United States. In the summer of 1916, as the controversy with Germany over its submarine warfare tactics momentarily calmed, relations with Britain became strained over the British decision to blacklist American firms that continued to trade with Germany. The violent suppression of the Irish Easter Rebellion also provoked an outcry from the Irish-American community.

The War Comes Closer to the United States: A Distracting Fight with Mexico

As the role of the United States in supplying the Allies escalated, the war crept ever closer to American shores. Wilson focused public attention on unconditional submarine warfare, but throughout the period of neutrality German agents engineered attacks against American factories, ships, and goods. The largest incident of internal sabotage occurred in July 1916, when German spies within the United States orchestrated a huge explosion along the Hudson River in Black Tom, New Jersey, which destroyed munitions awaiting shipment to the Allies. The strength of the blast sent shrapnel flying into the Statue of Liberty and shattered windows in lower Manhattan.

German agents also did their best to distract American attention away from the war in Europe by spending $12 million to support rebel factions in Mexico that were hostile to the United States.[5] In 1916, the real threat to peace for the United States came not on the high seas, but along its southwest border. In the spring, Mexican rebel Francisco "Pancho" Villa launched a series of murderous raids against American border towns. In pursuit of Villa and his forces, 12,000 American troops marched nearly 300 miles into Mexico. The Mexican government regarded the incursion as an invasion and American troops clashed with the Mexican army in Carrizal on 21 June 1916. Wilson prepared an address requesting permission from Congress to occupy northern Mexico, but abandoned this idea when he learned that American troops had attacked first at Carrizal. "Someday," Wilson told his personal secretary, "the people of America will know why I hesitated to intervene in Mexico...Germany is anxious to have us at war with Mexico, so that our minds and our energies will be taken off the great war across the sea. . . . It begins to look as if war with Germany is inevitable. If it should come, I pray God it may not, I do not wish America's energies and forces divided for we will need every ounce of reserve we have to lick Germany."[6] Mexican-American relations improved during negotiation in the fall of 1916, and in January 1917 Wilson withdrew all American troops from Mexico.

The reconciliation with Mexico came none too soon. The same month that American troops left Mexico, Germany decided to resume unconditional submarine warfare. Now in possession of a larger U-boat fleet to patrol British waters, Germany believed these vessels could sink enough Allied shipping over the next few months to bring Britain to the brink of starvation, thus forcing her to leave the war. Without British support, France would be unable to continue fighting. If Britain left the war quickly then the likely intervention of the United States on the Allied side would make little difference. Germany was well aware that in the short-term the American military and navy were unlikely to contribute much. In the time that it took for the Americans to organize and train its wartime force, Germany fully intended to win the war.

It is easy to see why Germany dismissed the immediate military potential of the United States. Despite several diplomatic showdowns with Germany and the possibility of war with Mexico, the nation had made few preparations for war during the period of neutrality. The army contained no fully organized divisions, corps or armies, and available active duty and reserve troops numbered fewer than 350,000. The nation had fifty-five planes in questionable condition and no tanks. The army had enough rifles stockpiled to arm 890,000 troops, but only enough ammunition to support 220,000 men in battle.

These deficits in preparation only became significant once President Woodrow Wilson decided to send an army overseas. There were many Americans who initially expected the country to offer mainly material and financial support to the Allies. If the goal had remained to only send a token force overseas, then the nation's industrial capacity and its ability to transport those goods overseas would have been the true measure of its readiness to enter the war. In either case, the ability to effectively to move goods and men overseas was critical and with their augmented U-boat fleet, Germany believed it could quickly rule the sea.

Unaware of Germany's decision to resume unconditional submarine warfare, Wilson made one final effort to suggest "a peace without victory." In a speech before Congress on 22 January 1917, Wilson outlined a set of "American principles, American policies" that he felt would end this war and prevent future ones. In this address, Wilson proposed that the world embrace democracy, freedom of the seas, and equality of rights among nations, while eschewing entangling alliances. These were, Wilson asserted, " . . . the principles and policies of forward-looking men and women everywhere, of every modern nation, of every enlightened community. They are the principles of mankind and must prevail."[7] Little did Wilson realize that within three months of uttering these words the nation would be at war.

The Zimmermann Telegram

Before announcing that Germany would resume unconditional submarine warfare, German Foreign Minister Arthur Zimmermann attempted to take advantage of the Americans' recent trouble with Mexico. On 16 January 1917, Zimmermann sent a telegram to the German ambassador in Mexico instructing him to "make Mexico a proposal of alliance on the following basis: make war together, make peace together, generous financial support and an understanding on our part that Mexico is to re-conquer the lost territory in Texas, New Mexico and Arizona" ceded to the United States in the nineteenth century.[8] Zimmermann also suggested that Mexico encourage Japan to threaten America's Pacific island possessions. British intelligence cryptographers scored a major triumph when they both intercepted and deciphered the telegram. Britain presented the telegram to the Wilson administration at the end of February and its contents were released to the public in March. To many Americans, Germany's hostile intent against the United States now seemed clear. Rather than fighting just to protect American trade or the rights of neutrals to travel in the war zone, the Zimmermann Telegram seemingly illustrated a clear and present danger that Germany posed to the territorial integrity of the United States. In March 1917, German U-boats sank three American merchant ships further underscoring that American lives were now at risk.

The Declaration of War in the United States

The tangible physical danger that Germany posed to the nation's territorial and economic security convinced Wilson to ask Congress for a declaration of war in April. Yet in his war address, Wilson did not dwell on these threats to the nation's borders or economy. Instead, he quickly summarized Germany's crimes on the high seas then went on to cast the war in broader, idealistic terms. The United States, he declared, had "no quarrel with the German people." Instead, the United States was fighting against the "little groups of ambitious men" who used the German people as pawns to aggrandize their power. The nation was fighting, he intoned, "for the rights of nations great and small and the privilege of men everywhere to choose their way of life and of obedience." In addition to underscoring the principle of self-determination in his war address, Wilson framed the war's purpose in a phrase that has resonated in American foreign policy ever since: the world, he declared "must be made safe for democracy."[9] In outlining the nation's war goals, Wilson took pains to emphasize that the United States had no selfish ends to serve in fighting the war, emphasizing that the country expected no financial or territorial compensation for its part in the war. "We are but one of the champions of the rights of mankind," Wilson pronounced.

The lofty goals that the president gave the country helped inspire many men headed into the army. Once there, however, they would often discover that the war developed its own logic. Overseas, the reasons that men fought usually differed dramatically from the initial vision outlined by the president and accepted by the majority of Americans in April 1917.

Congress overwhelmingly supported Wilson's request for a declaration of war against Germany, but approval was not unanimous. "I shall always believe we could and ought to have kept out of this war," House majority leader Claude Kitchin, a Democrat from North Carolina remarked during the Congressional debate over the war resolution.[10] The United States officially declared war against Germany on 6 April 1917. The nation did not enter the war against Austria-Hungary until 7 December 1917, mostly to prevent Italy from leaving the war after its defeat at Caporetto and never declared war against the Ottoman Empire or Bulgaria.

FIGHTING IN THE FIRST WORLD WAR

With the nation now officially at war, Wilson quickly resolved that the United States needed to play a definitive role on the battlefield both to ensure an Allied victory and to give the United States enough clout to influence the eventual peace settlement. Many Americans were uneasy about sending troops into the bloody morass that had produced cataclysmic casualties at the Somme and Verdun. This sentiment was expressed best by Senator Thomas S. Martin, who when he heard of the War Department's initial request for $3 billion to equip the wartime force, exclaimed, "Good Lord! You're not going to send soldiers over there, are you?"[11] The decision to send a large force overseas presented the country with a vast array of practical problems that included raising, training, and transporting a mass army, and coordinating the American war effort with the Allies. The decision to draft the majority of troops and divide their training between the United States and France had a direct impact on the lives of millions of American men now headed into the service, and so did Pershing's negotiations with the Allies to provide aid in transporting American troops to France and training these soldiers for combat along the Western Front.

"I hope you have not arrived too late." This was the greeting that General John J. Pershing received from the American Ambassador to France on his arrival in Paris two months after the American declaration of war.[12] When the war ended on 11 November 1918, the Americans looked back over the past nineteen months and marveled that they had managed to raise an army of over 4 million men, transport 2 million to France, and command a field army of 1.2 million in major offensive operations along the Western Front. Despite these significant achievements, the Americans paid a price for their inexperience and lack of preparedness. American-commanded operations in the last four months of the war (when the United States took over its own sector of the Western Front) were hampered by disorganization in the rear, high casualty rates, and constantly changing leadership; problems all symptomatic of an army forced by circumstances to fight before it was fully trained and formed.

Wilson made two critical decisions in the opening weeks of the war. The first was to send a large, conscripted American Army overseas. The second was to instruct General John J. Pershing to protect the independence of the American Army. Wilson dismissed another alternative, which was to amalgamate American troops into already formed British and French armies, essentially re-energizing these foreign armies with an infusion of fresh, eager American troops. Wilson rejected this idea partially out of concern that the Allies had already squandered millions of troops at their disposal. If Allied commanders so freely sacrificed the lives of their own citizens, how could they be trusted to safeguard the well-being of Americans under their command? Perhaps more importantly, Wilson felt that a strong American showing on the battlefield would assure him a major role in fashioning the eventual peace settlement. Reflecting these concerns, Pershing sailed to France with these instructions from Secretary of War Newton Baker: "In military operations against the Imperial German Government, you are directed to cooperate with the forces of the other countries employed against the enemy; but in so doing the underlying idea must be kept in view that the forces of the United States are a separate and distinct component of the combined forces, the identity of which must be preserved."[13] Baker later recalled that he gave Pershing no other orders except to go to France and come home. Wilson preferred to let military professionals handle the details of actually winning the war. As Pershing biographer Donald Smythe aptly notes, "perhaps no field commander in history was ever given a freer hand to conduct operations than was Pershing by Wilson."[14]

By the time Pershing arrived in France, warfare along the Western Front had already passed through several stages. In 1916, each side attempted massive assaults designed to break the trench gridlock. The Germans attacked the French at Verdun, initiating a ten-month battle designed to bleed the French white. Verdun had been one of the last forts to fall in the Franco-Prussian War of 1871. France was determined to prevent another humiliating loss on this spot, and Germany correctly guessed that France would defend it at great cost. The Germans miscalculated, however, in assuming only one side would pay the price for such a deadly assault. It was impossible for Germany to attack France so continuously without also feeling the consequences. The 720,000 casualties from the battle were shared nearly evenly between the two sides. On the Somme, the British orchestrated its own massive assault of the German line, which killed a staggering 19,000 British soldiers on the first day of the offensive. By the time the battle ended four and a half months later, over 400,000 British soldiers, 200,000 French soldiers, and 650,000 German soldiers were dead or wounded. Who won the battle? The British poet Edmund Blunden supplied the answer: "The War had won, and would go on winning."[15]

Americans Begin Fighting

Hoping to put these debacles in the past, both sides were in the process of developing a more sophisticated integration of artillery and infantry when the Americans entered the war. The Allies believed they now had the expertise to engineer a successful breakthrough and urged Pershing to provide the manpower needed to seize the battlefield advantage by funneling American troops into their exhausted armies. In accordance with his instructions from Wilson, Pershing refused, expressing his own concerns that the Allies might squander American lives.

Both sides had a point. Pershing only had to look as far back as April 1917, when a few days after the Americans declared war on Germany, French commander Robert Nivelle launched an ill-advised assault at Chemin des Dames that provoked a mutiny in the French army. The Allies were not wrong either however to insist that their increasingly sophisticated use of new tactics and technology, coupled with American brawn, would defeat the Germans. In the end, this was exactly the formula that gave the Allies the edge in the fall of 1918.

By the final year of the war, Allied commanders had increased faith in new tactics such as the rolling barrage, which was a complicated artillery plan that entailed moving the artillery barrage forward with advancing troops according to a time schedule. Ideally, the rolling barrage weakened resistance to an attack not only by destroying the first enemy trench, but also second and third line enemy trenches as attacking infantrymen approached them. In reality, however, without radio communication, the timed lifts in the artillery barrages were hard to change if a battle did not unfold exactly as planned. Unless the infantry was ready to immediately exploit the advantage given by a creeping artillery barrage, the Germans had time to regroup and prepare for the onslaught. Coordination between the infantry and artillery took a lot of practice—experience that the Americans would gain on the battlefield rather than in the training camp. The rolling barrage concept used artillery to improve the infantryman's performance, and gave the artillery a more prominent place in battle strategy than Pershing was initially willing to adopt.

The Allies also believed that the integration of new military technology such as tanks and airplanes into offensive plans would make operations more efficient and productive. The British developed the first tank in 1916, although its first battlefield appearance during the 1916 Somme offensive was unimpressive. Poorly chosen ground, crew inexperience, and mechanical breakdown doomed the experimental use of these initial forty-nine vehicles to failure. In November 1917, however, at the battle of Cambrai, the British demonstrated that if used on firm terrain in sufficient numbers with a properly trained crew, placing tanks at the head of an infantry advance to crush barbed wire and aim machine gun fire at German defenders could result in a major breakthrough. The success of the tank in penetrating five miles into German lines (a short-lived incursion that the British could not exploit because of limited reserve troops) demonstrated the potential of this weapon to support an infantry advance. These experiences provided valuable lessons for the Allies in 1918, when tanks would make more regular and effective appearances in battle. This was one technological advantage that the Allies retained throughout the war. The Germans developed several tank prototypes that were both too large and cumbersome and instead relied on captured British tanks to create its own tank corps.

Similarly, airplanes emerged as a multifaceted offensive and defensive weapon. Initially both sides used airplanes mostly to collect intelligence about the enemy's activities. To head off a successful reconnaissance mission, the other side would deploy its own fleet of aircraft armed with machine guns to intercept and shoot down the invading aircraft. These duels in the sky provided the only true romance and glory in fighting the war. Pilots became legendary for their dueling skills, evoking a past time when individual heroism meant something in battle. The German Manfred von Richthofen (the Red Baron) and Frenchman Roland Garros became international celebrities for their feats in the air. By 1916, however, even airplanes became absorbed into the industrialized warfare that dominated the Western Front. The air war shifted from relying primarily on the skill of individual ace pilots to the use of squadrons and squadron tactics. Commanders also developed multiple uses for the new airplane technology. Aircraft now helped direct artillery barrages, dropped bombs on opposing trenches, and strafed troops with machine gun fire.

Together, these technologies and tactical strategies provided a new direction for the war in 1918, giving the Americans both greater possibilities for victory and much more to learn. Yet, the Allies were not the only ones developing new sophistication in their military planning. Both Britain and Germany were simultaneously training specialized teams of infantrymen to pierce deeply into enemy lines through which reinforcements could pore. In the winter of 1918, however, Germany had one clear advantage over Britain and France. In March 1918, Russia signed a peace treaty with Germany that ended the war on the Eastern Front. This separate peace treaty freed millions of experienced German troops to join their colleagues on the Western Front. Allied commanders expected the German manpower advantage over the Allies to increase by as much as 60 percent and correctly assumed that Germany would try to exploit its manpower advantage by attacking in the spring before the Americans could arrive in force. The first challenge for the Allies and Americans in 1918, therefore, was withstanding these attacks.

This expectation of a German attack caused the British and French to increase their demands that Pershing abandon his plan to create an independent army and instead amalgamate his troops into already existing Allied units. Although Pershing made multiple temporary concessions that put American troops in the front lines alongside French and British troops, he never wavered in his commitment to create an independent American Army that fought in its own distinct sector of the Western Front. Pershing also developed an operational doctrine that he termed open warfare, which he felt differed sharply from the style of trench warfare fought by the Allies in the past. "It was my opinion," Pershing wrote in his memoirs, "that the victory could not be won by the costly process of attrition, but it must be won by driving the enemy out into the open and engaging him in a war of movement."[16] Trench warfare, the AEF (American Expeditionary Forces) commander concluded, had weakened the aggressive spirit of the Allied forces, and now their troops fought ineffectively when forced out of the trenches and into the open battlefield. He intended to train his army to fight differently. Pershing defined open warfare as including "scouts who precede the first wave, irregularity of formation, comparatively little regulations of space and time by the higher command, the greatest possible use of the infantry's own fire power to enable it to get forward, variable distances and intervals between units and individuals, use of every form of cover and accident of the ground during the advance, brief orders, and the greatest possible use of individual initiative by all troops engaged in the actions."[17] Pershing's concept of open warfare put a heavy emphasis on the role of the infantry, causing a lag in the Americans' embrace of the newer strategic ideas involving the use of artillery, tanks, and airplanes employed by the other warring armies. Nor was it the unique American doctrine that Pershing claimed. The elements of open warfare which Pershing identified as the most important—individual and line commander initiative in battle, using ground cover to advance, irregular formations, and rifle power—were used by both the British and Germans in 1918 to create the first major breaks in the trench lines since 1914.

The journey toward creating an independent American army and an American-controlled sector of the Western Front began in the summer of 1917. Pershing believed that the Americans would not be ready to make a decisive impact until 1919, when he expected to have three million troops in France. Besides establishing the basic parameters of his overseas force, Pershing and his small staff immediately set to work reading maps, touring the front, and studying supply routes to decide where the AEF would fight. The British held the northern part of the Western Front and the French occupied the south. In the end, the Americans settled on taking over the Lorraine sector of the front, exactly where the French wanted them. From the French perspective, placing American troops in this relatively inactive southern sector far

American tanks heading into battle during the Meuse-Argonne campaign. (*Courtesy of the National Archives*)

from the British would ensure French influence over training and even combat operations involving American troops. Railroads also connected this region to ports in Brest on lines running south of Paris, thus avoiding already overtaxed routes straining to supply the French and the British further north. For the Americans, the Lorraine sector offered advantages as well. Many of Pershing's staff officers were already intimately familiar with the terrain in Lorraine as a result of intensive pre-war study of the Franco-Prussian War. Perhaps more importantly, Pershing believed that the key German railroad lines and iron mines above Metz and the coal mines in the Saar gave the AEF the kind of targets that would help Pershing fulfill his goal of launching a definitive attack in 1919.

In retrospect, Pershing may have employed faulty reasoning in selecting Metz as a decisive target. The German railroad line that Pershing expected to cut at Metz actually turned west much further north at Thionville, while the coal and iron reserves in the Saar region only accounted for ten percent of Germany's available resources. Yet the selection of Metz as the AEF's key target supported Pershing's emphasis on open warfare. Breaking out of the trenches to resume a war of movement became a strategic necessity because attacking Metz meant fighting in the open terrain on either side of the Moselle Valley. In this way, Pershing was consistent in the strategic vision that he established for his army and the specific targets he set.

In June 1917, the first American troops landed in France. About two-thirds of the First Division consisted of raw recruits, and it would take months before the outfit was ready to enter the front lines. Both Wilson and Pershing appreciated, however, the symbolic importance of sending a contingent of American troops as quickly as possible to boost French morale. In an emotional July 4 ceremony before the Marquis de Lafayette's tomb in Picpus Cemetery, Colonel Charles E. Stanton declared, "Lafayette, nous voici!" (Lafayette, we are here!), a statement that suggested the Americans had come to repay their debt to the French for aid rendered during the American Revolution. A battalion of the 16th Infantry from the First Division traveled from Saint Nazaire to Paris for the ceremony, and joyful crowds cheered the troops, lavishing them with wreaths and bouquets. "Many people," Pershing recalled, "dropped on their knees in reverence as the column went by. These stirring scenes conveyed vividly the emotions of a people to whom the outcome of the war had seemed all but hopeless."[18]

After much feting and celebrating, the Americans settled down to train, not by themselves, but with the French 47th Division. The training regime of the First Division would seem downright leisurely compared to the often-rushed programs followed by divisions that arrived overseas in 1918, but ensconcing these troops with the French set an important precedent. Despite Pershing's insistence on developing an independent training regime, over the course of the war twenty-five American Divisions spent time training or fighting with the French while nine Divisions encamped with the British. The influence that Allied trainers exerted on American troops was a constant source of concern for AEF commanders who worried that their instruction would undermine efforts to develop a distinctly American training and combat doctrine. Brigadier General Harold B. Fiske, the head of the AEF training program encapsulated this view perfectly when he remarked, "an American Army can not be made by Frenchmen or by Englishmen."[19]

American Weapons

The United States grudgingly accepted Allied aid in training its troops, but eagerly requested help in arming them. In developing his training doctrine, Pershing placed heavy emphasis on the one weapon that the United States possessed in abundance—the Springfield Model 1903 rifle. Yet in 1918 most American troops ended up fighting with modified British Enfield rifles because American factories were already producing these rifles in large quantities for the British when the United States entered the war. For field artillery, both light and heavy guns, the United States quickly realized that it needed help from the French armaments industry to supply the American army. With the French offering the Americans an ample supply of 75mm guns and 155mm howitzers, as well an initial delivery of one million shells with subsequent daily allotments of 30,000 75mm shells and 6,000 155mm shells, the War Department officially adopted these as the field artillery pieces of the AEF on 9 June 1917. American armaments manufacturers received licenses to build these guns, but the war ended before any American-produced 75mm or 155mm guns reached the Western Front. Pershing also turned to the French to provide machine guns. In July, the French government agreed to provide Hotchiss machine guns and Chauchat automatic rifles for the initial AEF contingents. The Americans depended on these weapons until September 1918 when enough American-produced Browning machines guns and automatic rifles arrived at the front. In exchange for these munitions, the French received much-needed raw materials, especially steel, smokeless powder, brass, and high explosives.

By the end of 1917, Britain and France pressed for a more active role in helping prepare the American Army for combat. By then, the Second, 26th, and 42nd Divisions had joined the First Division in France, bringing the total to 200,000 of the 2 million troops who would eventually travel to France. These scant numbers were not enough, in the eyes of the Allies, to help repel the expected German spring attacks. The slow progress in forming the American army dismayed the Allies. "The raising of new armies is a tremendous task for any country," wrote General William Robertson to the British War Cabinet, "and although one might expect that America, with her two previous experiences, and her supposed great business and hustling qualities, would do better than other countries, the fact is she is doing very badly. My general impression is that America's power to help us win the war—that is, to help us to defeat the Germans in battle—is a very weak reed to lean upon at present, and will continue to be so for a very long time to come unless she follows up her words with actions much more practical and energetic than any she has yet taken."[20] General Philippe Pétain echoed these sentiments more diplomatically during a Supreme War Council Meeting in January, stating that "the American army, if it wished to retain its autonomy, would be of no use to the Allies in 1918, except, perhaps, along some quiet section of the front."[21] Even Pershing later professed "much embarrassment" over the failure to make a greater contribution to the fighting along the Western Front in 1917.[22]

When the expected German offensives came in March, the German Army put into practice many of the tenets of open warfare advocated by Pershing. In the days preceding the attack, the Germans limited their use of heavy artillery bombardments to destroy barbed wire entanglements and soften up the opposing army. The Germans realized that the massive bombing traditionally used to launch an attack effectively alerted the other side that an attack was coming and created huge craters in No Man's Land for attacking troops to negotiate. This time, small infantry teams advanced under artillery cover, and got past strongly defended front lines. Men then poured through the opening to assault weak rear defenses and encircle Allied lines before front-line troops had time to fall back. These attacks were spectacularly successful, resulting in the first major break of the trench lines since 1914. By May, the Germans once again came within forty miles of Paris. With German long-range shells raining down on them, one million people fled in panic.

The German spring offensives in 1918 ensured that the Americans did more than train with the French and British; they fought alongside them as well. Although Pershing had repeatedly resisted Allied demands to amalgamate American troops permanently into their armies, he realized that how close the Allies were to losing the war. Accordingly, on 28 March 1918, Pershing went to Marshal Ferdinand Foch, the newly appointed Supreme Commander of the Allied Armies on the Western Front and told him that in light of the seriousness of the situation, "all that we have is yours; use them as you wish."[23] For the next two months American troops occupied quiet sectors of the Western Front to free veteran French troops for the defense of Paris. Finally, from 28–31 May the First Division fought in the first offensive American action of the war at Cantigny, the farthest point of the German thrust toward Paris. In this battle, the Americans succeeded in seizing a plateau that gave the Allies an improved view of enemy movements. This first taste of active operations tempered any illusions about combat among these troops. After the battle, exhausted troops "could only stagger back, hollow-eyed with sunken cheeks, and if one stopped for a moment he would fall asleep," one colonel recalled.[24] The Second Division also played a key role in halting the German drive towards Paris at Chateau-Thierry by re-capturing Belleau Wood and Vaux. The appearance of Americans in battle at Cantigny and Chateau-Thierry provided a psychological boost for the Allied side and a corresponding fear in Germany that time was running out.

The initiative still lay with the German Army, however. In July the Germans launched their fifth and last offensive at Rheims. American troops fought alongside French and

Moroccan troops in the Second Battle of the Marne to stymie the advance. Pershing took particular pride in the counterattack at Soissons, which he considered the turning point of the war because the Germans never regained the initiative. The rout by British, Canadian, and Australian troops near Amiens on 8 August 1918 in which Allied soldiers penetrated five miles into German lines confirmed that the German spring offensives had failed.

American reinforcements were beginning to make a mark, funneling fresh troops into the battle just as the Germans had exhausted their reserves. With the German advances halted, the Allies now initiated a series of counterattacks over the summer that gradually pushed the Germans back to the original trench line by September. The American soldiers who received their initiation to combat during these battles experienced a type of fighting that bore little resemblance to the previous three years of trench deadlock. As they pressed the Germans into retreat, American and Allied troops did not pause to create permanent trenches. Instead, troops hastily dug shallow holes to provide immediate cover with the expectation of abandoning them as the general drive forward continued.

The American Sector of the Western Front

During these counter-offensives, American Divisions fought under the command of the French and British, where some remained for the duration of the war. At the end of August, however, Pershing recalled most of his troops to occupy the newly designated American sector of the Western Front. In September, the American First Army attacked the Germans holding the St. Mihiel salient, a bulge of German-held land jutting into Allied lines. This area was strategically important because German troops could use it to launch another attack on Verdun, as they had in 1916. With the help of over one hundred thousand French troops providing artillery and air support and guarding the flanks of the American Army, half a million American soldiers fought to push the Germans out of this salient that they had held since 1914 to straighten out the Allied line. The Germans had used their time in the sector to create a formidable defense of barbed wire up to 13 rows deep, elaborate trenches, and well placed artillery and machine guns. The Americans attacked while the 23,000 German troops holding the salient were in the midst of withdrawing to a more fortified position. In the face of a retreating enemy, the Americans captured the railroad lines as far as Nancy for the relatively light cost of 7,000 casualties. To win control of the skies during the battle, General Billy Mitchell, head of the AEF Air Service, assembled nearly 1,481 aircraft, the largest concentration of airpower in any single wartime operation. The British and French provided 130 and 742 aircraft respectively that helped Mitchell strafe and bomb first one side of the salient, then the other. Poor weather kept many aircraft grounded during the first two days of the battle, but on the third day Mitchell's overwhelming strength gave the Americans control of the skies as the Germans concentrated on protecting rear area installations.

The American victory against a retreating German enemy camouflaged numerous errors made by the American Army during the attack. Failures included lax discipline on the front lines, commanders located too far back from the front to respond to developments on the field, long and confusing orders, and traffic jams that prevented needed supplies from reaching the front. The Germans were unimpressed by the performance of the Americans at St. Mihiel, despite losing valuable terrain to this untested force. "The Americans have not yet sufficient experience and are accordingly not to be feared in a great offensive. Up until this time our men have had too high an opinion of the Americans," a German intelligence report surmised.[25]

To quiet Allied critics who doubted the ability of American commanders to orchestrate a major offensive on the Western Front, Pershing did his best to ensure victory in the St. Mihiel offensive by employing his most experienced combat divisions. Pershing got the overwhelming victory he desired, but soon paid a price. Just as the Americans were launching the offensive, word reached Pershing of his next assignment. A mere two weeks after attacking in St. Mihiel, the supreme commander of Allied forces, Marshal Ferdinand Foch requested that the Americans move into position sixty miles away to launch an offensive in the Meuse-Argonne region. Pershing agreed, but the short notice put the Americans at a distinct disadvantage. In the midst of the St. Mihiel campaign, Pershing was forced to begin moving many supply and command units to the new staging area. Perhaps even more importantly, having committed his best troops to the earlier battle, Pershing began his drive in the Meuse-Argonne with these men resting in the rear and five of his nine divisions fighting for the first time. Pershing had always expected the major contribution of the AEF to come in 1919, but circumstances now forced him to commit under-prepared troops to battle. Consequently, the Americans would fight their longest and most sustained wartime battle of the First World War with many under-trained and inexperienced troops and officers.

The Meuse-Argonne campaign was the American part of a much larger, coordinated Allied offensive. In the fall of 1918, the Allies for the first time had the manpower and willingness to launch four, synchronized assaults against the Germans from the North Sea to the Meuse River. At the southern end of the Western Front, the American attack in the Lorraine region shadowed the British and French attacks further west intended to disrupt a critical railroad line between Lille and Thionville that supplied the German Army in the north of France. Foch believed that losing this vital supply line while under attack on multiple fronts would break the German line and force a retreat out of France.

To prepare for the attack, the Americans funneled approximately 600,000 men, 4,000 artillery guns, and 90,000 horses into the region, moving mostly at night to avoid alerting the Germans that a buildup was underway. Supply units also streamed towards the Meuse-Argonne, setting up ammunition depots, evacuation hospitals, and light railways to carry men and supplies to and from the front. On 26 September 1918, the Americans attacked five weak, but well-placed, German Divisions. Despite their numerical advantage, the Americans were unable to make much headway before nearby German reserve Divisions arrived to reinforce the German line. Facing terrain and formidable German defenses likely to pose a challenge to even the most experienced and well-trained troops, the American offensive quickly ground to halt. The Americans attacked in a narrow strip of land between the hilly, densely wooded Argonne Forest on the west and the heights of the unfordable Meuse River on the east that housed strong German fortifications that further enhanced their favorable positioning. In the center a 13-mile long and 20-mile wide tunnel-like stretch of land gave the Germans a third entrenchment on high ground. The Americans battled for four days to reach the Kriemhilde Stellung, the strongest line of German fortification. There, the attack halted as terrific traffic jams in the rear prevented food or ammunition from reaching the front lines.

Hardships: Death, Injuries, Disease, Lack of Supplies

More American soldiers were killed or wounded in September and October 1918, than in any month of battle during either the Civil War or World War II, making this a

Congestion in the rear during the Meuse-Argonne campaign hampered the flow of supplies to the front, creating additional hardships for American troops engaged in the battle. (*Courtesy of the National Archives*)

costly period in American military history.[26] During these two months, nearly 27,000 men died of combat-related wounds.[27] In six months of active fighting, the American Army averaged 43,000 casualties a month, compared to 24,000 a month during World War II and 13,000 a month for the Union Army in the Civil War. The First Army saw 45,000 men killed and wounded in first four days of fighting in the Meuse-Argonne campaign alone.[28] The coincidence of this battle with the second wave of the deadly influenza pandemic that swept the globe in 1918 added to the stream of men headed to the rear. Over the course of the campaign, both enemy bullets and influenza germs seriously depleted the American forces and combined to overtax an already fragile supply system. During the six-week battle the numbers of men incapacitated by enemy fire (69,832 wounded; 18,864 gassed; 2,029 shellshocked) was only slightly higher than those felled by disease (68,760, mostly from the flu). "Influenza so clogged the medical services and the evacuation system, (and) rendered 'ineffective' so many men in the armies that it threatened to disrupt the war," Alexander N. Stark, chief surgeon of the First Army later noted.[29]

The official numbers do not tell the full story of the epidemic's impact on the fighting effectiveness of the AEF. Many men opted to stay away from army hospitals and instead chose to remain with their units and let their comrades care for them, or they hid away in bunkers or the woods until they recovered. For the time that they were absent from duty, their units received no replacements for them. Even after they felt better, many flu victims were severely weakened for weeks after their illness and therefore fought ineffectively.

Besides struggling to overcome illness, American soldiers faced other serious handicaps during the opening days of the battle. The lack of artillery support proved particularly troublesome. Implementing a rolling barrage required maintaining a good liaison between the infantry and artillery to keep the shells falling on the enemy as the infantry advanced, something that came from extensive practice or experience, neither of which the AEF had. For the individual soldier, this meant facing the risk of friendly fire when American artillery shells fell short or facing German machine guns that the artillery had failed to locate and destroy. Part of the problem was faulty communication between the infantry and artillery. Another difficulty was an early AEF decision to arm their units with heavy French 75mm and 155mm guns that improved their firepower, instead of light howitzers that were easier to maneuver in battle. Commanders found the psychological impact of supporting artillery fire as important as its actual effectiveness in reducing German resistance. "The officers of infantry battalions that were fortunate enough to have their accompanying guns or infantry batteries keep up with them," reported one AEF inspector general, "stated that their fire was very 'comforting' to the men and greatly increased their determination to advance upon the various strong points that started to hold up the line."[30] If men could not achieve safety by advancing under the cover of artillery fire, then they sought it by massing together on the battlefield. When enemy machine guns held up front lines, reserve units "could not be made to see that their crowding forward did not help the attack but merely fed the men to the machine guns," the AEF inspector general complained at the end of the war.[31]

Supply difficulties further hampered the American effort. Some soldiers went into battle without gas masks or overcoats, while rifles, helmets and gun oil were in short supply throughout the First Army. Under-equipped and inexperienced, many soldiers made mistakes on the battlefield that both raised the casualty rate and hampered the effectiveness of the entire army. "I am afraid that we had too many who were like me to fight a well-trained army, and it cost us dearly," one veteran sadly concluded in later years.[32] All divisions experienced widespread problems with straggling, and at the close of the campaign AEF Headquarters estimated that close to 100,000 of the 1.2 million men who took part in the battle lost contact with their units either intentionally or inadvertently.

The Lost Battalion

The dramatic experiences of the Lost Battalion provided a human face to the general hardships and travails facing American soldiers during the Meuse-Argonne campaign. On 2 October over five hundred men from the 306th, 307th, and 308th regiments found their advance stalled against a German force entrenched on a high slope. That evening, Major Charles W. Whittlesey sought a way around the barbed wire entanglements by heading up an undefended ravine. He led his men nearly one thousand yards into the ravine as he reconnoitered a way to flank the Germans. After alerting divisional headquarters of his discovery, Whittlesey had his men dig into a hillside while they waited for reinforcements to arrive. During the night, the Germans closed the gap in the ravine and surrounded Whittlesey and his men. Only a day earlier, Whittlesey and his battalion had been rescued after spending three days trapped behind enemy lines. Whittlesey resolved once again to wait for help. The men only carried one day's rations, and no blankets or overcoats. They were, however, amply armed with ammunition for their machine guns, rifles, and Chauchat automatic rifles. "Our mission is to hold this position at all costs," Major Charles Whittlesey told his officers. "Have this understood by every man in the command."[33] Throughout the day, the men fended off German attacks and sought protection from machine gun and artillery fire in their dugouts along the slope. These rudimentary shelters provided little defense from the trench mortar fire that the Germans soon directed into the ravine. Slowly the numbers of wounded and dead began to mount. "Situation is cutting into our strength rapidly. Men are suffering from hunger and exposure. Cannot support be sent at once?," Whittlesey messaged back by carrier pigeon.[34] The men soon abandoned efforts to bury the dead, who lay where they fell. Their comrades in the 77th Division mounted two rescue attempts on 4 October. Each failed and resulted in heavy casualties. Late in the day, the Americans tried shelling the Germans to ease the pressure on Whittlesey and his men. Whittlesey had sent his exact coordinates, but this did not prevent the barrage from going terribly wrong. "Our own artillery is dropping a barrage directly on us. For Heaven's sake stop it," Whittlesey wrote, using his last carrier pigeon to send this message to the rear.[35] Trapped in their dugouts by German snipers and machine gunners, the men waited for an anxious thirty minutes before the shells were redirected to fall on the Germans. Over the next two days, the men endured another friendly fire artillery barrage (this one from French artillery) and watched French and American planes miss the mark and drop much-needed food and ammunition into the German lines.

The men were nearing the end of their endurance. The delirious cries of the wounded rang out continuously, and many wounds turned gangrenous. At night, men often slipped down to the muddy stream below to fill canteens for the wounded. Men continuously asked Whittlesey to let them steal away under the cover of darkness so they could take their own chances making their way back to American lines. Whittlesey refused each request. On 6 October at 4 P.M., a blindfolded Private Lowell R. Hollingshead walked into the ravine carrying a white flag. Hollingshead and eight others had stumbled into German lines while trying to retrieve one of the errant food baskets dropped by American planes. The opposing German commander sent Hollingshead back with a message. "The suffering of your wounded men can be heard over here in the German lines, and we are appealing to your humane sentiments to stop. A white flag shown by one of your men will tell us that you agree," the note read.[36] In response, Whittlesey ordered white signaling panels hidden while his men screamed obscenities at the Germans.

Finally, on 7 October advances by the 82nd Division elsewhere along the front convinced the Germans to evacuate the area. As the Germans pulled back, a rescue party rushed to the ravine. "The relief felt by our men is indescribable," Whittlesey recalled.[37] Five days after being cut off, 194 out of the original 550 marched out on their own. "It was one of the saddest moments of the entire war," recalled one member of the rescuing party.[38] Overall, 111 died and 199 were wounded. Major Whittlesey walked out of the forest with his men, but the guilt of having survived these five harrowing days when so many of his men lost their lives never left him. Decorated for his bravery under fire with the Medal of Honor, Whittlesey never recovered from the ordeal. In 1926, he disappeared from a boat heading to Cuba, most likely leaping to his death mid-voyage.

Renewed American Offensive Strikes

The rescue of the Lost Battalion occurred as part of the renewed offensive that Pershing had begun on 4 October 1918. Before the Americans could advance, they needed to seize the high ground east of the Meuse and in the Argonne Forest. For six days, the Americans attacked entrenched German positions along a fortification called the Kriemhilde Stellung to little avail. The Meuse-Argonne now took on the character of previous Western Front battles. Instead of surging forward and driving the Germans from their bunkers and trenches, the Americans tried to weaken their opponent through

An American gun crew firing in the heat of battle along the Western Front where scarred trees and lingering smoke revealed the intensity of the fighting. (*Courtesy of the National Archives*)

steady artillery barrages. With these tactics, U.S. troops only made minor, incremental advances against this well-defended ground.

As the American effort stalled, the French and British armies further north had more success pushing the Germans back. Faced with accusations from Foch that inept American leadership had prevented the Americans from keeping up with the general Allied advance, Pershing responded angrily. He noted, with some justification, that both the terrain and German reinforcements sent to the area made the American task difficult and that the Americans had been given little time to plan their attack. Many of the problems that the Americans faced during the battle were symptomatic of an army forced to fight before its time. Yet Pershing was responsible for other problems encountered by the Americans. The AEF went into combat with divisions twice the size of their European counterparts, and in battle these double-sized divisions often proved unwieldy and difficult to maneuver. In the end, these larger divisions simply led to increased numbers of casualties. With a lack of confidence in their training, Pershing and his staff tended to give units carefully constrained instructions that deterred troops from exploiting unexpected successes on the ground. While units waited for further orders, the window of opportunity often closed.

Yet the fighting ability of the American Army also improved as the battle wore on and troops gained valuable experience. One example was the enhanced use of airplanes during the offensive. When the battle began poor coordination between the infantry, the artillery, and the air service made it difficult for these various arms to work together on the battlefield. Facing determined German resistance, infantry commanders requested additional help from the air service to secure needed intelligence on the location of machine gun nests and to strafe enemy front lines. Billy Mitchell agreed to reduce the numbers of planes harassing rear area depots to provide frontline support to the infantry. Ground troops, however, often did not know how to signal their requests to pilots, and pilots resorted to bringing infantry officers up in the air with them to demonstrate the kinds of information they could provide. In the largest single bombing operation of the war on 8 October the Americans borrowed nearly 500 bombers and escort planes from the French and dropped 32 tons of bombs on a counter-offensive force that the Germans were forming five miles behind their lines. Besides hampering the buildup, the attack also attracted hundreds of German pursuit planes and gave the Americans a chance to destroy some enemy aircraft. Although the employment of airplanes as offensive weapons remained in its infancy during the war, these innovations demonstrated the increasingly sophisticated tactics adopted by the American army as it gained battle expertise.

After three weeks, the campaign's original first day objective was finally met when the 32nd and 42nd Divisions made a limited dent in the Kriemhilde Stellung. The American forces now divided into two field armies, the First and Second Armies, and continued to expand its fighting capabilities. The new commander of the First Army, Major General Hunter Liggett began training of infantry assault teams to knock out the machine-gun nests that hampered the advance of the infantry. By November, infantry-artillery coordination improved, commanders became confident enough to approve night attacks, and aerial bombing and mustard gas attacks supported infantry troops' advance. In pursuit of a withdrawing German Army, the Americans were finally able to fight a war of movement. By the armistice of 11 November 1918, the First Army had reached Sedan and the Second Army was preparing to launch a drive towards Metz.

The German decision to seek an armistice came after a series of reversals along the Western Front threatened to bring the fighting into Germany. By November, the Allies had captured one-fourth of the German Army and half of its guns. Germany faced setbacks on the high seas as well. In 1918, the Allies implemented a convoy system that thwarted Germany's ability to use its U-boats to starve the British and French into submission. Merchant ships now traversed U-boat infested waters in groups under the watchful eye of Allied destroyers and battleships that made ready use of newly available depth charges and sonar. Convoys ensured a steady stream of men and material to the Allied side, while the Americans' help in laying a curtain of mines in the North Sea strengthened the Allied blockade that pushed Germany to the brink of starvation. With the naval and ground war going badly, the future only guaranteed the arrival of more and more American troops in France. Realizing its prospects were dim, the German government sued for peace before Allied troops set foot on German soil. Pershing always believed the Allies made a mistake in agreeing to this request. "What I dread is that Germany doesn't know that she was licked, had they given us another week, we'd have taught them," Pershing remarked.[39]

The American Contribution to the Overall Victory

When the war came to an abrupt end, the American military looked back with satisfaction at their army's final campaign. During the Meuse-Argonne offensive, the Americans advanced thirty-four miles against enemy lines. This forty-seven-day battle was a significant military and political achievement for the United States. In little more than a year, the military had raised, trained, and transported an army of two million men to France. Over a million men fought in the Meuse-Argonne campaign, more soldiers than had served in the Confederate Army during the Civil War. Yet the Americans also paid a heavy price for their inexperience and early commitment to battle. Throughout the Meuse-Argonne campaign, casualty rates averaged 2,550 a day and 6,000 Americans died each week during the battle.

Over the course of the war, 53,402 American soldiers lost their lives in combat, while 204,002 were wounded. Having fought for a longer period, the other major combatant nations experienced much higher casualty rates. France lost 1.3 million men in the war, Britain lost 900,000, Germany's casualties topped 1.6 million, and Russian deaths neared 1.7 million. Citing these disproportionate casualty rates, some postwar commentators viewed the United States as barely bloodied by the war. This flippant dismissal of the American war effort grossly underestimates the intensity of the American combat experience. It took nearly a year for the United States to raise, train, and transport enough men to France to make a substantial contribution to the fighting. From that point on, the Americans were fully engaged on the battlefield. Fifty-three thousand men died in what amounted to six months of battle, which is more than the number of men who died in nine years of fighting in Vietnam (47,355) or three years in Korea (33,746). Over the course of the war, France and Britain lost an average of 900 and 457 men a day, respectively. Once Americans began to fight in earnest through the summer and fall of 1918, deaths in the American Army averaged 820 a day, close to the wartime averages within the French Army and nearly twice as many as the British. These comparisons suggest that barely bloodied is hardly an accurate description of the American Army's experience during the war.

Besides sharing in the horrors of the war, the American Army contributed significantly to the overall Allied victory. The Americans had reason to be proud of the part they played in defeating Germany, but they did not single-handedly win the war for the Allies as American soldiers sometimes claimed in the postwar period. American military leadership had little influence on the overall strategic plan that won the war. Foch was the real architect of the eventual victory who devised the successful Allied attack that forced Germany to request an armistice. Yet American troops played a key role in 1918. Initially, American Divisions occupied quiet sectors of the front, thus freeing more experienced British and French troops to participate in active combat operations. The Americans soon made their own contributions on the battlefield to prevent Germany from winning the war. At crucial moments as the Germans advanced towards Paris in the spring of 1918, the Americans fighting in Chateau-Thierry and Belleau Wood helped halt the German offensive. If they did not win the war for the Allies at this point, the Americans certainly stopped them from losing it. Throughout the summer, American troops provided the additional troop strength needed to slowly push the German army back to the original trench line. On the high seas, American sailors provided key help in mining the North Sea and protecting convoys headed overseas with men and supplies. During the final Allied assault, the Americans held nearly 21 percent of the Western Front, and without their presence it is difficult to imagine the Allies prevailing at that moment. Finally, the specter of a million more fresh and eager troops arriving to bolster Allied lines in 1919 was a major factor in convincing Germany to sue for peace.

THE PEACE

Wilson had sent American soldiers to France to help the Allies defeat Germany and to secure a prominent place for the American president in the peace negotiations. The army succeeded in both endeavors. Now it was up to Wilson to fashion a peace that met the high expectations he had created when he led the country into war and declared that the United States was fighting for "the ultimate peace of the world." In many respects, the challenges that Wilson faced in creating this lasting peace were as daunting as the ones the country had faced eighteen months earlier in mobilizing its resources to send a mass army overseas. Rather than sending his Secretary of State or trusted advisers to hammer out the details of the peace treaty, Wilson became the first sitting president in American history to travel to Europe where he engaged personally in the peace process. How well he succeeded in the quest to fashion a lasting and just peace settlement became the yardstick Americans used to decide if their sons and husbands had sacrificed their lives in vain.

Wilson outlined his view of a just peace settlement in 1917 through his "peace without victory" and war addresses. In the middle of the war, Wilson refined the nation's war goals even further with a speech known as the Fourteen Points. Wilson's prescription for peace in the Fourteen Points reflected both his idealistic views and his desire to protect the interests of the United States. In his address, Wilson repeated his call for freedom of the seas and self-determination. He now linked these ideas to the spreading of laissez-faire capitalism, a stand that seemed more imperative in light of recent Bolshevik advances in the Russian Revolution. The principles of free trade and freedom of the seas advanced by Wilson offered more than an antidote to communism. They were also likely to advance American trading interests at the expense of imperialist powers like Britain and France. In the Fourteen Points Wilson also urged the world to disarm. To some, this appeared as naïve idealism, but there was a pragmatic element to Wilson's suggestion. The United States had traditionally maintained a small peacetime military, and Wilson had every reason to expect Congress to continue this pattern after the war. Convincing other nations to disarm was a practical way to ensure the safety of the United States, especially since Wilson was unlikely to persuade Congress to authorize an arms buildup at home. The Fourteen Points also used the principle of self-determination to re-draw the map of Eastern and Central Europe along ethnic lines. Wilson further proposed that colonial populations have a voice in determining their futures. After the difficulty the United States had experienced subduing the Philippines in the wake of the Spanish-American War, Americans had no interest in acquiring any more colonies. Wilson's efforts to curtail the growth of British and French colonial empires was a way to protect American access to international markets and remain true to his principle of self-determination. Finally, Wilson endorsed the establishment of a League of Nations that would implement a system of collective security to maintain world peace.

Hinting at the trouble Wilson would face convincing the Allies to accept these ideas, French Prime Minister Georges Clemenceau did not even bother to read the Fourteen Points until Germany requested an armistice based on them in October 1918. France and Britain only agreed to accept the Fourteen Points (minus the provision for freedom of the seas) as the basis for the armistice after Wilson threatened to sign a separate peace agreement with Germany. On the eve of peace negotiations, Clemenceau quipped, "God gave us his Ten Commandments and we broke them. Wilson gave us his 14 points—well, we shall see."[40]

By the time Wilson arrived in Paris, he was no longer opposed to dealing harshly with Germany, having become convinced over the course of the war that the German people actively supported the war and their Kaiser. When Germany defeated Russia in 1918, it inflicted a harsh peace settlement that forced Russia to cede one-third of its arable land (including the Ukraine, Finland, Estonia, Lithuania, Latvia, and parts of

Poland which became satellite states of Germany) and most of its coalfields. The Germans also demanded that Russia demobilize its army, disarm its navy, and pay reparations to Germany. To Wilson this punitive peace settlement revealed the full scope of German territorial ambitions, and he now believed that maintaining peace in Europe required weakening Germany militarily and economically. Wilson, therefore, supported depriving Germany of its navy and colonies. Wilson, however, disagreed with the French insistence on completely eviscerating Germany. He also parted company with the French over the best way to prevent another war from occurring in Europe. Wilson hoped that a new League of Nations could take the place of the traditional defensive alliances that France hoped to establish with Britain and the United States to protect its borders.

Beset with political difficulties at home that forced him to leave the peace conference temporarily in February and exhausted by the sheer length of the negotiations, Wilson lost many key battles during the peace negotiations. In the end, the Versailles Treaty required that Germany admit guilt for starting the war, pay reparations to the Allies, and disarm. Germany also lost its colonies, the territory ceded by Russia, as well as Alsace and Lorraine (two French provinces taken by Germany during the Franco-German War in 1870). When Foch read the treaty, he exclaimed, "this isn't a peace, it's a twenty year truce."[41]

Although the treaty's excessive harshness dismayed Wilson, he remained hopeful that the provision to establish a League of Nation would usher in a new chapter in world history. Once war passions cooled, Wilson believed that the League could modify some of the treaty's more egregious features. He also expected the pledge that member nations made to aid one another in the event of an attack to provide a powerful deterrent against war. Wilson, however, encountered some opposition at home over this dream of a powerful League of Nations constructing and implementing a system of collective security. Skeptics in Congress noted that Wilson had proposed a dramatic realignment in the nation's foreign policy, which until this point had avoided formal alliances or international commitments. Isolationists who preferred no ongoing involvement in world affairs joined forces with advocates of the traditional balance-of-power approach to maintaining peace in Europe. Both factions questioned whether joining the League of Nations deprived Congress of its power to declare war. The pledge that member nations made to defend each other if attacked, which Wilson saw as essential to creating a more peaceful world, League critics feared gave the League too much power to control American foreign policy. "Are you ready to put your soldiers and your sailors at the disposition of other nations?," Senator Henry Cabot Lodge, the leading Republican opponent of the treaty, asked the American people.[42] To resolve this impasse, Lodge proposed adding fourteen American reservations to the treaty. The most important one explicitly stated that "the United States assumes no obligation to preserve the territorial integrity or political independence of any other country or to interfere in controversies between nations" unless Congress gave explicit approval to send American troops overseas.[43]

Unwilling to accept any modification that might re-open negotiations with other signatories, Wilson refused to accept any alterations to the treaty. From the standpoint of American jurisprudence, renegotiation was only necessary if the Senate demanded the addition of amendments rather than reservations to the treaty. In taking this stand, Wilson somewhat willfully ignored hints from abroad that France and Britain would accept some American reservations if they ensured American

President Woodrow Wilson and Gen. John J. Pershing. (*Courtesy of the Library of Congress*)

participation in implementing the provisions of the treaty. Instead of compromising, Wilson resolved to take his case directly to the American people.

Over the course of three weeks, Wilson made forty speeches and traveled ten thousand miles before the huge crowds that thronged to hear him speak. Wilson's powerful defense of the treaty made an impact and public opinion began to build in support of ratification. Wilson dismissed his critics' concerns as wrongheaded and impractical. "If you want to stamp out the smoldering flames in some part of Central Europe, you don't send to the United States for troops," Wilson contended. The League of Nations had no ability to force any nation to send troops against its will, he claimed. The League, he assured his audiences, would only choose "the powers which are most ready, most available, most suitable, and selects them at their own consent, so the United States would in no such circumstances conceivable be drawn in unless the flames spread to the world."[44]

In conveying this message, Wilson used his considerable rhetorical skills to bring audiences to tears as he reminded them of the sacrifices made by American soldiers on the Western Front. "What of our pledges to the men that lie dead in France" to fight the war to end all wars, asked Wilson in the last public speech he gave in Pueblo, Colorado. "Nothing less depends upon this decision, nothing less than the liberation and salvation of the world," he warned.[45] Having pushed himself to the limit in defense of the League, an exhausted Wilson soon paid the price. Hours after giving this speech, Wilson fell ill and his doctors rushed him back to the White House where he suffered a stroke. For weeks, Wilson lay in bed fighting for his life. As he recovered, his wife and physician shielded him from over-exertion. He spent only a few hours a day out of bed and his wife conducted much of his formal business. Permanently paralyzed on his left side, Wilson remained ensconced in the White House for the rest of his presidency. Wilson was "as much a victim of the war as any soldier who died in the trenches," observed British Prime Minister David Lloyd George.[46]

The president's inner circle kept the extent of Wilson's illness a secret, assuring the public that he was simply recovering from exhaustion. With Wilson now absent from the public stage, the doubts raised by opponents of the League began to gain momentum. Rejecting all suggestions that he resign, Wilson also refused to consider any compromises that might ease Senate ratification of the treaty. The Senate consequently rejected both the original treaty and one with the reservations attached. The United States never ratified the treaty that its president had worked so hard to negotiate, and never joined the League of Nations that he championed as the harbinger of world peace. Instead, the United States signed its own separate peace treaties with Germany, Austria and Hungary in October 1921. The rejection of the treaty did not, however, signal a complete rejection of Wilsonian ideals. Throughout the 1920s, the United States used traditional diplomacy to negotiate multinational treaties through which signatories pledged to disarm and renounced war.

CONCLUSION

In 1914, Europe rushed to war. By contrast, the United States took two and a half years to enter the First World War, and only did so after deciding that Germany posed a distinct military threat to the nation's wellbeing. Although there was little chance of Germany directly invading the United States, Germany's policy of unconditional submarine warfare threatened the lives and property of Americans engaged in the thriving war trade with France and Britain. In addition, Germany's clumsy attempt to prod Mexico into war with the United States exacerbated anti-Germany sentiments in the country and seemingly demonstrated Germany's ill-will toward the United States. During the period of neutrality, the United States made few preparations for war and consequently the declaration of war initiated a frenzied effort to raise, train, equip, and transport a mass army capable of fighting on the Western Front.

Once overseas, Pershing faced distinct challenges in coordinating the American war effort with the British and French. Resisting the Allied request to amalgamate their armies, Pershing insisted on forming an independent American force that would eventually control its own sector of the Western Front. While this remained the steadfast goal of the American military, Pershing also bent during moments of crisis and willingly lent American units to the Allies to stop the German drive towards Paris in the spring of 1918. By the fall of 1918, the Americans were in control of their own sector where they engaged in their biggest campaigns at St. Mihiel and the Meuse-Argonne. Although victorious in both battles, American inexperience led to high casualties and much hardship for front-lines soldiers, especially in the Meuse-Argonne campaign. By the end of the war, the fighting abilities of the American military had vastly improved as it absorbed lessons learned on the field of battle. Although many American soldiers perished in these final campaigns, thanks to their efforts, the overall victory came much sooner than expected thus saving the lives of men slated to head overseas in 1919.

The United States made a substantial military and financial contribution to the overall victory, and that participation won Wilson a prominent role in the peace negotiations. Wilson led the country into war proclaiming that the defeat of Germany would usher in a future of peace, democracy, and free trade. At the end of the war, he traveled to Europe to build these principles into the Versailles Treaty. He only partially succeeded. The treaty inflicted harsh, punitive terms on Germany (which it may or may not have deserved), and Wilson came home only completely satisfied with the clause establishing the League of Nations. Within the United States, however, Wilson soon faced strong doubts about the wisdom of joining the League. The treaty failed to win ratification after a stroke interfered with the president's ability to advocate publicly in its favor and his refusal to endorse any compromises proposed by the Senate.

Ultimately, all the decisions made by American politicians and generals from 1914–1918 had a dramatic effect on the average soldiers who did the fighting and dying overseas. The president and the Congress determined much of their fate by deciding to enter the war, draft an army, and send it overseas. In France, Pershing decided where, how and when enlisted men fought, literally making life and death decisions for some. Even the eventual failure of the peace treaty influenced American veterans, causing some to feel disillusioned about the overall outcome of the war.

NOTES

1. Martin Gilbert, *The First World War: A Complete History* (New York: Henry Holt and Co., 1994), 22.

2. Gilbert, *The First World War,* 24.

3. Walton Rawls, *Wake-Up, America! World War I and the American Poster* (New York: Abbeville Publishers, 1988), 81.

4. William Dudley (ed.), *World War I: Opposing Viewpoints* (San Diego: Greenhaven Press, 1998), 82.

5. Arthur S. Link, *Woodrow Wilson and the Progressive Era, 1910–1917* (New York: Harper and Row, 1954), 200.

6. Norman Gordon Levin, *Woodrow Wilson and World Politics: America's Response to War and Revolution* (New York: Oxford University Press, 1970), 311.

7. Otis L. Graham, Jr., *The Great Campaigns: Reform and War in America, 1900–1928* (Englewood Cliffs, NJ: Prentice Hall, 1971), 326.

8. Zimmermann Telegram reproduced at http://www.archives.gov/education/lessons/zimmermann/

9. Graham, *The Great Campaigns: Reform and War in America*, 330–2.

10. Jeanette Keith, *Rich Man's War, Poor Man's Fight: Race, Class and Power in the Rural South during the First World War* (Chapel Hill: University of North Carolina Press, 2004), 14.

11. Keith, *Rich Man's War, Poor Man's Fight,* 42.

12. John J. Pershing, *My Experiences in the World War*, vol. 1 (New York: Frederick A. Stokes Co., 1931), 60.

13. *United States Army in the World War, 1917–1919*, vol. 1 (Washington, D.C.: Center for Military History, 2001), 3.

14. Donald Smythe, *Pershing: General of the Armies* (Bloomington, IN: Indiana University Press, 1986), 11.

15. John M. Merriman, *A History of Modern Europe: From the Renaissance to the Present* (New York: W.W. Norton & Co., 1996), 1063.

16. Pershing, *My Experiences in the World War*, I, 152.

17. *United States Army in the World War, 1917–1919*, II , 491.

18. Pershing, *My Experiences in the World War*, I, 92.

19. Brig. Gen. H. B. Fiske, assistant chief of staff, G-5, AEF, "Report of G-5, " June 30, 1919, 31–33, folder # 215; Entry 22, Record Group 120, National Archives, College Park, Maryland.

20. "American Battalions for British Divisions," 12 January 1918, in *United States Army in the World War, 1917–1919*, III, 16.

21. Minutes of Supreme War Council Meeting, 3rd session, 30 January 1918 in *United States Army in the World War, 1917–1919*, II, 186–7.

22. Pershing, *My Experiences in the World War, I*, 278.

23. Smythe, *Pershing: General of the Armies,* 101.

24. Smythe, *Pershing: General of the Armies,* 128.

25. Smythe, *Pershing: General of the Armies,* 189.

26. Carol R. Byerly, *Fever of War: The Influenza Epidemic in the United States. Army during World War I* (New York: New York University Press, 2005), 110.

27. Leonard P. Ayres, *The War With Germany: A Statistical Summary* (Washington, D.C: Government Printing Office, 1919), 120.

28. James Seidule, "Morale in the American Expeditionary Forces during World War I," Ph.D. diss., Ohio State University, 1997, 130.

29. Byerly, *Fever of War*, 108.

30. Jennifer D. Keene, *Doughboys, the Great War and the Remaking of America* (Baltimore, Md.: Johns Hopkins University Press, 2001), 42.

31. Keene, *Doughboys, the Great War and the Remaking of America*, 43.

32. Keene, *Doughboys, the Great War and the Remaking of America*, 44.

33. Meirion and Susie Harries, *The Last Days of Innocence, America at War, 1917–1918,* (New York: Vintage Books, 1997), 375.

34. Harries, *The Last Days of Innocence, America at War, 1917–1918*, 376.

35. Harries, *The Last Days of Innocence, America at War*, 1917–1918, 376.

36. Harries, *The Last Days of Innocence, America at War*, 1917–1918, 378–9.

37. Harries, *The Last Days of Innocence, America at War*, 1917–1918, 385.

38. Christopher M. Sterba, *Good Americans: Italian and Jewish Immigrants during the First World War* (New York: Oxford University Press, 2003), 181.

39. Smythe, *Pershing: General of the Armies*, 232.

40. W.C. Widenor, "The United States and the Versailles Peace Settlement," in J.M. Carroll and G.C. Herring (eds.), *Modern American Diplomacy* (Wilmington, DE: Scholarly Resources, 1996), 40.

41. Merriman, *A History of Modern Europe: From the Renaissance to the Present*, 1151.

42. Widenor, "The United States and the Versailles Peace Settlement," 49.

43. Dudley, *World War I: Opposing Viewpoints*, 211.

44. Arthur S. Link, (ed.) *The Papers of Woodrow Wilson*, vol. 63 (Princeton: Princeton University Press, 1986), 453.

45. Link, *The Papers of Woodrow Wilson*, vol. 63, 500–13.

46. David Kennedy, *Over Here: The First World War and American Society* (New York: Oxford University Press, 1980), 361.

2   DRAFTING AND TRAINING THE ARMY

In World War I, the United States broke with tradition by immediately implementing a wartime draft. In previous wars, the government had waited until enlistments began to wane before introducing conscription. This time, Congress agreed to institute a draft without delay before the American Expeditionary Forces (AEF) commander General John J. Pershing had determined exactly how many men the army would need. The effect of the draft was felt throughout the nation as each community assembled registration and draft boards to decide who went into the army and who stayed home. The demand for men, economic imperatives at home, racial prejudice, and medical concerns all influenced these decisions. The entire process resulted in a "typical recruit" who stood 5'7" tall, weighed 141 1/2 pounds, was in his early twenties, and unmarried. The army reflected the diversity of the American population as well. Nearly thirteen percent of the wartime army was black and eighteen percent was foreign-born.

When the United States declared war on Germany, the Regular Army consisted of 121,797 enlisted men and 5,791 officers. The National Guard, whose units were controlled by state governors until President Woodrow Wilson drafted them into federal service, stood at 174,008 enlisted men and 7,612 officers. The total force raised during the war numbered 4,412,533, including 462,229 sailors, 54,690 marines, and 2,294 Coast Guard troops. Of the 3,893,340 soldiers inducted during the war, 2,810,296 (72 percent) were conscripted. Overall, 20 percent of the draft-eligible male population (aged 18–45) served in the military.

Congress made the decision to raise the bulk of the army through conscription, but Pershing dictated how the men would be trained once they were inducted. In formulating his overall strategic vision, Pershing embraced the concept of open warfare. He wanted infantry troops to leave the safety of the trenches and fight on the open battlefield. Pershing's strategic doctrine influenced the training program implemented in the camps, but other factors also affected the American soldiers' training camp experience. Many men arrived at camps still under construction as the government struggled to clothe and equip them. There, men from all walks of life came together for the first time and faced the distinct challenges of adjusting to a completely new way of life.

CONSCRIPTING THE WARTIME ARMY

When the nation entered the war, the government faced the choice of relying primarily on volunteers, instituting an immediate draft, or waiting until enlistments began to flag before turning to a draft to bring men into the army. When Congress authorized the draft, the legislators initially intended to maintain the traditional American practice of using conscription to spur enlistments. An expanded Regular Army and National Guard continued to accept volunteers, while a new yet-to-be formed National Army was reserved for conscripts. Wilson, however, had concrete economic, political, and military reasons for accepting the draft as the most logical way for the United States to raise the bulk of its wartime force. Economically, Wilson worried that the rush to the colors might rob essential wartime industries of their workers and managers. Politically, the offer by former president Theodore Roosevelt to raise a regiment of volunteers and take them to France threatened to undermine the government's control of the war effort. The draft solved both these problems by allowing the government to grant deferments to needed workers and prevent enthusiastic individuals from raising independent forces to send overseas. Militarily, the draft would also ensure that the army continued to receive the numbers of men that it needed, even after the initial enthusiasm for war subsided. The road to war had been long and full of controversy, and Wilson was unsure how firmly committed the nation was to fighting. Fully aware of the mass slaughter underway along the Western Front, Wilson took steps early on to prevent the inevitable sag in enlistments once long casualty lists became a reality.

Conducting the Draft

The past weighed heavily on nearly every decision that the government made on how to conduct the draft. The nation's last experience with conscription had been in the final two years of the Civil War from 1863–1865. In that conflict, opposition to the draft became the catalyst for race riots and much anti-government sentiment. Hoping to prevent another violent reaction to the draft, Provost Marshal Enoch H. Crowder eliminated past practices that Americans had found particularly objectionable such as allowing men to pay a substitute to serve in their place. Instead of using its own agents to register and select men, the federal government funneled its requests for troops through 4,647 local boards. These "friends and neighbors" granted exemptions and chose soldiers for the wartime army. Communities formed registration and draft boards, each with three members who served without pay. To register men for the draft, again in deference to lessons learned from the past, Crowder eliminated the individual house visits by federal agents, which many Americans had resented as intrusive. Instead, men were required to appear before registration boards in person on selected days to complete their paperwork. To popularize the draft among the American people, the government took heed of the common perception that a draft forced reluctant men into the army. The government renamed conscription as "selective service," and insisted that it bore little resemblance to drafts of the past. Selective Service, the government repeatedly told the American public, was a modern management technique designed to place men where they could best serve the war effort. The caption on one wartime propaganda poster perfectly encapsulated the government's message: "Selective draft and service not like the old-time conscription of the unwilling, the President says. It is rather a selection from a Nation which volunteers in mass." [1]

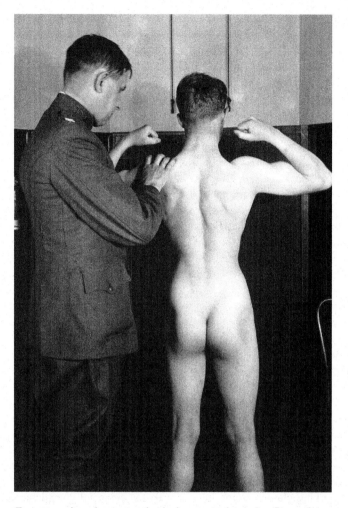

Every recruit underwent a physical exam to determine fitness for
military service. (*Courtesy of the National Archives*)

On 5 June 1917, 10 million men between the ages of 21 and 30 registered amid
patriotic festivals throughout the nation. Ship horns, church bells, and factory whistles
rang out in cities and towns to announce the start of registration, and many families
accompanied their sons, husbands, and brothers to the designated registration sites.
Officials had focused so much attention on potential resistance to the draft that they
were unprepared, yet pleasantly surprised, to discover that complaints instead came
from men who had to wait for hours in long lines to complete the registration process.
In some areas, men camped out overnight to be the first to register from their neigh-
borhoods, with much shoving, pushing, and occasional fistfights in the morning over
who would receive this honor.

Registering for the draft proved quite different, however, than expecting to go to
war. Although 24 million men eventually registered for the draft without incident,
millions then took advantage of their right to request a deferment because of their occupation or support of dependents. Eventually, over 65 percent of those who registered

received deferments or exemptions from service. The Selective Service system contained five classifications. Class I was composed of men eligible to serve immediately. Classes II and III included temporarily deferred married men and skilled workers in industry and agriculture; Class IV contained married men with economic dependents and key business leaders, while those unable to meet physical and mental requirements were placed in Class V.

After receiving a white postcard scheduling him for a physical exam, a man had seven days to file a claim for a deferment. A second white postcard in the mail alerted a man that the claim was approved, while a green postcard indicated that the draft board had rejected his application and ordered him to report. Men requesting a deferment had to complete a daunting twelve-page questionnaire that was often beyond the capabilities of recent immigrants with imperfect English skills or barely literate workers and farmers. Selective Service regulations exempted foreign-born men who had not declared their intention to become citizens. Because the burden of receiving any exemption lay with the recruit, men who barely spoke English or were unknowledgeable about Selective Service regulations often found themselves caught up in the net of the draft. Nearly 200,000 nondeclarant immigrants served during the war. A few thousand contended that they had been drafted against their will. Once in the training camps, despite the pressure to stay, these men went to court or appealed to their embassies to contest their conscription. Over the course of the war, the War Department received 5,852 diplomatic protests over the drafting of nondeclarant aliens, and the army released 1,842 of these men.

The largest proportion (43 percent) of deferments went to married men who were the sole providers of their families. As one applicant succinctly noted, "No one wants to take care of another man's wife."[2] Not all married men with dependents received deferments, however. Crowder left it up to local draft boards to determine which wives could work to support themselves and which could not. Local boards all included a physician to conduct medical examinations. Other members were generally a mix of county clerks, sheriffs, lawyers, or businessmen. The composition of these boards put the local professional elite firmly in control of deciding the fate of each community's lower and working classes. Some local boards put financial considerations aside and instead focused on preserving family stability in time of war. These boards often bragged of convincing alcoholic or wayward husbands to renounce their irresponsible ways and return home. In a few isolated instances, wives provided testimony against their husbands to ensure their induction and a steady income for the family. Most wives, however, supported their husbands' claims for deferment. "My George ain't for sale or rent to no one," one farmer's wife told his draft board. "If he goes, I got to go too. I don't want your money—I jist wants George."[3]

In the South, the ability of local boards to issue deferments became yet another vehicle to support white supremacy. White landowners sometimes exerted their considerable social influence to persuade local draft boards to defer their black tenant farmers, thus protecting their labor force. Black farmers without the support of powerful white patrons often found that local boards viewed their claims unsympathetically. Few southern boards balked at the prospect of putting black women to work while their husbands served in the military, especially, as an Arkansas board noted, "in cases where the wife had always worked by her husband in the crops."[4] Sending impoverished black men into the military might even improve their families' circumstances, one Alabamian board argued. In its deliberations, this board concluded "that the husband in the army could send the wife more than he had heretofore contributed, and further, that negro women are always in demand as cooks . . . the matter of loneliness during the absence of the husband was not taken into consideration."[5] In many cases, the thirty dollars a month that a soldier received was actually more than a sharecropper, white or black, earned. Even if military service would impose a financial hardship on the family, another draft board's supposition that "it is a matter of common knowledge that it requires more for a white man and his wife to live than it does a negro man and his wife, due to their respective station in life" helped draft boards justify their willingness to disproportionately call black men into service.[6] Nationwide, over one-third of all black registrants were drafted, compared to one-fourth of all white registrants.

Yet the impoverished condition of white tenant farmers in the South also hurt their ability to prove that entering the military posed a financial hardship for their families. Selective Service regulations granted deferments for occupation, but the government did not initially consider agriculture a critical wartime industry and left it to local boards to determine if a soldier's pay of $30 a month would be enough to support a man's family. In the end, these rules worked against the rural poor, white and black. Deferments for black farmers sponsored by rich white landowners, coupled with the delayed induction of most black draftees until March 1918, meant that poor whites were the ones primarily sent to fill the southern states' draft quota in 1917.

Refusing the Draft, Conscientious Objectors, Deferments, and Draft Board Rejections

Not everyone abided by Selective Service regulations. Overall, nearly 3 million, or 11 percent, of the draft-eligible male population refused to register or report to induction centers once called into service. Nearly a third of reported draft-dodging occurred in the South where impoverishment actually helped men evade the draft. Thousands of men throughout the southern states successfully evaded the draft because the state did not have the written documentation that it needed to place them in the draft-eligible category. With notations in family bibles often the only testament to a person's age, local draft boards and federal agents found it impossible to contradict a man's claim that he fell outside the 21- to 30-year-old age range of the first draft law. Letters to family members that established the whereabouts of young men who had joined the hordes of migrant wartime workers were also scarce among this barely literate population. Isolated cases of armed resistance resulted in a few dozen gun battles between local police and draft resisters. A handful of men also appealed their inductions through the courts. The most famous incident of mass protest took place during the Green Corn Rebellion in eastern Oklahoma when the police arrested 500 sharecroppers and day laborers for protesting their impending induction into "a rich man's war, poor man's fight." But more commonly, southerners seeking to evade the draft discovered that their impoverished lifestyles provided them with an effective way to evade state officials.

The Selective Service law provided a way for conscientious objectors to avoid fighting without resorting to draft-dodging. Initially only those with long-standing ties to a religious order that espoused pacifism were eligible, but in 1918 Secretary of War Baker extended conscientious objector status to include anyone with "personal scruples against war."[7] Over the course of the war, 20,000 men were classified as conscientious objectors and were therefore liable only for noncombatant service. On arriving in the training camps, these men faced strong pressure from officers and their peers to reconcile the war with their religious convictions. Nearly 80 percent of conscientious objectors eventually abandoned their initial stance against the war and agreed to serve in combatant branches. Those who held fast to their convictions performed noncombatant duties such as driving ambulances at the front. Others received furloughs to work on farms near the training camps. Another 1,500 refused to perform any service that aided the war effort and were imprisoned for the duration of the war. Scorned and abused within the military prison system, several conscientious objectors complained of beatings, being forced to stand shackled for hours, and guards forbidding them to talk.

Occupational deferments became more common during the second year of the war. In 1917 when the most pressing issue was raising a mass army quickly, boards proved reluctant to grant exemptions for vocational reasons. In doing so, local boards threatened to undermine one of the administration's reasons for implementing an immediate draft. By 1918, in response to increased pressure from Congressional and business leaders, the War Department urged local boards to grant more industrial and agricultural exemptions to protect the national economy. With congestion and breakdowns on the nation's railway lines threatening to bring the war effort to a standstill, Wilson granted a blanket exemption for all railway workers and men in the merchant marine. Otherwise, local boards still determined who received a deferment and who went to war.

The Provost Marshal also began explicitly using occupational deferments as a way to funnel needed workers into war-related industries when he issued a "work or fight order" on 17 May 1918. This order stated that any man who received an occupational deferment risked induction into the military if a local board discovered he was either unemployed or working in a nonessential sector. Crowder claimed that this order forced 137,000 men to switch jobs in the final months of the war, a negligible number in a workforce of nearly 35 million.

The public perception that large numbers of men had either abused the draft process or successfully evaded the draft eventually led to demands that the government capture and punish these "slackers." Seeing multitudes of able-bodied men walking the streets of every American city provoked a sense of injustice among the relatives of those serving overseas. Anger that immigrants had migrated to benefit from the economic opportunities available in the United States, yet then refused to serve in the military bolstered anti-immigrant feelings in some inner cities. "While the flower of our neighborhood is being torn from their homes and loved ones to fight," one Brooklyn draft board reported, Russian nondeclarant immigrants "remain smugly at home to reap the benefits of the life work of our young citizens." When "these miserable specimens of humanity" appeared before the board, they "shrug their shoulders, laugh at us and say, 'What are you going to do about it?'"[8] Although these immigrants were asserting their rights under the law, many native-born Americans seethed over such acts of defiance and in their eyes, ingratitude. Taking advantage of public anger, the Justice Department orchestrated a series of "slacker raids" throughout major metropolitan areas in the spring and summer of 1918. Additional manpower for the raids came from ultrapatriotic organizations like the American Protective League and Council of National Defense that had demonstrated their loyalty in 1917 by coordinating illegal vigilante attacks against opponents to the war. A dragnet of federal marshals, local police, and their civilian allies descended on movie theaters, ball parks, restaurants, train stations, and even union halls in search of any man who appeared of draft age. Men who could not produce a draft card or deferment were herded, sometimes at bayonet point, into detention centers where inmates often remained for weeks before officials determined their draft status. Nearly 40,000 men were illegally imprisoned in the slacker raids. The attorney general claimed that loyal Americans were willing to submit to the inconveniences of wrongful imprisonment if it helped the government catch genuine draft evaders, but many of those jailed disagreed and vocally protested the government's violation of their civil liberties.

Receiving a draft notice did not guarantee that one would serve in the military. Millions of men were drafted, but then rejected as physically unfit for service before being sworn into service. Medical examinations by local draft boards revealed the impact of poor housing and unsafe work environments on the nation's young men. Northern middle- and upper-class men who lived in suburban areas were the healthiest population reporting for service, reflecting their generally favorable living and working conditions. Yet, as one medical officer in Camp Fuston, Kansas noted, "it is quite apparent that the physical condition of the men as they file past, stripped, is poor. Many have been office workers or indoor salesmen, and their pale skins and flabby tissues bespeak lack of tone, and indicate the absence of any kind of exercise."[9] Laborers and farmers performed manual work on a daily basis that in theory prepared them for the physical challenges of soldiering. In their early twenties, many men from working class or farming communities started working as children. Workplace accidents and backbreaking work had left already its mark on many young men, revealing the dangerous and difficult conditions in which many labored. Stripping the men to perform these medical exams served the other useful purpose of undermining the self-confidence of those attempting to feign illness or faulty hearing to avoid military service. "With few exceptions, these men lost all guile with their clothes. They appeared helpless and could, with a little tact, be handled like school children," one examiner noted.[10]

Approximately one-third of the men called into service were judged unfit physically to serve. As with nearly every other decision regarding the draft that was left to local boards, the definition of physical fitness varied considerably. The fluctuating demands from Washington, D.C., for men also influenced medical examiners' decisions. The Surgeon General reported that in December 1917, for instance, the fewest men were rejected and the greatest number accepted as mobilization reached its zenith. In 1918, some men who had tried earlier to enlist but had been rejected for medical reasons found themselves drafted and inducted into the army.

Volunteers

Not every registrant waited to be drafted. For a while, men could volunteer for any branch of the army. After 15 December 1917, Class I registrants with the appropriate skills could still volunteer for Surgeon General, Engineers, Signal Corps and Quartermaster units. Draft-eligible men could also enlist in the navy or marines until 27 July 1918. When Congress expanded the draft to include men from the ages of 18–45, the War Department stopped accepting any volunteers into the army, navy, or marines in August 1918.

For those who agreed with Congressman James Beauchamp Clark that "there is precious little difference between a conscript and a convict," volunteering was more appealing than the draft as a way to enter the wartime military.[11] One volunteer offered another practical reason for enlisting, "You can pick any branch you want *now*, later they pick you."[12] Yet during the short window available for enlistment, men did not flock to the colors and the army had to fill many spaces reserved for volunteers with conscripts. Enlistments came in fits and bursts, as individuals weighed their chances of being drafted with their desire to control where they served. "When America entered the war I knew if I didn't go they would get me so I enlisted right away," explained Louis Popolizio.[13] Alongside the national efforts to register, exam, and select draftees, the Regular Army and National Guard launched massive recruitment drives to bring their volunteer units up to war strength. Volunteering fell off throughout the late summer and fall of 1917 after the War Department decided the order in which numbers assigned to draft registrants would be called. "If they'd come and got me I would have grabbed a flag and yelled 'Hurray!' and 'Let's go!' but they didn't come around so I didn't go. I wasn't mad at anybody," said Huey Long, the infamous governor of Louisiana, to explain his decision to sit out the war as a young man.[14] In September 1917 when the army began inducting 324,248 of the 687,000 slated for the first draft round, only 24,367 men volunteered. Enlistments for the army then picked up dramatically in December as the deadline for volunteering neared. That month, 141,931 men voluntarily entered the army ranks. As the Provost Marshal noted, "there persisted always, for many at least, the desire to enter military service, if needs must, by enlistment rather than by draft—that is, to enter voluntarily in appearance at least."[15] Over the course of the war, the Regular Army and National Guard enlisted 230,509 and 296,978 men, respectively. By contrast, over 2.8 million men were drafted into the military.

The lackluster pace of enlistment throughout most of 1917 took Army officials by surprise, and the army eventually revised its initial decision to maintain three distinct military entities within the AEF. At first, War Department planners intended to form Regular Army divisions solely out of volunteers who enlisted for the duration, National Guard divisions from men who represented distinct states or regions, and then National Army divisions that drew their personnel from the draft. In 1917, well before the need to replace battle casualties played any role in diluting the makeup of the Regular Army and National Guard, the War Department found itself forced to funnel conscripts into these divisions to bring them up to war strength. By the end of 1917 the American wartime army was already well on its way to becoming a national mass army, although it took the War Department until April 1918 to formally eliminate Regular Army and National Guard designations. From this point on, all divisions carried the insignia of the U.S. Army on their clothing and equipment.

ENTERING THE ARMY

Before a man entered the service, he received a copy of the *Home Reading Course for Citizen-Soldiers* in the mail from the War Department. This pamphlet explained the purpose of taking up arms against Germany and attempted to instill a sense of higher purpose in the men who would soon come together to fight for their country. Americans, the pamphlet asserted, had "no taste for warfare and no lust for territory or power" but only fought wars to preserve liberty. These men now had the chance to become part of the pantheon of American heroes who had served the country bravely in past conflicts such as the American Revolution and Civil War. Besides giving men a romantic and glorious reason to fight, the pamphlet also addressed potential concerns that recruits might have about military service. Although the military demanded

Drafted men from New York City arrive in camp carrying flags and signs from the festive send-off given to them by their friends and relatives. (*Courtesy of the National Archives*)

unquestioning obedience from its troops, the pamphlet assured recruits that the army honored the nation's egalitarian traditions by giving all an equal chance for promotion (certainly news to the African American recruits who received the home study course). The course passed relatively quickly over the realities of war. A man might feel afraid at first in combat, the pamphlet admitted, but he would soon learn to conquer these feelings in "the great game of war." The home study course concentrated mainly on the daily living skills that new recruits would have to master including military courtesy, drilling, military equipment, and personal hygiene. The lessons offered for this final category made no assumptions about previous living conditions and included detailed advice on how to chew food and brush teeth.[16]

When the moment to depart arrived, community celebrations marked the event. On 31 August 1917, which Wilson designated the "day of the Selected Man," communities across the nation gathered to watch as recruits, many dressed in their best clothes, marched past their friends and neighbors to the trains waiting to transport them into their new army lives. In Washington, D.C., President Wilson and members of Congress marched with local draftees, while in New York City, Theodore Roosevelt sat in the reviewing stand as seven thousand newly inducted soldiers paraded up Fifth Avenue. Processions leading men to the train stations were common, as were luncheons and gifts to honor the departing troops. "The local Board did things up mighty well," one draftee exclaimed. "I find myself possessed of a razor, razor strop, wrist watch, two pocket knives, unbreakable mirror, drinking cup and a lot of other things that I never expected to own or need."[17] Others left with boxes of their mothers' cookies and doughnuts handed out by the Red Cross to sustain them on their journey. In one Pennsylvanian town, recruits marched by a bonfire of burning German textbooks, while the local band played the song "Keep the Home Fires Burning." Not everyone in the crowd cheered. Small groups of weeping relatives added a more somber note to the process of sending men off to war. On the Lower East Side, wives and sweethearts clung to their men folk as they paraded past and screamed in anguish when the men tore themselves away and began boarding the train. Because men left for the training camps over a staggered series of dates to avoid overwhelming transportation and processing facilities, departing celebrations replete with cheers and tears occurred continuously throughout the war.

After the noise and festivities surrounding their send-off, the sudden quiet that descended about an hour into the journey to their training camps became a time of reflection for many men as they pondered what lay ahead and what they had left behind. Others continued their celebration until the liquor ran out. To set a more disciplined tone on the trains, the Provost Marshall instructed local officials to give men armbands that technically put them in uniform and made them subject to military regulations forbidding uniformed troops from possessing alcohol. Men often carried banners from their towns all the way from their points of departure to the training camp gates. Painted with slogans like "We're from Hell's Kitchen, We'll Keep the Kaiser Itchen" and "Gas Bombs for the Kaiser from the Boys of the Gas House District" evinced the high spirits with which many entered service. Unfortunately, their first few days in service often squashed this initial enthusiasm. One morale officer in Camp Meade, Maryland, complained to his superiors after observing the harsh treatment meted out to incoming recruits. The men entered the camp carrying suitcases, satchels, and bundles, which they placed at their feet after receiving orders from the noncommissioned officers who greeted them to stand in columns of two. During the long wait, the morale officer observed some draftees "laughing, joking, etc; others (many, many of them) were sullen, subdued, sad—and I saw a good many of them who were having a hard time (and not always successfully) in keeping the tears back." Oblivious to the fragile emotional state of the men, the noncoms walked up and down the columns taking away the flags that some held under their arms, "evidently flags used by groups of drafted men from the same respective towns when they marched down to the depot amid the cheers and applause of their fellow townsmen, who gave them a 'good send-off.'" Appreciating the need to instill immediate discipline in the men, this particular morale officer nonetheless deplored the army's failure to extend "at least some element of cordiality and welcome" to entering conscripts. [18]

Camp Life

When the men arrived, each took possession of a few blankets and a mattress sack. They then filled the sack with straw and placed it either on a bunk in a newly constructed barrack or found a place in one of the tent cities erected in camps still under construction. They then spent their first night in the midst of a sea of other men, some from their hometown and others strangers, who coughed, snored, and tossed and turned their way through the night.

The next morning began promptly at 5:30 A.M. when the blast of a bugle awoke the men. The famous musical composer (and soldier) Irving Berlin used this unpleasant part of army life as the inspiration for a popular wartime song he wrote in 1918 that

A bugler blows into a megaphone to wake up sailors in a naval training camp. (*Courtesy of the National Archives*)

found its way into many soldiers' wartime diaries, titled "Oh, How I Hate to Get Up in Morning," whose clever lyrics referred to murdering the offending bugler, including "I'll amputate his reveille and stomp upon it heavily." It ends with the soldier looking forward to getting back to the United States and spending the rest of his life in bed.

The song proved a showstopper in the wartime Broadway show that Berlin created called, *Yip Yip Yaphank*. A lifelong insomniac, Berlin found the army routine impossible to master and convinced his camp commander to let him skip drilling and instead devote his energies to writing a Broadway musical that raised funds for a camp community building in Camp Upton, New York. The show, which included some recruits from Camp Upton in the cast, ran for six weeks on Broadway in the spring of 1918. While at Camp Upton, Berlin also wrote "God Bless America," a song that he put aside at the last minute because it seemed "just a little too sticky."[19]

Few other recruits could rely on unique gifts, musical or otherwise, to help them avoid the tedium and exhaustion of the military regime. Instead, these men had a quick rinse with cold water, ate breakfast, and cleaned their quarters according to military standards, which included placing their polished pair of extra shoes under the edge of their beds and folding their blankets correctly. The recruits then headed off to the "school of the soldier" to receive instructions in saluting and the manual of arms for an hour or so. Next came "school of the squad," which consisted of marching and drilling. Inspection of quarters followed, then more drills or group calisthenics, and perhaps some lectures. The afternoon schedule differed depending on how far along a recruit was in his training, ideally progressing from rifle and bayonet practice to tactical maneuvers in small units on the open battlefield with occasional hikes included to offer some variation and build physical fitness.

Clothing, Food, and Medical Care in Camp

If they were lucky, recruits also received their army uniform during these initial days in camp. In 1917, it took many weeks before camps had enough uniforms to go around, resulting in a piecemeal distribution of clothes and kits. Most men initially received at least a campaign hat and pullover khaki shirt that they wore with civilian pants and shoes. Over the next few weeks, recruits lined up for the rest of their standard

This cartoon from *The Stars and Stripes*, a military newspaper published for soldiers, spoofs soldiers' frustration with leggings, a standard part of the army uniform. (*Courtesy of the Library of Congress*)

army entire, including olive drab wool pants and jacket. Recruits were quickly learning by this point that standing in line was a major part of military life. "I never waited so much, so long, or so often in my life," complained one man to his family.[20] The coat was lined with cotton where the wool might touch the skin along the neck. Soldiers were also given a pair of brown boots and gaiters, which were cloth leg coverings that they tied with a cord at the top, over their pants, and at the bottom, over their boots, to prevent mud and dirt from entering the top of the boot. When they got to France, the army replaced gaiters with leggings, a bandage-like cloth that soldiers wrapped around their calves over their pants and boots. Soldiers often found it difficult to master this unfamiliar item of clothing, but most learned to prefer them to gaiters.

Clothing might have been in short supply, but stateside recruits generally ate well. The army's daily ration provided a whopping 4,761 calories a day to provide sustenance for the physical demands of basic training. A typical breakfast consisted of fruit, cereal, fried liver, bacon, toast, and coffee. Lunch was the heaviest meal of the day consisting of meat, potatoes, a vegetable, bread and dessert, while dinner was a lighter meal of meat and biscuits with something sweet to finish off the day. Overall, the heavy meat allowance that troops became accustomed to while training contrasted sharply with the eating habits of Allied troops who relied more heavily on soups and bread to sustain men in the field. Catholic soldiers received a dispensation from the church to eat meat on Fridays (with the exception of Good Friday), but observant Jews could still not touch pork any day of the week.

Within the first few weeks, recruits were interviewed about their skills and intelligence, given shots, learned some basic drills, and awaited assignment to a unit. Vaccinations were now a routine part of the soldier's entry into the military. Medical advancements promised to reduce the outbreak of contagious diseases in the training camps—a debilitating problem in past wars. In the First World War, troops received shots for tetanus, typhoid, and smallpox. For men from rural areas, the inoculations that they received in the army were the first shots of their lives. These mandated shots provoked more immediate fear than the thought of charging against German machine guns on the Western Front. In his war memoir, *Stretchers*, Frederick Pottle recalled the trepidation of those advancing in a slow moving line towards the needle. "The recruit in front is white; as he moves up to the man with the needle he suddenly crumples up in a faint," Pottle recalled. Turning to meet his fate heroically, "our recruit's arm is dabbed with alcohol on a swab of absorbent cotton. He passes a little beyond the man with the needle. He feels a sharp sting in the back of the arm; the needle goes in still farther. All over. It was not much, after all, but he will dread it the second time just as much as the first."[21] Besides inoculating soldiers with proven serums, the army also experimented during the war with other vaccines; essentially using soldiers as guinea pigs to assess their effectiveness.

Insurance Programs for Soldiers

Recruits soon learned that completing paperwork was a large part of army life. On arriving in the camps, soldiers received their first offer to subscribe to the government's War Risk Insurance program. The government promised to aid disabled veterans or families of deceased soldiers, but allotments topped out at $200 a month. To supplement these government payments, soldiers were urged to purchase a renewable one-year insurance policy that guaranteed a disabled soldier or a deceased soldier's beneficiary between $1,000 and $10,000, depending on the policy that a soldier selected. Rates varied according to age, ranging between $.63 and $1.08 per $1,000 of coverage. The insurance policy was valid whether a soldier was killed in combat or in a traffic accident.

Low rates and the heavy advertising of the program among enlisted men and officers resulted in the purchase of policies by ninety percent of the wartime force. Most purchased the maximum amount of $10,000 and the premium payments were automatically deducted monthly from their paychecks.

Taking out an insurance policy was optional, but providing for dependents at home was not. In October 1917, Congress mandated that enlisted men send at least $15 of their army pay home to care for any relatives who relied on them for support. The government then supplemented these allotments by sending the wife another $15 to support herself, $10 for her first child, $7.50 for the second child, and $5 for every additional child. The subsidies topped out at $50, so families with more than six children still only received $80 a month from the government including the money sent home by the husband. Wartime deductions from the soldiers' pay ensured that men did not forgo their responsibility to provide for their families even while in uniform. Army officials also hoped that giving soldiers a reduced amount of cash at the end of each month would lessen the gambling, drunkenness, and carousing that usually marked payday. If single men decided against sending money home to their parents, the army took a portion of their pay and deposited it into interest-bearing savings accounts. "The fact that the commanding general of the American Expeditionary Forces believes that receipt of full pay is subversive of discipline is the strongest possible argument in favor of compulsory deposit of at least part of the soldier's pay," a General Staff officer noted when enacting this decision.[22]

CLASSIFYING SOLDIERS FOR WAR DUTY

A soldier often purchased a war risk insurance policy before he even knew if he was headed to the front lines. To help the army match the masses of men pouring into the camps with the positions that suited them best, the Committee on Classification of Personnel designed forms that queried a man on his occupational background. Knowing whether a man could type, fix a truck, had training as an engineer, or could operate a telegraph was useful information. Compiling this data for each individual was a time-consuming process, however, and by the time classification cards reached camp commanders, field assignments had often already been made. Officers relied mostly on their own interviews with individual men and their personal judgment about a man's physical or mental abilities to fill available positions in the infantry, artillery, or quartermaster corps.

Intelligence Tests

The four hundred psychologists spread throughout the nation's domestic training camps tried to convince camp commanders that newly designed intelligence tests provided a more scientific and accurate way to assign men to specific branches or tasks. Over the course of the war, army psychologists administered nearly 1.7 million intelligence tests to incoming recruits, thanks to the early intervention of Robert M. Yerkes, a Harvard professor and president of the American Psychological Association who convinced the Surgeon General to adopt the tests. Army psychologists developed two sets of tests, an Alpha series for literate recruits and Beta exams for illiterate recruits or those with poor English-speaking skills. There were immediate problems with these exams. First, many commanders did not trust them. "I am not convinced that the stupid man, with proper training and leading, is necessarily going to give way in the trenches," wrote one officer.[23] Wartime psychologists never presented any direct evidence linking intelligence with performance on the battlefield, and many officers resented this intrusion by so-called experts into a domain traditionally under their control. Second, the tests tended to measure one's educational background and familiarity with middle-class values and lifestyles rather than native intelligence. One Alpha exam asked soldiers to correctly identify a dictaphone as a phonograph, Nabisco as a food product, and spare as a term used in bowling. Queries about brand name products and urban middle-class leisure activities resonated poorly with rural and urban working class men. Yet even illiterate men received a version of these same questions in a pictorial exam that asked them to draw in the missing features of particular scenes. Questions included adding a horn to a phonograph, a ball to the hand of a man in a bowling alley, and the filament to a light bulb. Men also completed exams that asked them to replicate patterns, solve math word problems, and recognize antonyms and synonyms. Other tests demanded that they unscramble words in a sentence to determine whether a phrase was true or false such as translating "certain some death of mean kinds sickness" to "some kinds of sickness mean certain death" and then determining that the statement was true. There was also a test of common sense that asked a soldier to decide if he won a million dollars whether he would pay off the national debt, contribute to various worthy charities, or give it all to some poor man (the correct answer was to contribute to various worthy charities). The testing conditions were also far from perfect. Examiners shouted instructions in English as they demonstrated the required task such as completing a maze. Soldiers had to change tasks every two minutes, making no allowances for men who had often left school at a young age and therefore read and wrote slowly. The resulting intimidation and confusion no doubt caused many poorly educated and foreign-speaking soldiers to score poorly.

Unsurprisingly, given the contents of the exams and the testing protocol, American soldiers performed poorly on these intelligence exams. Test results released after the war purported to show that the average white American soldier had a mental age of thirteen. This low score caused widespread concern throughout the country about the future of the nation. Few commentators questioned the validity of test results that seemingly provided scientific evidence for the superior intelligence of native-born white Americans. Widely reported figures claimed that the average mental age was 11.01 for Italians, 11.34 for Russians, 10.74 for Poles, and 10.41 for American-born blacks. Overall, nearly eighty percent of African Americans scored poorly enough to be labeled feeble-minded or, in the parlance of the time, as morons. The geographical distribution of scores indicated that Western and Northern states held more intelligent people than the Southern states, an area rife with children working in the fields at the expense of their education.

Because familiarity with mainstream American culture, a secondary school education, and a middle-class economic background were not necessarily the prerequisites for a successful military career, intelligence test results had limited usefulness for the army. After the war, however, public schools throughout the nation embraced intelligence testing as a useful way to measure the potential of their students. Measuring student aptitude has been a staple of the American school system ever since.

The army could dismiss the importance of intelligence test scores, but by revealing the limited educational background of many soldiers, intelligence tests uncovered an important deficiency that the army had to address. Literacy was essential to function in the modern army. Nearly 20 percent of the men tested took the Beta exam for illiterates. The majority of native-born white men had completed only seven years of school, while foreign-born and Southern black men averaged 4.7 years and 2.6 years of schooling respectively. Civilian reformers had long been aware of the relationship between child-labor and poor school attendance, and as the war was underway the Progressive-era campaign for mandatory schooling ended when Mississippi became the final state in the nation to pass a compulsory school attendance law. Absorbing a high concentration of semi-literate or illiterate men who could not read basic orders, understand signs in the trenches, or send letters home presented a thorny dilemma for the military. Army officials expected to teach men how to drill and handle firearms; they were surprised to discover that in many camps men also required instruction in reading and writing English. Some camp commanders established base schools for men to attend in their off-duty hours, while others turned to the Young Men's Christian Association (YMCA) to instruct soldiers or help them write letters home.

Selecting and Training Officers

Selecting and inducting enlisted men into the military was pointless if there were no officers there to lead them once they arrived in the training camps. During the war, there were several ways to become an officer. Men who had held commissions in the Regular and National Guard before the war provided the wartime army with a nucleus of trained leadership. They were not plentiful enough, however, to officer the entire wartime army. Consequently, the army had no choice but to quickly train the officers it needed to lead troops into battle. There was a limited precedent to follow in turning civilians into officers. In 1915, the War Department had supported General Leonard Wood when he ran a series of semi-official volunteer summer boot camps for 1,300 college students, bankers, and businessmen in the wake of the *Lusitania* sinking. Others had enthusiastically attended summer training camps organized by private groups such as the Military Training Camps Association. These pre-war camps held in Plattsburgh, New York, identified a contingent of upper and upper middle-class men eager to lead men into battle if the nation went to war. Before a single enlisted man stepped foot in a training camp, these men were among the 30,000 civilians and 7,957 Reserve Corps officers who headed off to attend one of sixteen Officers' Training Camps opened by the War Department in the spring of 1917. By the end of the war, the army had trained 182,000 officers, nearly half in three-month officer training camps. In addition, the army promoted 16,000 qualified enlisted men and the Medical Department and other specialized branches commissioned nearly 70,000 civilians, including doctors and engineers who possessed much needed expertise.

Most of the men attending officer training camps were college graduates or university students who abandoned their studies to volunteer for military service. The three month course primarily introduced these future officers to the rigors of military life and the rudimentary skills that they would soon have to impart to men under their command including close order drill, marksmanship, scouting, patrolling, elementary tactics, and for those headed to artillery or cavalry units, horsemanship. Their instructors, frequently just recently commissioned themselves, were often just one step ahead of their students. Charles L. Bolté had attended three pre-war summer training camps, but the young second lieutenant found himself staying up all night with the manual of a 45 automatic pistol to learn how to take it apart and put it back together so "that the next day I could sit down as if I knew all about it and try to teach this company how to do this very complicated task. It was a case of the blind leading the blind."[24]

Many an idealistic recruit discovered, as Frederick T. Edwards did, that "getting ready for war isn't all brass buttons and cheering." Instead, Edwards described an exhausting routine of marching, drilling, and studying that began at 5:15 A.M. in the morning and lasted until 10:00 P.M. at night. Edwards struggled to find some analogies to civilian life to help his sister understand his new military life. Imagine, he told her, hoeing in the rain and lying down in the mud every few minutes, "then, when you get tired, come in the house and sit on the edge of a bed and read a few columns of Webster's Dictionary (that's the nearest layman's book to a 'Drill Regulations')."[25] Not every officer candidate worked himself into exhaustion to perfect his military skills. At a later camp held in Fort Leavenworth, F. Scott Fitzgerald found time to write his first novel but often dozed off during lectures given by his unit commander, Captain Dwight D. Eisenhower.

Most officers continued their training in France where an elaborate system of officers' schools honed the skills of these "90-day wonders." At the end of the war, Brigadier General Harold B. Fiske, who ran the AEF training program, felt compelled to justify his decision to take officers away from their men for long stretches of time to complete these rigorous courses. Because the AEF fought its major battles in the fall of 1918, rather than in 1919 as Pershing initially expected, some of the army's most talented officers ended up spending much of the war behind the lines taking courses rather than leading men into battle. These unforeseen circumstances did not in Fiske's view diminish the importance of thoroughly training officers. "We frequently hear it said that the best school for war is war. No idea could, however, be more fallacious," Fiske wrote. "One has only to visualize the conditions at the front to appreciate how limited is the view of any man and how little opportunity he has to understand what is actually occurring and why . . . . If he cannot understand the how and the why of what is happening on the battlefield, he cannot there learn to make successful war. Service in battle hardens officers and men, an important part of training, but it does not school them."[26]

African American Officers and Segregated Divisions

The issue of commissioning African American officers also proved contentious throughout the war. In 1917, 622 men graduated from a hastily convened black officer training camp at Fort Des Moines, Iowa. Bowing to political pressure from the civil rights community, the War Department agreed to hold a camp for black officer candidates despite much internal disagreement over the leadership abilities of black men. Civil rights leaders also divided over the wisdom of supporting a segregated officers' training camp, which was at odds with their general insistence on integration. In the end organizations like the National Association for the Advancement of Colored People agreed to back the camp when it became clear that it was the only path open to black men who wanted to become officers. While these potential officers trained, the War Department debated what to do with the black enlisted men about to enter the army. After considering multiple proposals, the Secretary of War finally approved a plan that created one black combatant division from the 40,000 black conscripts scheduled to enter the army in October and another one from the National Guard units mobilized into federal service. Establishing black combatant divisions created a place for black officers to serve, because no one in the War Department ever considered letting black officers command white troops. As civil rights leaders suspected, there was a noticeable lack of official enthusiasm for black officers to lead even black troops into battle. Within black units, War Department policy mandated that white men fill all vacancies for generals, headquarters officers, regimental adjutants, supply officers, commanding officers of engineer, ammunition, and supply trains, and captains of field artillery units. For the duration of the war, black officers battled charges that they were unfit to command and more concerned with advancing their race than winning the war.

African American officers and men often developed strong bonds because they faced similar challenges as black men fighting for equal opportunity in a white man's army. Close ties between officers and men were also a hallmark of the National Guard, especially in units that had drilled or served together before the war. In peacetime, governors appointed commanding officers and the men often elected their line officers. When the federal government federalized the National Guard, the War Department assumed responsibility for selecting officers. Now, for the first time in American history, political clout was not enough to secure a commission.

The National Guard

Rather than respecting the traditions of the National Guard, the Regular Army professionals who controlled the planning and organizing of the wartime army wanted to use the war to weaken the National Guard's autonomy. Since the turn of the century, the Regular Army's drive to control or eliminate the National Guard had dominated army politics. The mandate to build a wartime army now gave the Regular Army an opportunity to fulfill its dream of professionalizing the National Guard. In their eyes, this primarily meant introducing a more professional relationship between officers and troops in National Guard units either by reducing fraternization between officers and their men or replacing National Guard officers.

Army inspectors visiting National Guard units inevitably attributed poor discipline to deficiencies intrinsic to the citizen-soldier ideal of the National Guard. These men, inspectors felt, were too familiar with their officers who failed to maintain an appropriate distance from their men. Common complaints about National Guard officers in official inspection reports criticized their tendency to explain orders to men, their willingness to let men walk by without saluting, and their tendency to look the other way if men went absent without leave for a few days. One inspector was particularly incensed when a battalion in the 31st Division simply failed to report for trench training the day after the Thanksgiving holiday and the unit's officers did nothing but express sympathy for the men's claim that they deserved the traditional long week-end holiday. French advisors working in the training camps offered a similarly dismissive appraisal of the National Guard, claiming that "false democratic sentiment" created lax discipline within these units and led to too much socializing between ranks after hours.[27] Although investigators tended to single out National Guard officers as lax disciplinarians, in reality many inexperienced National Army officers were also often too lenient with their men until they became more confident in their command.

Building Morale

One of an officer's primary duties was to build morale within his unit and cultivate faith in his abilities to lead. These two goals were sometimes at odds with one another. While men might like and appreciate a commander who called them by their first name and was not a harsh task master, they at the same time expected good leadership under fire. Many officers found other ways besides relaxing standards of discipline to build a strong bond with their units. Throughout the training camps, for instance, officers engaged their units in a series of competitions to create *esprit de corps*. Some regiments competed against each other to see who could reach a 100 percent subscription rate to the War Risk Insurance or Liberty Loan campaigns. Regimental boxing champions squared off against one another in camp boxing tournaments with their entire units cheering for them. Regiments also developed their own emblems, songs, and mascots that helped distinguish them from others.

TRAINING FOR ENLISTED MEN

If learning to give orders was an essential part of being an officer, then learning to obey orders unquestionably was the first requirement of military training for enlisted men. Recruits discovered that much of their army life was spent marching in unison around fields executing maneuvers such as "squads right" and "squads left." "I didn't know there were so many people on earth who didn't know their right hand from their left," one soldier wrote home after his first few weeks in camp.[28] In an earlier period, close order drill helped accustom soldiers to the formations that they would use in battle where marching shoulder to shoulder helped maintain discipline within the ranks and eased communication between an officer and his men. No Americans would go marching onto the Western Front in a tightly packed company of men, but the army still maintained the tradition of incessantly drilling its troops. Rather than learning specific drilling maneuvers essential to combat operations, the army now maintained that close order drill taught men to obey orders unquestionably and instilled the discipline that they needed for the long marches ahead in France. Despite the purported benefits of close order drill, soldiers were relieved when long awaited trips to the firing range interrupted their endless days of drilling.

Rifle Training

Pershing's operational preference for open over trench warfare set the tone for the training that American soldiers received during the war. The AEF commander believed that too much emphasis on trench warfare taught soldiers to cower defensively as they waited to fend off assaults. To force combat out of the trenches and onto the open battlefield where maneuver could make a decisive difference, Pershing advocated training American soldiers to rely on their rifles in combat. Like all Western Front commanders, Pershing believed that an army needed to go on the offensive to win. In outlining the general principles governing the training of the AEF, Pershing underscored that the aim of all training was to undertake a vigorous offensive. He acknowledged the "special features" of combat along the Western Front but maintained that the rifle and bayonet remained the principal weapon of the infantry soldier. "An aggressive spirit must be developed until the soldier feels himself, as a bayonet fighter, invincible in battle," Pershing directed.[29]

Pershing's emphasis on rifle training reflected his assumption that the rifle, rather than the machine gun or artillery, was the decisive weapon in combat. In his formulation, artillery support merely helped infantrymen advance but was not itself a key offensive weapon. To maximize the firepower of riflemen, Pershing formed divisions that were twice the size of their Allied counterparts, each with nearly 28,000 men. The hope was that their increased strength would give these units greater staying power in the field as the American Army surged forward. "With the deep and very powerful defense developed in the World War, no decisive stroke could be secured in battle without a penetration necessitating several days of steady fighting," Brigadier General James Harbord, Pershing's chief of staff, later wrote in his memoirs. "It was thus reasoned that the infantry of the division must be of such strength as to permit it to continue in combat for such a number of days that the continuity of battle would not be interrupted before decision was reached."[30]

Reflecting Pershing's emphasis on marksmanship, his training program put American recruits on the rifle range for long stretches of time. The increased urbanization and industrialization of the nation since the Civil War had an obvious impact on the shooting skills that recruits brought into the military. Harking from the mountains in Tennessee where he had grown up hunting wild turkeys, Alvin York was appalled by what he saw on the rifle range. "Them there Greeks and Italians and even some of our own city boys . . . missed everything but the sky," he noted after watching target practice in the 82nd Division.[31]

Bayonets, Boxing, and Other Preparations for Trench Warfare

Bayonet training supplemented rifle practice as another way to foster confidence and aggressiveness in troops. Killing from a distance with bullets was one thing, but bayonet fighting required training a soldier to put a blade of cold steel into the body of another human being. One training officer tried to prepare soldiers by explaining the situation thus:

> When you drive your bayonets into those dummies out there, think of them as representing the enemy. Think that he began the practice in this war of running bayonets through wounds, gasping-on-the-ground and defenseless prisoners.... They will crucify some of your men like they crucified the Canadians. So abandon all ideas of fighting them in a sportsmanlike way. You've got to hate them.[32]

Boxing instruction that mimicked the motions of using a bayonet in battle was another popular training camp exercise. Besides preparing men for hand-to-hand combat, time

Army officials used bayonet practice to create an aggressive fighting spirit among troops. (*Courtesy of the National Archives*)

in the ring improved a soldier's physical fitness and self-confidence. "After a man has boxed a few rounds he knows what this means and he stands up and takes what is coming to him if he is any kind of man," explained one boxing instructor to his class in Camp Custer, Michigan.[33]

The ideal program outlined by Pershing early in the war envisioned troops completing three months of training in rudimentary drills and maneuvers and becoming expert shots before heading to France to undertake another three months of more specialized training in trench and open warfare under the tutelage of experienced units before entering the line independently. Model training schedules called for soldiers to train seven hours a day, Monday through Friday, and four hours on Saturdays for sixteen weeks. The actual amount of training that an individual soldier received varied tremendously. Shortages of supplies and barracks forced the War Department to stagger new camp arrivals, meaning that men trickled into the camps unevenly for months. Recruits sometimes arrived at camps still under construction and spent their first days in the service building their own training trenches and rifle ranges. Many others in the fall of 1917 and winter of 1918 found themselves marching around fields carrying wooden rifles or sticks. While they still learned the basic maneuvers required by Pershing's training schedule, the experience did not make too many "feel" like soldiers. Even more importantly, equipment shortages lessened the amount of rifle practice a unit received before its deployment to France. In frustration, Congress launched five investigations into the functioning of the War Department. After a major re-organization in 1918, the chaos and confusion that characterized the first eight months at war lessened considerably, but not completely.

Men experienced constant interruptions to their training throughout the war. Hundreds of thousands of troops found themselves reassigned in the first few months of their military service. The army shifted men around to fill up Divisions about to leave for France, to keep the racial balance in camps at an acceptable level, or to provide specialist training. The steady flow of men in and out of units wreaked havoc with the training schedule. Men were either welcoming an infusion of new recruits, leaving to join new units themselves, being placed under quarantine to stop the spread of infectious diseases, getting new officers as former ones left to attend various officer training schools, or falling ill and being reassigned to a new unit once they regained their health. As if these obstacles were not enough, unusually harsh winter weather in 1918 brought training to a standstill throughout much of the country. For these reasons, the amount of training that a soldier received fluctuated greatly from troops in the First and Second Division who had nearly a year of training before entering the front lines to troops in 1918 who claimed that they entered battle after only firing a few shots on the rifle range in preparation. Remarkably, the AEF Inspector General reported, few untrained men refused to fight. Instead, "when issued rifles they asked to be shown 'how to work this thing so that they could go up and get a *boche* [the derogatory French term for German soldiers].'"[34] How many paid for such bravado with their lives or realized their mistake and joined the ranks of stragglers is unclear.

Besides creating competent marksmen, stateside training ideally introduced troops to using firepower, maneuver, cover, and concealment to advance. The training camp experience did not, however, completely ignore the realities of trench warfare. Soldiers received their first introduction to gas masks, and had to perform drills wearing them to overcome any feelings of claustrophobia. Childhoods filled with neighborhood baseball games proved apt preparation for learning to throw hand grenades. In some camps, commanders even took the initiative and relied on the advice of visiting British and

French instructors to construct elaborate trench systems where they taught troops the rudimentary skills of trench warfare such as protecting oneself from machine gun and artillery fire. When Pershing got word that camp and divisional commanders were training troops in these defensive tactics, he quickly ordered them to cease any instruction that interfered with his plans to emphasize open warfare. The usefulness of such training would become apparent to many troops soon enough.

Alongside this emphasis on developing individual marksmanship and combat skills, Pershing stressed the need to instill strict obedience in troops. The standards of discipline in the American Army must be those of West Point, he announced, setting a goal that his officers would never achieve. With so much to teach in such a short amount of time, a rigorous application of professional military disciplinary standards proved too burdensome in the face of stiff resistance from newly inducted citizen soldiers. Pershing predicted the problems that the army would face when he noted in September 1917 that "a prompt military salute is often misunderstood by our people (as a sign of subservience) but it simply emphasizes an aggressive attitude of mind and body that marks the true soldier."[35] Changing ideas about the role of an enlisted man in combat also helped convince the army that simple obedience was not enough. Increasingly, the army expected soldiers to do more than obey in battle. The 1917 version of the Infantry Drill Regulations, for instance, simply required a soldier to memorize the answers to questions asked during inspections. By May 1918, however, lessons from the limited fighting experiences of the AEF came trickling back to the United States, and now Infantry Drill regulations cautioned soldiers that during inspections they would have to learn to think for themselves when asked hypothetical questions about tactical situations, and to give the solution that "advances the line farthest with the least loss of men, time, and control."[36]

CONCLUSION

Overall, Pershing's training program reflected his belief that open warfare would break the trench deadlock and his heavy emphasis on infantry over artillery firepower put the American training regime at odds with the lessons that the Allies had learned in the three previous years. In France, troops received more exposure to trench warfare methods but in the end soldiers learned as much from their own experiences as they did from training camp lessons. The abbreviated nature of many soldiers' training programs guaranteed that learning in the field from more seasoned soldiers or from their own mistakes proved an essential component of every soldier's military education.

NOTES

1.   Walton Rawls, *Wake-up America! World War I and the American Poster* (New York: Abbeville Press, 1988), 112.

2.   D. Clayton James and Anne Sharp Wells, *America and the Great War, 1914–1920* (Wheeling, IL: Harlan Davidson, 1998), 34.

3.   James and Wells, *America and the Great War, 1914–1920*, 34.

4.   Jeanette Keith, *Rich Man's War, Poor Man's Fight: Race, Class and Power in the Rural South during the First World War* (Chapel Hill: University of North Carolina Press, 2004), 73.

5.   Keith, *Rich Man's War, Poor Man's Fight*, 72.

6.   Keith, *Rich Man's War, Poor Man's Fight*, 72.

7.   Robert H. Zieger, *America's Great War: World War I and the American Experience* (Lanham, Md. Rowman & Littlefield, 2000), 61.

8. David Kennedy, *Over Here: The First World War and American Society* (New York: Oxford University Press, 1980), 157.

9. Jennifer D. Keene, *Doughboys, the Great War and the Remaking of America* (Baltimore, Md.: Johns Hopkins University Press, 2001), 26.

10. Fred Baldwin, "The Enlisted Man During World War I," Ph.D. diss., Princeton University, 1964, 27.

11. John Whiteclay Chambers, II, *To Raise an Army: The Draft Comes to Modern America* (New York: The Free Press, 1987), 165.

12. Keene, *Doughboys, the Great War and the Remaking of America*, 15.

13. Christopher M. Sterba, *Good Americans: Italian and Jewish Immigrants during the First World War* (New York: Oxford University Press, 2003), 46.

14. Baldwin, "The Enlisted Man During World War I," 19.

15. Office of the Provost Marshal General, *Second Report of the Provost Marshal General to the Secretary of War on the Operations of the Selective Service System to December 20, 1918* (Washington, D.C.: GPO, 1919), 224.

16. Ronald Schaffer, *America in the Great War: The Rise of the War Welfare State* (New York: Oxford University Press, 1991), 178.

17. Sterba, *Good Americans*, 106.

18. Memorandum for Captain Perkins, Aug. 30, 1918, Camp Meade file; Entry 377, Record Group 165, National Archives, College Park, Maryland.

19. Sterba, *Good Americans*, 110.

20. Baldwin, "The Enlisted Man During World War I," 134.

21. Carol R. Byerly, *Fever of War: The Influenza Epidemic in the U.S. Army during World War I* (New York: New York University Press, 2005), 52.

22. Keene, *Doughboys, the Great War and the Remaking of America*, 73.

23. Jennifer D. Keene, "Intelligence and Morale in the Army of a Democracy: the Genesis of Military Psychology during the First World War,"*Military Psychology* 6 (1994): 237.

24. Edward Coffman, *The War to End All Wars: The American Military Experience in World War I* (New York: Oxford University Press, 1968), 57.

25. Coffman, *The War to End All Wars*, 55.

26. Brigadier General H. B. Fiske, "Report of the G-5," American Expeditionary Forces, France, June 30, 1919, Entry 22, Record Group 120, National Archives, College Park, Maryland.

27. Jennifer D. Keene, "Uneasy Alliances: French Military Intelligence and the American Army during the First World War," *Intelligence and National Security* 12: 1 (Spring 1998): 20.

28. Baldwin, "The Enlisted Man During World War I," 92.

29. "The General Principles Governing the Training of Units of the American Expeditionary Forces," October 1917, file #7541–60, Entry 296, Record Group 165, National Archives College Park, Maryland.

30. James G. Harbord, *The American Army in France, 1917–1918* (Boston: Little, Brown, 1936), 103.

31. David. D. Lee, *Sergeant York: An American Hero* (Lexington: University Press of Kentucky, 1985), 18.

32. Schaffer, *America in the Great War*, 179.

33. Keene, *Doughboys, the Great War and the Remaking of America*, 41.

34. Keene, *Doughboys, the Great War and the Remaking of America*, 47.

35. Pershing to Adjutant General, Telegram No. 178-S, September 24, 1917, in "Report of G-5," June 30, 1919, Appendix no. 31, 10; folder 246, Entry 22, RG 120, National Archives, College Park, Maryland.

36. Kenneth E. Hamburger, *Learning Lessons in the American Expeditionary Forces* (Washington, D.C.: U.S. Army Center of Military History, 1997), 23–24.

3 MORALS AND MORALE

The willingness of men to risk their lives in defense of their country often depended on maintaining good morale in the ranks. The army sought to build morale by educating men about the war, cultivating *esprit de corps* to create a sense of community in the ranks, and providing spiritual reassurance that God was on their side. The army clearly saw the benefits of leading men into battle who believed in the cause. The general public, however, worried about more than winning the war. In the past, military service exposed soldiers to a host of vices such as drinking, gambling, and prostitution. Social reformers hoped to replace these traditional leisure activities with more wholesome pursuits. During the First World War, therefore, the army worked hard to safeguard both the morale and morals of the men under its command. As the army worked to develop sound minds and bodies, soldiers often devised their own ways to bond with one another and enjoy their off-duty hours. The programs that army officials created and soldiers' reactions to them formed an important part of daily life experiences in the wartime army.

BUILDING MORALE

Training American soldiers to fight effectively on the battlefield meant more than instilling proper respect for military authority and conveying critical technical skills; American soldiers also needed a reason to fight. By 1917, low morale and mutiny plagued the British and the French armies. Allied advisors suggested that the Americans learn from their mistakes and institute a comprehensive political education program to ensure that troops went to war with the proper political convictions. Faced with the overwhelming task of formulating its basic training program, the army pushed these suggestions aside and instead concentrated on perfecting the military expertise of incoming troops. It took until May 1918 before a core of reformers within the army finally convinced the War Department to follow this advice and create the Morale Division.

Recruitment and War Propaganda

Well before the creation of a formal agency charged with promoting a high sense of purpose among the troops, the War Department and army trainers recognized the importance of giving men a reason to fight. Initially, the War Department relied on recruitment posters to encapsulate the nation's wartime goals for soldiers. The short, pithy phrases that adorned these posters were often less significant than the imagery they conveyed. These posters served the dual purpose of both enticing men into the service and underscoring why men needed to serve at all. Even those who waited for the draft, therefore, ended up receiving their first dose of political indoctrination from the recruitment and war bond posters that soon became an omnipresent part of the American urban landscape.

Wartime propaganda posters relied on messages of patriotism, shame, manliness, hate, and sympathy to rally young men to arms. A 1917 Army recruiting poster titled "Destroy this mad brute" depicted the Germans as savage beasts who raped, pillaged, and killed. In the poster, Europe lay in ruins behind a gorilla-like German soldier who carried the limp and partially clothed figure of lady liberty as he walked across the Atlantic and reached American soil. This bestial image of Germany linked the German soldier's crimes against civilians with his government's violation of international law. In addition to breeding hate for an uncivilized enemy who threatened the very fabric of Western civilization, this poster also suggested that men needed to fight to protect the United States from invasion. Although the idea that German troops were on their way across the Atlantic was far-fetched, German U-boats were patrolling American waters on the lookout for merchant and troop ships. The club of *kulture* that the ape-like soldier carried also reminded Americans to stay alert for the contaminating influences of German culture (music, language, literature) within the United States.

Many propaganda posters depicted honorable military service as a way to demonstrate healthy masculine virility. One recruitment poster asked men to consider "On Which Side of the Window Are You?" The image of a well-dressed, but slightly effeminate, man hiding behind the curtain of his darkened home as he watches a group of robust, uniformed men march proudly together in the bright sunlight played on the fears of many middle and upper-class men that the comforts of modern life had robbed them of their masculinity. Before the war, a rash of articles in popular magazines fretted over the emasculating effect of urban and industrial life on American men. Rather than celebrating this man's willingness to stand against the crowd, this poster depicts him as shamefully missing his chance to take his proper place alongside his countrymen. As one Princeton-educated pilot put it, within the social circles he frequented "to be young and not in uniform in those days was a disgrace."[1] This poster accurately depicted the cultural malaise that had set in among the nation's well-to-do and the ways that peer-pressure induced college students to enlist immediately.

Another recruitment poster made a clear offer to those concerned about manliness by declaring "The United States Army builds Men" above the image of a uniformed soldier who stood deep in thought before a globe, undoubtedly contemplating the worldwide adventures in store for him. Behind the soldier stood ghostly figures representing skilled crafts, knightly character, and manly physique, presenting a perfect trilogy of the physical, moral, and financial benefits one gained from military service. One sergeant admitted that like many others, he had given little thought to the Kaiser or German U-boat attacks when he enlisted. "We men, most of us young, were simply fascinated by the prospect of adventure and heroism. Most of us, I think, had the feeling that life, if we survived, would run in the familiar, routine channel. Here was our one great chance for

Tell That to the Marines! Poster by James Montgomery Flagg (*Courtesy of the Library of Congress*)

excitement and risk. We could not afford to pass it up."[2] Before these men settled into lives as farmers, mill hands, or accountants, they resolved to see the world and partake in the great adventure that the war seemed to offer.

Propaganda posters also relied heavily on patriotism to motivate men to fight the Germans. The ubiquitous image of Uncle Sam pointing his finger at the viewer above the slogan "I Want You" was introduced during the war. Ostensibly intended to entice men to enlist, the image and slogan worked equally well to generate acceptance of the draft. When the army closed voluntary enlistments in December 1917, the navy, marines, air service, and various specialized branches continued to accept volunteers until August 1918. The recruitment posters designed to attract men to these more specialized branches reiterated the reasons why men should join the fight, and indirectly sent their messages to conscripts waiting for their induction notices. "Tell That to the Marines," proclaimed a poster designed by James Montgomery Flagg, which depicted a man angrily taking off his jacket in preparation for a fight after reading in the newspaper that "Huns Kill Women and Children!" A Naval recruitment poster emphasized civilian support for the war by showing a mother who willingly offered her son to Uncle Sam with the simple statement, "Here he is, Sir." The expectations of Americans at home often influenced more than a soldier's initial decision to enlist. As Sergeant Norman Summers lay in a hospital bed recovering from a gas attack, he contemplated why soldiers fought. Summers concluded, "it is because our people back home expect it of us." His parents, he continued, "wouldn't want to say after the war is over that their son didn't go into the front lines and now they won't have to say it."[3]

Propaganda posters aroused feelings of hate and patriotism that army instructors continued to stoke during a recruit's indoctrination into military life. From the moment that a soldier passed through the training camp gates, he was subject to nearly constant exhortations to hate the enemy. Daily lectures underscored the inhumanity of the Germans, informing recruits that

> We know that in certain Belgian towns young girls were dragged out of their homes into the streets and publicly violated by . . . German beasts. We know that Belgian children clinging to their parents had their hands cut off and their parents murdered before their eyes. . . . We know that the German soldier commonly cut off the breasts of the woman he or someone else had violated and murdered. He wanted them as souvenirs. . . . We know that wounded men have been mutilated and in at least one instance, crucified.[4]

From lectures like these, it was no surprise to hear veterans later recalling, as Arthur E. Yensen did, that American solders were "brainwashed into thinking all Germans were rats that ought to be killed."[5]

Teaching Soldiers about the War

Fighting to avenge crimes against civilians, fulfilling the expectations of relatives, or carrying out one's patriotic duty gave soldiers only a partial understanding of why the nation fought. The administration's overall war goals remained remote to many soldiers. Private Henry Van Lauginham wrote somewhat sheepishly to his family that he spent more time worrying about himself than thinking about the larger purpose of the war. It was easy, he admitted, to lose sight of the larger issues "in the days' petty worries."[6] Officers censoring soldiers' letters continually lamented the absence of any ideological convictions. Soldiers instead concentrated on relating details about their health, minor discomforts of military service and family gossip. "Do you think this business is being brought home as strongly as possible to our people?," Second Lieutenant Donald Dinsome wondered after reading a batch of such letters. "I know that nine out of every ten of our enlisted men do not know what they are fighting for, the idea is simply to kill the Boche."[7]

To some army officials, simply building hate was not enough. "The citizen-soldier of a democracy is entitled to understand the cause in which he fights, and the reasons and principles underlying the policy of the government," Colonel Edward L. Munson asserted.[8] Throughout the winter of 1918, Munson worked with like-minded officials in the War Plans Division and Intelligence Division to create a formal morale program that placed a morale officer in every combat unit. In the spring, these officials convened an "Informal Conference on Morale" that included Assistant Secretary of War Frederick Keppel. Keppel subsequently ordered the War Plans Division to examine morale programs within the Allied armies. At the end of this comprehensive study in May 1918, the War Plans Division created the Morale Division, which became an independent bureau in the fall of 1918.

The Morale Division only worked in stateside training camps, where it tried to expand soldiers' ideological commitment to the war. Morale officers disseminated propaganda through camp newspapers and prepared numerous lectures for officers to give their men. Judging from veterans' postwar recollections, soldiers at least memorized a few key phrases from presidential addresses that seemed to sum up the nation's war goals. When asked why they fought in the war, these veterans replied that they were engaged in a crusade "to save the world for democracy" or that it was a "war to end wars."[9]

Yet soldiers did not rely solely on military officers to provide them with reasons to fight. Once a man was under fire, a new logic began to take hold about why one was fighting. "I was hesitating," one private admitted, the first time he was in combat "because I didn't really know if I wanted to kill someone. Then I heard a bullet whistle by my head."[10] In France, investigators behind the lines routinely questioned wounded and ill soldiers on their feelings about the war and the Allies. Interviews with recovered soldiers revealed a wide range of feelings about their imminent return to the front. Some, an investigator reported, wanted to go back because "they have personal scores to settle with the Germans now that they have been wounded or gassed, while others want to go back on general principles and still others because they feel they have greater

Camp commanders often had troops create formations like this human Statue of Liberty for souvenir photos of their training camp experience to remind them that the war was a crusade "to save the world for democracy." (*Courtesy of the National Archives*)

liberty and more privileges at the front than they have enjoyed behind the lines."[11] The desire to prove one's bravery or not let down comrades in arms also became strong inducements to fight. Going into combat for the first time, one private looked around and decided that "since the other fellows were not showing yellow" he would stick together with them. "All of us were afraid in a sort of way, in that we didn't know what we were getting into and didn't know what to expect. But in order to keep our personal reputation up . . . we were more afraid to go to the rear than to the Front."[12]

The superstitions and rumors about the enemy that circulated among the troops also gave them ample reason to hate the Germans and fight to avenge their supposed wrongs. American soldiers quickly appropriated many tales of German treachery initially popularized by British soldiers. Stories about underhanded German battlefield behavior reinforced the treacherous image of the enemy first introduced to troops in the training camps. These soldiers' tales recounted incidents of German soldiers who disguised themselves as wounded French soldiers or Red Cross workers then lay on the battlefield and called for help to lure rescuing Allied troops into the direct range of German machine guns. Another tale described German soldiers who pretended to surrender in order to draw Allied soldiers out into the open. Besides keeping their fighting spirit up, American troops used these stories to pass valuable information to one another that helped them survive at the front. It was handy to learn, for example, that German troops booby-trapped dugouts or poisoned wells as they withdrew.

The network of morale workers who filtered out throughout the training camps in the summer of 1918 never crossed the Atlantic. With few officers to spare and skeptical that morale officers did much good, Pershing instead maintained that it was an officer's responsibility to cultivate the proper frame of mind among the men under his command. In his view, the YMCA provided ample recreation for the soldiers while their unit officers maintained morale in the ranks. Morale officers remained at home, but some vaudeville performers did cross the Atlantic to offer free entertainment for the troops. An evening of diversion, preferably one that included American women, was in Pershing's view a good tonic for the homesickness that often created low spirits among the men. Out of the 700 entertainers who traveled overseas, the most famous was Elsie Janis, dubbed the "Sweetheart of the AEF." Janis performed anywhere from two to seven shows each day for American troops in Paris, treating them to a musical comedy revue that included songs, dances, impersonations, and acrobatics. Janis connected well with her soldier audiences by beginning every show with the shout, "Are we downhearted?" to which the audience always roared in response: "No!" and incorporating the song "All We Do Is Sign The Payroll, And We Never Get a God Damned Cent" into her act. In appreciation of Janis's hard work, Pershing provided her with an army limousine driven by a soldier chauffeur and an unlimited pass to visit troops wherever she liked. "If you can give our men this sort of happiness, you are worth an Army Corps," Pershing told her.[13] By the fall of 1918, Janis could no longer afford to perform for free in Paris and accepted an extended engagement in London. She continued to send messages to the troops in France, however. "Congratulations on your big show," Janis wrote as the Meuse-Argonne campaign began. "Sorry not to be in the cast. Hope to join the company in Berlin."[14]

The Soldiers' Newspaper: *The Stars and Stripes*

Pershing refused to let the Morale Division operate overseas, but he did make one concession to those officials who wanted to build morale systematically in the AEF. He agreed to let Brigadier General D. E. Nolan, who headed the AEF's Intelligence Bureau, circulate a soldier's newspaper called *The Stars and Stripes*. Nolan expected the paper to keep morale high in the AEF by giving men the news they wanted from home and a bird's eye view of military operations. By helping soldiers see that they were part of something bigger than themselves, Nolan hoped to counter soldiers' tendency to become consumed by the day-to-day challenges and discomforts they faced. The editorial staff of *The Stars and Stripes* consisted of a sergeant, three privates, and an officer. Many of the soldiers who worked for the paper went on to become famous newspapermen including the theater critic Alexander Woollcott and sports writer Grantland Rice. Harold Ross who later founded *The New Yorker* magazine and Stephen Early, a press secretary to President Franklin Delano Roosevelt, both worked for *The Stars and Stripes* during the war. From the beginning, *The Stars and Stripes* urged soldiers to write with contributions and comments. This "is your paper," the editor told readers in the first edition, promising that *The Stars and Stripes* would be "lively, slightly irreverent, [and] plain-spoken." It was not a propaganda sheet, he assured soldiers, "as Yanks are all skeptics who can smell bunk a mile off."[15]

The Stars and Stripes began publication on 8 February 1918 and appeared every Friday until 13 June 1919, for a total of seventy-one weeks. At the height of its popularity, the eight-page newspaper boasted a circulation of 560,000, including 70,000 copies distributed in the United States.[16] Eventually a staff of over 300 produced the paper's content and layout, receiving help from the *London Daily Mail*, which printed the paper at its Paris plant, and a French association that supplied the paper. The paper was not free (except for hospitalized soldiers), but cost fifty centimes in France, sixpence in Britain, or ten cents in the United States. Charging for the paper added to its legitimacy, the editorial staff contended, since "no American ever did or ever will respect reading matter that is thrown at him like a department store bulletin."[17] The funds collected made *The Stars and Stripes* self-sufficient and bolstered the editors' claims that the paper truly belonged to the soldiers who funded its operations.

The Stars and Stripes contained mostly sports news, humorous stories about the absurdities and inconveniences of army life, and vignettes that highlighted the accomplishments of individuals and units. To a remarkable degree, the paper remained editorially independent during the war. Every Monday, the editors were required to send that week's copy by courier to a GHQ Board of Control that reviewed the material. Few controversies over copy arose during the war, but the paper did face occasional pressure to adopt a more serious and formal tone. When the commanding general of the Paris district complained about the large amount of slang in the paper, he received a quick rebuke from Nolan. "*The Stars and Stripes* is essentially by the soldiers and for the soldiers . . . ," he replied. "The use of slang in the interpretation of subjects in themselves serious is the surest way of getting the average soldier to read the article."[18] With Nolan's support, the paper remained written in doughboy vernacular.

The newspaper provided its readers with constant reminders of the war's larger purpose to help build pride in the Allied cause. The Allied purpose was underscored by cartoons like "Now-all together boys" which showed figures representing Britain, France, and the United States getting out a car marked democracy to roll the boulder of autocracy off a mountain road called civilization. *The Stars and Stripes* sometimes adopted a preachy tone when trying to encourage soldiers to tow the line. In one such editorial titled "How to Lengthen the War," the paper's editors lambasted an enlisted man for siphoning off some gas from a reserve tank to wash his pants. "The private in question would probably fight if you accused him of betraying his friends in the trenches," the editors preached, "Yet gasoline means airplanes, and airplanes mean dead Germans, and dead Germans mean live Americans."[19]

Attacks against the Kaiser were commonplace; *The Stars and Stripes* usually referred to him as "William the Coward." Initially, the paper's editors readily reprinted rumors of German atrocities including a story that Americans had found German

American soldiers' disdain for the German Kaiser is well-represented in this cartoon published in *The Stars and Stripes*. (*Courtesy of the Library of Congress*)

machine gunners chained to their guns at Chateau-Thierry. When GHQ subsequently prohibited the paper from publishing unverified accounts of atrocities, the paper grudgingly admitted that the story had proven false. Nonetheless, the paper's editors asserted, "that is only a minor detail. The main fact is that all Germany is chained to Kaiserism, chained to a wild madness without a parallel in the world's history."[20]

The normal news "beats" covered by the paper included collecting General Orders and other official information from Pershing's headquarters in Chaumont. Written in a legalistic style that was often incomprehensible to the average soldier, the paper's reporters rewrote these orders in language that most soldiers could understand. The editors of *The Stars and Stripes* did not restrain themselves from putting an occasional irreverent spin on official orders. "'Soldiers who are married and do not state the fact are subject to penalties,' says an American dispatch to the *Daily Mail*. Especially, we surmise, if certain parties find it out," one item read.[21] Reporters also paid a weekly visit to the Service of Supply headquarters in Tours. From these visits, reporters might "emerge with the exciting announcement of a new overseas cap, of a contemplated tobacco ration, or of a change in the construction of imported toilet paper from the cylindrical to the rectangular as an essential step in the conservation of tonnage," joked Corporal John T. Winterich, a founding member of *The Stars and Stripes* who had worked in civilian life as an editor of the *Springfield Republican*.[22] Despite the tongue-in-cheek nature of Winterich's comment, these possible changes to their daily routines did interest troops. Besides tapping official military sources for information, *Stars and Stripes* reporters published news about the activities of the social welfare organizations working overseas with American troops such as the YMCA, American Red Cross, Salvation Army, Knights of Columbus, the Jewish Welfare Board, and the American Library Association.

Next in importance, after instilling hate of the enemy and informing soldiers about military matters, was keeping men connected to events at home. A stateside correspondent sent domestic news to the paper's editors in Paris, including updates regarding Congressional investigations into overseas mail delays, progress in the suffrage movement, and the spread of prohibition throughout the United States. For a while, the paper published sports news from home but dropped the coverage when controversy arose over draft-age sports stars freely pursuing lucrative sports careers. The sports idiom remained, however, as articles repeatedly linked prowess at baseball with hand-grenade throwing, boxing thrusts with bayonet fighting, and compared the nervousness that a soldier felt when heading to the front with "a sensation much like that just before you go into a football game-the same nervous tension, the same doubts about whether you will be able to hold your bit of the line."[23] Sports coverage in *The Stars and Stripes* resumed after the armistice, but focused on sporting competitions with the AEF.

The morale-building goals of the paper were apparent in the coverage given to rear-area units. Throughout the war, poor morale in laboring and stevedore units was a pressing problem. To improve the flow of supplies through the ports and to the front, GHQ launched a contest among all stevedore companies to see which unit could handle the most supplies within a set period of time. Charts showing the progress of the competing units appeared in *The Stars and Stripes* for weeks. The winners received front-page coverage for their feats, along with special arm bands to wear, leaves, and a host of camp privileges.

The editors of *The Stars and Stripes* filed away any serious complaints that they received, but they did print petty and minor gripes from soldiers. Without them, editor

Captain Mark Watson argued, troops would start seeing *The Stars and Stripes* as nothing more than an official bulletin board. By providing a way for men to harmlessly let off some steam, the paper gained credibility as a true voice of the average soldier and perhaps prevented grumblings from taking a more mutinous turn. To that end, the paper mounted minor campaigns to protest unjust army policies or capricious officers whose actions appeared to infringe on the rights of enlisted men. Hearing that company officers in one overseas camp forbid their men from writing more than one letter a week, *The Stars and Stripes* angrily denounced the officers' attempt to relieve themselves of constant censorship duties. This prohibition, *The Stars and Stripes* noted with satisfaction, countermanded an AEF general order stating that writing "home frequently and regularly, to keep in constant touch with family and friends, is one of the soldier's most important duties."[24] The paper also criticized officers who failed to properly return enlisted men's salutes.

Indignant protestations were the exception rather than the rule. More commonly, *The Stars and Stripes* relied on wit to make good-natured jabs at enlisted men's superiors. The mess sergeant and the unappetizing food he served at most meals were regularly mocked in both prose and poetry. "An army cook is known by the mess he makes," quipped the editors.[25] Corned beef, a staple of army cooking, was detested by most soldiers, who employed a host of derogatory nicknames when referring to the canned meat such as "corned Willie," "monkey meat" or "slum" in the disparaging verse they wrote. Second Lieutenants, known as "2d Loots" or "shavetails," were another favorite target of ridicule. A shavetail's position in the army was particularly difficult jibed one article, "with mere majors and captains ranking him out of his bed or girl at every turn."[26] Noncommissioned officers received their fair share of comeuppance. Soldiers reveled in trading stories of hard-boiled sergeants, or "Tops," who verbally abused their men. These jibes often contained a modicum of grudging respect for a demanding sergeant who set high standards. When Sergeant Ben Gold was killed in September 1918, the 306th Infantry Regiment memorialized him in the pages of *The Stars and Stripes* with this tribute: "As strict as iron, as tough as rust,/A bulging bean, a hard-boiled crust,/ He growled like hell, he cussed like smoke,/Some woof/Was our top-kicker."[27]

The paper never, however, criticized the highest-ranking levels of leadership within the AEF or the strategy pursued. Instead, the paper tended to lionize the army's commanding generals. One published anecdote recalled a general's surprise visit to the front lines where he chatted amicably with privates and sergeants. Major-General Joseph T. Dickman of the Third Division (who went unnamed in the story) proved to have a heart of gold. "That division did its share, and paid its price for the doing, when it helped drive the Hun back across the Marne. That night someone softly opened the general's door, and then as softly closed it. And the word went around that he sat with his face buried in his hands, and his frame quivering with sobs," the paper revealed.[28]

In the wake of the armistice, the paper became bolder and published a host of soldiers' complaints concerning officer privileges and poor living conditions in the embarkation camps. This increased criticism touched a nerve in GHQ. In January 1919, the paper's editors received word that "the Commander-in-Chief has noticed recently that *The Stars and Stripes* is criticizing the AEF. Some of these criticisms have appeared in a humorous vein. You will take proper steps to the end that no article containing a criticism of any kind appears in *The Stars and Stripes*."[29] Captain Mark Watson (who would later win a Pulitzer Prize for his reporting for the *Baltimore Sun*) ably defended the paper's editorial freedom, noting that as soon as the paper stopped printing the "humorous, harmless grouches of the soldiers just at that time will *The Stars and Stripes* be regarded as a GHQ organization." To fulfill its purpose, the paper had to remain "a means of free expression for the soldier." Watson won this round, yet the editors did agree to cease their criticism of sanitation in the embarkation camps. AEF Headquarters argued that by repeatedly printing the same concerns about disease in the camps, *The Stars and Stripes* was creating unnecessary apprehension among troops headed to the camps. With a third wave of influenza sweeping the muddy and dirty camps, soldiers had good reason for concern. The editors, however, accepted official assurances that the improvements in sanitation and housing were imminent.

Using the paper to give soldiers a voice involved more than airing their complaints. *The Stars and Stripes* mostly published doughboy verse, letters from troops, and cartoons that focused on the lighter side of military life. Private William Hunter wrote to inquire whether he should mimic the style of military orders in his letters home to his sweetheart, providing an example of such a missive:

From: William Hunter, Private.

To: Miss Katie Cullin.

Subject: Regards.

1. Attention is called to the fact that since my arrival in France my feelings have undergone no change. I am still yours.
2. Answer, by indorsement [sic], at once, if my photo is still on your bureau.
3. I hope George Goldfish is drafted.[30]

The editors advised Hunter to stick to the traditional love letter format.

The discomforts and strangeness of French culture and language elicited many humorous poems and limericks from American troops, including one that mocked Americans' efforts to pronounce the surname of the Allied Commander in Chief, Ferdinand Foch.

> "It's Pronounced Foch"
> The French will think it is a joke
>   When bungling Yanks pronounce it Foch,
> Yet will we make a sadder botch
>   If we attempt to call it Foch;
> Nor can we fail to pain and shock
>   Who boldly try to say it Foch.
> In fact, we have to turn to Boche
>   To find the word that rhymes with Foch.[31]

Speaking in doughboy vernacular also had its downside, especially when it led to the inclusion of racist dialect jokes. *The Stars and Stripes* offered contradictory commentary on the contribution of black soldiers to the war effort. Informing its readers that several black soldiers had received the French *croix de guerre*, the paper's editors expressed admiration for the "slaves of a century ago [who] are defending their American citizenship on a larger battlefield. Now is their first chance to show themselves before the whole world as good and brave soldiers, all."[32] If this story reaffirmed that African American soldiers were making speedy progress in realizing that goal, the dialect stories that the paper regularly featured sent exactly the opposite message. *The Stars and Stripes*, complained First Lieutenant Charles L. Holmes, "when speaking of the American Negro Soldier, seems to find space only for ridicule, degrading remarks, and prejudicial propaganda."[33] Holmes was objecting to stories like "Around the Sibley Stove" in which

> One Negro soldier in the Argonne was as pale as circumstances would permit, and visibly shaken.
> "It's de tawkin' shells what gits me," he confided to a lieutenant.
> "Nonsense, Sam; shells don't talk."
> "Don' you tawk that away to me.I kin hear 'em plain as day. Four dese old G.I. cans jus' whizzed by and I heard 'em say: 'Niggah, you ain't going back to Ala-BAM!'"[34]

Major Guy Viskniskki, the officer in charge of *The Stars and Stripes*, rejected Holmes's contention that such stories degraded black soldiers. These vignettes, he insisted, were conceived "just in the same spirit that no one is making fun of the white man when we print letters of Henry's Pal to Henry. In these stories Henry and his pal are both made to appear ridiculous, but no one thinks that there is any desire to degrade." Dialect stories did not hurt black troops he contended because they improved race relations within the army by giving whites "a larger liking for the colored man."[35] Viskniskki declined to consider the impact of dialect stories on black troops.

The paper was more than a joke-sheet, however. As the army began fighting, more coverage focused on conditions at the front. One soldier wrote to ask if a gas victim was entitled to a wound stripe, receiving an affirmative reply. The tone of these articles was unsentimental but remained generally positive. Reporters reflected on the hardships that soldiers had overcome on the battlefield, the strong friendships they had made with French families along the way, and their overall determination to achieve victory. One reporter ventured out to visit the 26th Division as it completed its training in trench warfare in Seicheprey. Traveling in the rain by car, First Lieutenant Charles Phelps Cushing set out along a pitch-black road with no headlights to illuminate the path. After an hour's drive, Cushing and his driver reached the crest of a hill where small lights flickered like fireflies in the distance. "Those are the big guns," the driver explained. He paused; then whistled. 'Lots of 'em tonight. Something on, I guess.'" They pushed on to a ruined village square, where an officer told them to abandon the car and seek immediate cover in a sheltered part of the ruins. Likening the ensuing shell bursts to Fourth of July celebrations at home, Cushing put on rubber hip boots and followed a wooden board sidewalk into the trenches. Following his guide, Cushing quickly lost all sense of direction in the maze of trenches and contented himself with fleeting glimpses of trench life: snipers at work, men carrying coffee to the front lines, and silent doughboys waiting with hand grenades and automatic rifles in case the barrage signaled the beginning of an attack. Cushing made it to within 200 yards of the German trenches, and with strict instructions to remain silent, he peered out at No Man's Land through a periscope. "The scenic features were simple, consisting chiefly of tangles of wire and a few flashes of gun fire from the dark background," Cushing reported.[36] Early touristy accounts like this from the trenches helped soldiers training or working in the rear visualize the conditions at the front, while the straightforward style underscored that war was serious business.

Once the Americans began taking heavy casualties, anecdotes and features focused mostly on the manly courage that soldiers exhibited under fire. In a typical incident related by the paper, a soldier with seven machine-gun bullets, one in his leg, three in his chest, and three in his side asked for a pen and paper to write a letter to his family. "Dear Mother," the soldier wrote, "We made an attack on the Germans today and drove them five miles. I am in a hospital tonight. I was slightly wounded in the leg."[37] The paper provided little detail on wounds or treatment, focusing instead on the stoic demeanor of men undergoing painful treatments. "'What's this fellow got, lieutenant?' asked someone peering over the surgeon's shoulder. 'Guts,' said the lieutenant respectfully," read one such item.[38] The most explicit mention of the war's toll came through the tributes that units paid to their fallen comrades in the pages of the newspaper. These memorial letters or anecdotes did more than honor individual bravery; they also imbued these deaths with broader significance. The desire to die a meaningful death ran strong throughout the ranks, best expressed by the poem that Sergeant John Fletcher Hall submitted for publication titled "A Prayer From the Ranks."

Grant us this prayer: that the toll that we pay
    Shall not have been levied in vain;
That when it is sheathed, the sword of the world
    May never see sunlight again
When the roses shall climb o'er the crumbling
       trench
    And the guns are all silenced in rust,
May War find a grace where none shall disturb
    Through the ages his mouldering dust![39]

The war inspired many other soldier poets to put pen to paper, and every day brought a fresh delivery of poems for *The Stars and Stripes* to consider for publication. At the end of the war, *The Stars and Stripes* published *Yanks: A Book of A.E.F. Verse*, revealing that poetry remained a potent vehicle of expression for this generation of soldiers. Most soldier poets were unknown writers whose wartime poems were their first and only published works. *The Stars and Stripes* also published the poems of better-known writers such as Joyce Kilmer and Rudyard Kipling. Before Kilmer was killed in August 1918, he had penned a poem titled "The Woods Called Rouge-Bouquet" to commemorate the nineteen men killed by a shell blast during his regiment's first stint in the trenches. Read at their memorial service and published in *The Stars and Stripes*, the poem championed the heroic sacrifice made by the men.

The Stars and Stripes worked hard to instill pride in hard-won American victories on the battlefield, although the paper warned troops against over-confidence. "Let us not claim to more than we can, but to let our performance surpass our claims," the editors advised.[40] Throwing caution to the wind at the war's conclusion, *The Stars and Stripes* gave free rein to a bit of hyperbole. "The story of American valor along the Meuse and in the Argonne will shine radiantly through the ages. It will glow in the printed word as long as men read the deeds of their fathers, as long as the passion on liberty swells in the bosom of mankind," the editors proclaimed.[41]

The paper proved so lucrative that it boasted $700,000 in profits at the end of the war—money that the paper's editors wanted to donate to an orphan relief fund. The AEF judge advocate, however, ordered the money returned to the U.S. Treasury because the profits came from labor and material provided by the U.S. government. Advertisement fees helped fill the paper's coffers during the war. The Board of Control prohibited any ads for liquor, patent medicines, or political causes. Companies selling tobacco, personal hygiene products, and clothes eagerly promoted their products in *The Stars and Stripes*, submitting more ads than the paper could print. Besides doing their patriotic duty, American firms saw an opportunity to attract new customers and reach a national readership.

Advertisements reflected soldiers' distinct needs for soap, razors, socks, shoes, and foot powders. Companies marketed new devices such as the "Army-Navy Ear-Drum Protector" that shielded the eardrum during shell attacks. Wyse Pipe advertised its specially designed trench pipe that allowed soldiers to smoke contentedly when out in the rain and wind. Boston Garters held up socks wonderfully, the company assured soldiers, reminding them that "wrinkled socks make sore feet, sore feet make poor hikers, poor hikers never get there."[42] The new popularity of the wristwatch as a practical replacement for pocket watches was reflected in the number of advertisements devoted to displaying the wide array of available styles. Numerous ads for tobacco and chewing gum, both favorites among the troops, appeared. Bull Durham sold sacks of tobacco that soldiers could roll to make their own cigarettes. The company assured the troops that its complete stock was headed overseas, a sacrifice willingly made by people at home. British and French restaurants, clothing stores, and portrait studios also advertised in *The Stars and Stripes*. Many companies designed entertaining ads that fit well with the offbeat humor of the newspaper. Lowneys Chocolates developed a unique list of slogans such as "Lowney's Chocolates–Dig In!"; "Not a 'dud' in the box!"; "Get some before they Argonne! Ouch!"[43] When the war ended, advertisers began to seek new customers for cars and appliances, items of little use in the trenches but perhaps essential once men resumed their civilian lives.

The popularity of *The Stars and Stripes* among the troops attested to its success in printing stories that reflected the daily concerns of American soldiers during the war. By writing in language that they could understand, the editors opened up a dialogue with men in the field who enthusiastically embraced the invitation to send their thoughts, letters, and verse for publication. Begun to raise morale in the overseas army, *The Stars and Stripes* helped forge a sense of community among the men stationed in France.

Mascots

Occasionally soldiers and units adopted mascots, both as a way to create unity within a platoon or company and to simply provide a reliable source of comfort and friendship while overseas. Dogs were particular favorites for American soldiers. The British Army trained dogs to carry supplies to wounded men in the field and to lead first aid workers to the site where wounded men lay, but the Americans simply saw them as pets. Alexander Woollcott recounted the story of one dog, Verdun Belle, in both *The Stars and Stripes* and various civilian publications, and the tale soon became a favorite one within the AEF. A white setter with splotches of brown appeared in the trenches one day. Taking a fancy to her, an American Marine resolved to adopt the dog and named her Verdun Belle. She followed her owner to listening posts, wore a gas mask that he fashioned for her, and knew to avoid No Man's Land at all costs. By the spring, Verdun Belle presented the Marine unit with seven puppies. When the unit received orders to move, Verdun Belle's master found a basket to carry the puppies. With Verdun Belle trotting by his side, the Marine carried the basket along with all his normal gear for forty kilometers. When at last carrying the basket became too much, the Marine killed four of the puppies and put the other three in his pockets to continue the march. One died along the way, and in the mass of men and machines clogging the road, Verdun Belle was lost as well. Unable to feed the puppies, the Marine convinced some ambulance workers to take them to a field hospital, where Verdun Belle also appeared two days later. When the German advance forced an evacuation of the field hospital, the workers brought Verdun Belle and her two puppies with them. "Then one evening they lifted out a young Marine, listless in the half stupor of shell shock. To the busy workers he was just Case Number Such-and-Such, but there was no need to tell anyone who saw the wild jubilance of the dog that Belle had found her own again at last," Woollcott wrote.[44] Verdun Belle and her puppies stayed with her owner through his subsequent evacuation to a base hospital and throughout his entire recuperation in France.

In March 1918, *The Stars and Stripes* initiated a campaign asking units to adopt a French child as a mascot whose father had died in the war or sustained injuries that left him unable to work. The brainchild of Private Harold Ross (the future founder of *The New Yorker*), the program aimed to improve the lives of war orphans and to create a lasting bond between Americans and the French. It took 500 francs, or eighty-eight dollars, to "adopt" a child. The money that men donated to support a particular child was funneled through the Red Cross, which provided updates on how the money had furthered the youngster's education. Each week, the paper listed those units or individuals who had "adopted" a needy French child. Some men made specific requests for the kind of child that they wished to support. One unit wanted a red-headed, freckled face child, but had to settle for a blond after the paper reported, a bit tongue in cheek that "there had been a red-headed, freckled-faced boy in France once, but that his father had taken him back to Ireland."[45] By the end of the war, American soldiers were helping support 3,444 French children, including two aided by General Pershing, with nearly two million francs in donations.

RECREATION

"We quote Kipling these days, 'Take your fun where you find it'" quipped one nurse in describing how she and her colleagues in Little Rock, Arkansas, spent their off-duty hours. The fear that too many young men and women had adopted this attitude prompted much concern among Progressive reformers and military officials who worried that wartime excesses would undermine the moral fiber and physical health of American youth. Drinking had long been a hallmark of military service, and soldiers notoriously liked to prove their virility through both sexual escapades and battlefield heroism. A reputed ladies man, Pershing nonetheless took a hard line against sexual adventurism to prevent venereal disease from crippling his army. To keep men fit to fight, officials worked hard throughout the war to deter soldiers and young women from drinking and engaging in extramarital sexual relations. Besides protecting their virtue, the military also hoped to lessen its manpower losses by keeping its troops free of sexually transmitted diseases.

Measures to Promote "Healthy Living"

The wartime anti-venereal campaign was spearheaded by the Commission on Training Camp Activities (CTCA).The civilian reformers who worked for the CTCA were charged with enforcing sections 12 and 13 of the Selective Service Act that

The Commission of Training Camp Activities urged soldiers to keep themselves free of veneral disease during the war through propanganda posters, films, and sexual education lectures. (*Courtesy of the National Library of Medicine*)

prohibited the sale of liquor to men in uniform and allowed the president to outlaw prostitution around training camps. Under the direction of Raymond Fosdick, the CTCA tried to instill middle-class principles of clean living by creating vice-free zones around training camps. "Young men spontaneously prefer to be decent, and . . . opportunities for wholesome recreation are the best possible cure for irregularities in conduct which arise from idleness and the baser temptations," stated Secretary of War Newton Baker, a progressive reformer who had previously served as mayor of Cleveland.[46]

The CTCA, in partnership with army medical officers and community welfare organizations such as the Young Men's Christian Association (YMCA), Jewish Welfare Board and Knights of Columbus, launched a multifaceted attack on vice. Active in the social hygiene and park reform movements before the war, the middle-class Progressive reformers who joined the CTCA encouraged the mostly working-class soldier population to eschew traditional forms of urban recreation. Replacing saloons and brothels with athletics promoted middle-class values of healthy living that reformers expected to outlive the war. Beyond keeping soldiers healthy enough to fight for their country, CTCA reformers wanted these men to return home resolved to banish drinking and womanizing from their lives.

"What are those soldiers going to do in the towns, and what are the towns going to do to the soldiers?," asked Secretary Baker, setting out the basic dilemma facing the CTCA. To answer that question, the CTCA worked with the War Camp Community Service (WCCS), a group that employed 2,700 workers and established a presence in 615 towns. Apprehensive about leaving thousands of soldiers to fend for themselves on a nightly basis in their towns, many local communities happily welcomed these reformers into their midst. The situation facing Hattiesburg, Mississippi, mirrored the challenges experienced by local officials throughout the nation. The small city of 15,000 lay just eleven miles from Camp Shelby, a camp that housed 28,000 troops. The sudden influx of soldiers seeking off-duty diversions threatened to overwhelm the town's two movie theaters, handful of pool halls, and a lone public restroom located in its one hotel. In Hattiesburg, the WCCS worked with local churches to coordinate a series of weekend socials, created four soldiers' clubs, convinced the local YMCA to open its door to soldiers, and helped the town install more restrooms and drinking fountains.

Nationwide, the WCCS helped found 342 clubs for soldiers, sailors, and marines to visit when they went to town, many of which contained canteens, dormitories, showers, and recreation rooms filled with books, pool tables, pianos, and tobacco and candy stands. The WCCS also sponsored community dances, dinners, and festivals to ensure that soldiers interacted with the young women of the town under the watchful eyes of WCCS chaperones. The group sponsored a "Take a Soldier or Sailor Home to Dinner" program, reasoning that having dinner with a local family would encourage soldiers to respect area womenfolk. Thanks to the efforts of the WCCS, communities throughout the country invited soldiers to use their swimming pools, skating rinks, tennis courts, and bowling alleys on their trips off-base.

The CTCA's effort to organize Sunday afternoon entertainments for troops in town occasionally met opposition in the South. Many southern states prohibited concerts, dances, or showing movies on Sunday, but the CTCA handbook advised workers to do their best to convince local officials that "to leave these hours empty is to play into the hands of the illicit liquor seller, the woman of the streets, and all who prey upon the idle brain."[47] Some rural church congregations remained unmoved by this argument. "We sympathize with the boys' need for recreation and entertainment, but we do not believe that such things are suitable for our soldier boys, any more than for private citizens, on the Sabbath day," wrote one Texas congregation to Secretary Baker.[48]

In sponsoring town dances for soldiers, CTCA officials faced their own concerns about promoting physical contact between the soldiers and young women in attendance. Urban social reformers had long viewed public dance halls as disreputable establishments where tired female workers seeking diversion from their dull lives were frequently led astray. To avoid similar pitfalls, WCCS dance halls instituted strict standards of conduct, including appropriate dress, lighting, music, and types of dances allowed. Social welfare workers also took pains to keep working-class girls away from these dances, notably shifting in their attitudes towards these women who metamorphosed from innocent victims into women of easy virtue likely to lead soldiers into temptation. To take their place, the WCCS asked middle-class women's clubs to only invite girls with excellent character references and to personally chaperone these dances. In many locales, middle-class women wanted little contact with working-class soldiers, and these directives had the unintended consequence of turning WCCS dances into officers-only affairs.

The women's auxiliaries formed by officers' wives in many regiments also helped bridge the gap between the home front and battlefront. An officer's responsibility to care for his men often extended to his wife as well. These groups often distributed parting gifts of tobacco, knitted garments, and candy, all donated by the community, to troops headed overseas. In addition, these auxiliaries offered important welfare services to destitute families of departed servicemen by helping them cope if allotment checks were delayed. Women's auxiliaries helped families negotiate governmental red tape and in some cases even paid the rent, bought coal and food, or settled hospital bills for families in need.

Within the training camps, the CTCA promoted the virtues of healthy living through its recreational athletic program. Athletics developed both a pragmatic and ideological value during the war. Boxing matches helped men burn off sexual energy while spectators spent their free time watching tournaments rather than prowling the streets around training camps. The CTCA also promoted instruction in boxing as a way to perfect bayonet fighting skills. Through boxing, the military training that troops received during the day melded perfectly into the nightly entertainment provided on most camps throughout the nation. Besides boxing, baseball proved a popular evening pastime. Baseball games built unit morale and camaraderie while simultaneously teaching troops that athletics was a much safer way to demonstrate masculine prowess than picking up women. Many camp social welfare reformers were surprised to discover how many men had only passing familiarity with organized games. Reflecting the realities of child labor, urban living, and recent immigration, men had to learn a host of middle-class childhood games like tag and tug-of-war in the army before graduating to baseball and football.

CTCA reformers also presented singing as a group activity with a distinct military purpose. "Patriotism is no hollow thing," declared one CTCA worker, "It wins battles. And the music, be it instrumental or vocal, that awakens it and feeds it is scarcely less potent than high explosives."[49] The lyrics of many songs selected for inclusion in the formal singing program complimented the CTCA's moral uplift campaign, but CTCA workers also claimed that singing conveyed physical advantages such as strengthened back and chest muscles and improved mental agility. Singing identical songs helped mold men into a national army by exposing them to similar patriotic sentiments. The nationalistic and Christian songs included in the *Official Army Song Book* included "America, the Beautiful," "Battle Cry of the Republic," "Dixie," "Onward, Christian Soldiers," "Roll, Jordon, Roll," "*The Stars and Stripes* Forever," and "When Johnny Comes Marching Home." The song book contained Allied nations' national anthems and ditties made popular by British troops like "Pack Up Your Troubles in Your Old Kit Bag" and "There's a Long, Long Trail." These songs were often introduced into the English curriculum of foreign-speaking troops as part of their civic education. By "slowly repeating the words and injecting a plea for loyalty" as they sang, immigrant soldiers "fully sensed the meaning of true patriotism . . . making them true Americans through song," one CTCA music director concluded.[50]

The signature song of the AEF was "Over There" by George M. Cohan. Out of the flood of patriotic tunes unleashed by the nation's declaration of war, only "Over There" caught on with the troops. From the CTCA's perspective, the song perfectly emphasized the democratic purpose and resolve of the American soldier, making it an appropriate anthem of the war.

First verse:

> Johnnie get your gun
>> Get your gun
>> Get your gun
> Take it on the run
> On the run, on the run
> Hear them calling you and me
> Ev'ry son of liberty
> Hurry right away
> No delay go today
> Make your daddy glad
> To have had such a lad
> Tell your sweetheart not to pine
> To be proud her boy's in line

Chorus:

> Over There
> Over There
> Send the word
> Send the word
> Over There
> That the Yanks are coming
> The Yanks are coming
> The drums rum-tuming ev'rywhere
> So prepare
> Say a pray'r
> Send the word
> Send the word
> To beware
> We'll be over.
> We're coming over
> And we won't come back
> Till it's over
> Over There.[51]

Soldier musicians also provided the AEF and American people with some popular ragtime tunes based on the experiences of fighting men. After he was injured in a concussion blast during his first patrol of No Man's Land, the famed band leader James Europe penned "On Patrol in No Man's Land." His band recorded the composition in 1919 replete with instruments mimicking the sound of incoming shells and the chaos of battle as fellow veteran Noble Sissle sang:

> What's the time? Nine? Fall in line
> Alright boys, now take it slow
> Are you ready? Steady!
> Very good, Eddie
> Over the top, let's go!
> Quiet, lie it, else you'll start a riot
> Keep your proper distance, follow 'long
> Cover, brother, and when you see me hover
> Obey my orders and you won't go wrong

Chorus:

> There's a Minenwerfer [German mortar] coming—look out (bang!)
> Hear that roar (bang!),
> There's one more (bang!)
> Stand fast-there's a Very light [flare]
> Don't gasp, or they'll find you all right
> Don't start to bombin' with those hand grenades (rat-a-tat-tat-tat)
> There's a machine gun, holy spades!
> Alert! Gas! Put on your mask!
> Adjust it correctly and hurry up fast
> Drop! There's a rocket from the Boche barrage!
> Down, hug the ground,
> Close as you can, don't stand
> Creep and crawl, follow me, that's all
> What do you hear? Nothing near?
> Don't fear, all's clear
> That's the life of a stroll
> When you take a patrol
> Out in No Man's Land
> Ain't it grand?
> Out in No Man's Land[52]

Like all armies in the First World War, the American Army was a singing army. CTCA reformers led soldiers in official sing-alongs, and soldiers enthusiastically continued the practice while traveling on trains, marching, and in bars behind the lines. Belying the hopes of CTCA workers, many of the most popular song choices celebrated soldiers' less-than-wholesome adventures overseas. One particularly well-circulated song, "The Mademoiselle from Armentières," was appropriated from the British. The Armentières initial song lyrics made a humorous jab at a British soldier's bad French and the rebuff he received from a local woman.

> Oh, Mademoiselle from Armentières,
> Parley-vous
> Oh, Mademoiselle from Armentières,
> Parley-vous
> Mademoiselle from Armentières,
> She hasn't been kissed in forty years!
> Hinky-dinky, parlez-vous?

The song soon took on a life of its own, however, among British and American troops who constantly changed the song's fifth and sixth lines to convey completely different sentiments. American soldiers soon infused the traditional version with verses that reflected their own particular experiences overseas. Some verses questioned the mademoiselle's character ("You didn't have to know her long/To know the reason men go wrong" or "She'll do it for wine, she'll do it for rum/And sometimes for chocolate or chewing gun!").Other versions criticized officers' privileges ("As soon as she'd spy a Colonel's Brass, She'd take off her skirt and roll in the grass!") or questioned officers' contribution to the overall victory ("The colonel got the Croix de Guerre/The sun-of-a gun was ne-ver there").Other lyrics, commented on the frustrating experience

James Reese Europe, who gained fame for bringing jazz to France, composed the song "On Patrol in No Man's Land" after being wounded during a raid. (*Courtesy of the Library of Congress*)

of serving behind the lines ("Twelve long, rainy months or more/I spent hunting for that war"). Still another reflected the general disdain that soldiers felt for the YMCA (The YMCA, they saved my soul/Yes they did–in a pig's arse hole!]. Regardless of the version that men sang, this was not the kind of song that CTCA envisioned soldiers singing when they organized group sing- alongs in the training camps.

Besides censoring songs in official group singing, CTCA workers also carefully selected the films and books that made their way into stateside training camps. As with songs, many approved silent films, with titles like *The Kaiser's Shadow, Firefly of France,* and *I'm a Man* underscored the just purpose of the conflict. A handful of comedies and farces also made the cut, ones that screeners felt would not lower the moral tone of camp life. Books placed in camp libraries were also vetted for content. Pro-German and pacifist works were banned, including Henri Barbusse's *Under Fire: The Story of a Squad* which offered a realistic depiction of trench warfare and disillusionment within the French Army that critics deemed defeatist. Many libraries also sought foreign-language versions of approved books to offer to immigrant soldiers. If soldiers did not feel like reading or watching a film, then they often also had the option of attending a concert or play in one of the Liberty Theaters erected by the CTCA. Soldiers often had to pay a small admission fee, ranging from five to twenty-five cents for this entertainment. Thousands of civilians purchased Smileage ticket books for soldiers which were filled with coupons granting them free admission to Liberty Theaters.

MORALS

Overall, the CTCA tried to provide wholesome recreational activities for troops, both in the surrounding communities and on base, which promoted the values of clean living and raised morale. In this respect, organized recreational programs served the war effort every bit as much as the normal training regime. Controlling what soldiers did in their off-duty hours proved more challenging than dictating how they spent their working hours. Soldiers, one man recalled, talked nearly constantly in the barracks about sex, "as if it were a problem of physics rather than morals."[53] Bowing to the reality that not all soldiers would accept athletics and organized social activities as substitutes for sexual adventuring, the CTCA also instituted a comprehensive sex education program that taught soldiers how to practice safe sex.

Sex Education and the War on Vice

The CTCA and army medical corps offered many soldiers their first course in sexual education. These officials created a series of pamphlets, films, and lantern slide lectures designed to clearly establish the link between alcohol, prostitutes and venereal disease in soldiers' minds. Patriotic appeals were common as social welfare reformers tried to set a high morale tone for the army. Keeping sexually pure, CTCA propaganda maintained, was more than a way for troops to safeguard their own health or do their duty. It also elevated American troops above their German enemies. As one pamphlet entreated,

> You are going to fight for the spirit of young girlhood raped and ravished in Belgium by a brutal soldiery. You are going to fight for it in this country, too, where you yourselves are its protectors, so that it may never need to submit to the same insults and injuries. But in order to fight for so sacred a cause you must be worthy champions. You must keep your bodies clean and your hearts pure. It would never do for the avengers of women's wrongs to profit by the degradation and debasement of womanhood.[54]

CTCA educational materials often sent soldiers mixed messages. Many pamphlets and films strongly advocated abstinence, but then in recognition that soldiers were unlikely to heed this advice, encouraged them to seek immediate treatment if they slept with a woman other than their wife. Officially charged with ensuring that these men remained eligible for overseas service, the CTCA had to develop a pragmatic, as well as ideological, approach to handling the problem of venereal disease transmission.

A silent film, with dialogue cards, titled *Fit to Fight*, for instance, followed the adventures of five draftees who each reacted differently when faced with the opportunity to purchase sex with a prostitute. One soldier withstood temptation and went on to serve with distinction overseas. The others yielded and three paid for their sexual transgressions by becoming mired in disease and disgrace. The only one who escaped this fate was the soldier who visited a camp prophylactic station. The cleansing that he received did more than rid his body of germs; it also prompted him to renounce any further dalliances with prostitutes. Frightened about the possible ramifications of his mistake, this soldier resolved to keep his body clean and healthy so he could continue to serve his country. This happy ending presented available treatment as a way to get a second chance, and not as license to engage in illicit sex without fear of the consequences. The true intent of the film, however, was initially lost on foreign-speaking soldiers with a limited command of English, who could not read the dialogue written on the screen, and complained about being shown "a smutty exhibition."[55] The Foreign-speaking Soldier bureau quickly located bi-lingual officers who spoke Russian, Polish, Bohemian, Serbian, Italian, Spanish, German, and Magyar. In subsequent showings, camp officials stopped the film at key moments so these officers could translate the true intent and meaning of the film.

Shame sometimes induced soldiers to seek out private treatment rather than advertise their transgressions by visiting the camp medical facilities. CTCA literature stressed that the humiliation would be much greater if soldiers contracted venereal disease and were forced to serve out the war in a venereal unit permanently stationed stateside. The CTCA produced another silent film with dialogue cards titled "Damaged Goods" that warned soldiers about trusting the cures of "quack doctors." The film portrayed the misfortunes of a man who got drunk at his bachelor party, tried some ineffective medicine, and infected his wife, who then passed syphilis onto their unborn child. One psychologist who sat with a group of men watching the film expressed concern that some scenes played more like soft-core pornography than an anti-venereal lecture. "When men make remarks concerning the 'Girl in the Streets' such as 'That would make a man catch somethin' . . . 'By God, Some Stuff' . . . 'Go to it boy' . . . they are not at the same time susceptible to social hygiene instruction," he concluded. The most effective scenes in the film, however, were the graphic images of syphilis sores that flashed on the screen as the young man investigated his condition. "The hospital scenes silenced them all," the psychologist conceded.[56]

The Instruction Laboratory of the Army Medical Museum also developed lantern slide lectures for both white and black troops that made practically every argument officials could devise to ensure soldiers did their best to stay healthy. One such presentation began by posing the question "why should a man expect a woman to be decent if he is not?"[57]After considering the double standard that allowed men to sow wild oats but labeled women who engaged in risky sexual behavior as whores, the slides quickly moved to key mistakes that men made. A parade of "heeza" vignettes followed, "heeza" being a slang term used for "he's a." One slide showed a character named "Heeza boozer" who went home with a prostitute after a night of drinking. Another told the story of "heeza wiseguy," an overly confident young man who disregarded all warnings. Crippled from venereal disease, heeza wiseguy learned the hard way that "whiskey makes men weak, whores cause the 'bad leak.'" If soldiers ignored, as these characters had, the advice to abstain, then lecturers urged them to avoid compounding their mistake by turning in desperation to the "cures" sold by disreputable pharmacists. "What Fools These Mortals Be," proclaimed one lantern slide above the scene of a hobbled venereal disease victim buying "fixisit," a potion that claimed to cure gonorrhea in five days. Graphic photographs showed soldiers how to identify venereal disease sores on their genitalia and summarized

Army medical officers used lantern slide lectures to warn soldiers of the dangers of venereal disease. This slide emphasized the innocent victims harmed by venereal disease, depicted here as working on the devil's behalf. (*Courtesy of the National Museum of Health and Medicine*)

the cleansing treatments available in army medical facilities. A few slides even demonstrated how a soldier could inject a purifying solution into his penis. Medical officers, however, had no intention of ending the lecture on the positive note that some treatment was available. Instead, the final slides hit hard to discourage soldiers from sleeping with prostitutes. Where do prostitutes come from, asks one slide? The business constantly required new recruits. Were these men willing to sacrifice their sweethearts or sisters? Another image showed the devil keeping a scorecard of how many innocent babies were born blind and women diseased by men who had engaged in extramarital intercourse with prostitutes. The lecture concluded with the admonishment that each soldier owed it to his father, mother, sweetheart, and his country to stay clean for the duration of the war as a final image of Uncle Sam pointing his finger at the audience flashed on the screen.

Realizing that soldiers were only one side of the equation, the CTCA closed down red light districts throughout the nation and organized patrols to walk the streets looking for prostitutes or working-class girls seeking some excitement in the vicinity of training camps. Initially, CTCA workers only jailed the prostitutes, choosing to lecture teenage girls about the consequences of losing control at the sight of a uniform before taking them home to their mothers. Before long, however, both these "charity girls" and prostitutes faced the prospect of time in jail or a detention home for their transgressions in the anti-vice zone.

The CTCA produced a feature film for women living in the vicinity of military training camps titled *The End of the Road*. This film sent much the same message as

Fit to Fight by following the divergent paths of two childhood friends, Vera and Mary. Mary takes her mother's warning to heart and by keeping herself pure wins the heart of a successful doctor. Vera takes up with a slacker, contracts venereal disease, and suffers public disgrace and humiliation. Mary summed up the film's message by noting "I know . . . how hard it is to think of the consequences now, when we're young . . . unless we do we shan't find happiness at the end of the road."[58] To help occupy their time and keep their minds off the boys, the CTCA created girls clubs and organized social events through churches for young women who lived near training camps. CTCA workers also tried to steer girls towards valuable charity work that they could perform for the war effort such as volunteering for the Red Cross or creating a Victory Garden.

Removing temptation by clearing the streets of women willing to sleep with soldiers, either for money or for fun, was not an option once troops arrived overseas. Secretary of War Baker believed that the social hygiene instruction they received in the camps would serve soldiers well in France where both wine and women were readily available. Overseas, "they are going to face conditions that we do not like to talk about, that we do not like to think about," said Baker, referring, not to trench warfare, but to the licensed houses of prostitution that the French used to ensure that soldiers had access to women certified as disease-free.[59] Baker hoped that indoctrinating American troops with the importance of wholesome living would provide "an invisible armor" that gave them the strength to maintain a vice-free lifestyle overseas.

The anti-vice work of the CTCA met approval from army authorities because it helped preserve much needed manpower for the front lines. The social welfare workers in the CTCA, however, had much grander ambitions. They expected to set new standards of social hygiene and sexual purity that would improve the morale fiber of the nation for generations to come. The men who returned home safely at the war's end, contended one reformer, "will be better citizens than they were before they went in (to the service) . . . They will have learned the meaning of concerted effort, obedience, loyalty, cheerfulness, courage and generosity. They will come back with a new set of ideals, as men who have been tried by fire and found good metal."[60]

The YMCA's Role in World War I

The YMCA contributed heavily to programs run by the CTCA and WCCS, but also had an independent presence in the training camps. Overseas, the YMCA had complete control of recreational programming, and the Y man became a permanent fixture in the memoirs of nearly every American soldier who served overseas. The YMCA emerged in the mid-nineteenth century amid concerns that young men migrating to urban areas quickly lost their way without the guiding influences of family and church. To dissuade these young men from sampling the array of tempting vices readily available in every city, the Protestant-oriented YMCA created a homelike environment meant to remind young men of their moral upbringing. The array of enticements luring wartime soldiers away from a morally upright lifestyle presented a remarkably similar situation, and the YMCA eagerly replicated its civilian programs in a military setting.

The YMCA-approach placed particular importance on reminding soldiers of their home ties by creating a series of YMCA huts where soldiers could spend their free time playing or listening to music, reading, writing letters, watching movies, playing pool or learning to read. Some even included showers and gymnasiums. The YMCA fully participated in the CTCA's anti-venereal disease campaign, and a soldier might likely find

The YMCA offered sightseeing tours for doughboys visiting Paris on leave. (*Courtesy of the National Archives*)

the walls covered with posters reminding him that "A German bullet is cleaner than a whore" or "You wouldn't use another man's toothbrush. Why use his whore?"[61] On most camps, the YMCA also constructed larger auditoriums where soldiers could attend lectures, engage in mass singing, listen to concerts, attend religious services or watch plays performed by the amateur companies that formed in the camps or professional touring troupes. Male Y secretaries formed bible-study groups and gave lectures on the causes of the war. By the end of the war, the YMCA had constructed nearly 3,000 buildings, including 952 huts, and employed over 12,000 Y secretaries to oversee these recreational activities. On many camps, the YMCA also ran canteens that sold cigarettes, candy, and various items to soldiers. A YMCA-produced camp newspaper, *Trench and Camp*, kept soldiers informed about the latest war news and the regular sports competitions on base. Each camp received four standard pages printed in Washington, D.C. Camp editors then added four more pages of local news including the upcoming week's recreational offerings. Letters to the editor and a regular column by Ring Lardner exploring the adventures of a rookie writing to his buddy Al focused on the hardships of basic training and the humorous mistakes made by naïve recruits. *Trench and Camp* began a series of French lessons for soldiers in March 1918, which YMCA huts supplemented with nightly classes on many bases. By the end of the war, the YMCA estimated that 200,000 men had taken evening language classes.

On many bases, camp commanders delegated the task of teaching English to foreign-born soldiers to the YMCA. In the lessons that they gave, YMCA instructors took full advantage of the opportunity to inculcate valuable lessons about hygiene, patriotism, and civic responsibility as they taught new vocabulary. The *Camp Reader for American Soldiers* included lessons for soldiers to recite such as: "I will write a letter to my brother Jack. I will tell him how proud I am to be an American soldier." In lesson fifteen, soldiers read, "Last week I went home to vote. I am very glad that I went. I voted to rid the city of vice." Soon, soldier-students were learning that "I take a shower bath at least three times a week. A cold shower gets you awake quick. I like to shave every day. A good shave makes a man feel clean" and "a good soldier keeps his teeth clean and white."[62]

YMCA facilities were segregated on many camps, although in Northern camps several camp commanders insisted that Y huts welcome all soldiers regardless of race. The YMCA employed nearly 300 black Y secretaries to staff their "separate but equal" facilities that often suffered from a lack of funds. In many southern camps, Y huts set aside for white troops refused to even sell a postage stamp to a black soldier. The YMCA's tendency to create segregated huts also followed the army overseas. Eventually, the YMCA sent 61 black secretaries to France but most arrived after the armistice. Many black secretaries also encountered difficulties securing the needed supplies and cooperation from their white colleagues to properly minister the needs of black enlisted men. In the postwar period, several black Y secretaries offered scathing testimony regarding civil rights abuses within the wartime military.

To fulfill its mission, the YMCA had to follow the men. Male Y secretaries boarded the trains that transported troops throughout the nation and sailed on the same ships with them overseas. In transit, the Y secretary was there to provide paper and pens, postcards, magazines, newspapers, first aid kits, and social hygiene pamphlets. Y secretaries carried portable huts to the front that they could erect and then pack up quickly if a unit pulled out. Y secretaries and Red Cross workers close to the front handed out hot coffee or tea, candy, crackers and cigarettes to passing troops, provided a warm and dry place for them to compose what might turn out to be a last letter home, and sometimes even dressed minor wounds as men waited for ambulances to transport them to base hospitals. Army commanders often expressed mixed feelings about the presence of Y canteens so close to the front, especially when men snuck away to indulge in a free cup of hot chocolate. Many Y secretaries also had their own trucks, and often drove to the rear trench lines to offer these luxuries to cold and tired men. Having to pay for coffee and candy in rear YMCA canteens, after receiving these items mostly for free near the front, caused much consternation among soldiers. Soldiers' complaints about illicit profiteering were so vitriolic that the government launched an investigation into soldiers' claims that the YMCA was selling donated items. Congress eventually absolved the organization of any wrong-doing. The YMCA also made money from the postal services that it offered troops.

The YMCA also established huts in the towns that billeted American soldiers. "The YMCA have a representative here too, in fact wherever I have been," wrote one soldier to sooth his family's concerns about how he spent his off-duty hours. "In the town a house is set aside for the men to read, write and play and everything quite up to date and attractive. Religious services are held there and also here in the barracks, which keep the men close to things they were taught in their particular churches."[63]

For soldiers on leave, the YMCA maintained hostels in most major French cities and London that offered cheap, clean, and safe places to stay. Besides offering affordable lodging, the YMCA also produced slim guidebooks for soldiers, treating them to concise and pithy insights on the importance of various sites. The Place de la Concorde was summed up with the phrase "Marie-Antoinette and many others guillotined," while the Louvre was described as "formerly king's palace, largest in world, now the finest Art Museum in the world."[64] Y secretaries also offered guided motor tours around Paris and walking tours of the Latin Quarter. By keeping soldiers' attention focused on the buildings and history, the YMCA hoped to limit the contacts that American soldiers had with French civilians, particularly women, while visiting the capital city.

American soldiers were eligible for a seven-day furlough every four months, but the army preferred that troops take those leaves in resorts run by the YMCA, rather than head to big cities where they would be hard to recall in the event of a massive German attack and where they were likely to seek out women and wine. The YMCA established leave areas in picturesque resort towns that contained enough hotels and recreational facilities to handle a sudden influx of American troops. The first leave center opened in Aix-les-Baines in February 1918, and by the end of the war, the YMCA had established nineteen other resorts in France, five in the Rhine Valley, two in Italy, and one in England. The soldier-tourists who visited these areas could rest, hike, attend dances, play games, or tour the local sites with a guide. Soldiers were granted free entry into resort casinos, had access to bicycles to tour the nearby countryside, or could enter one of the numerous athletic or board game competitions organized by the YMCA. Nearly half a million soldiers passed through these official leave centers, staffed by 866 Y secretaries. Separate leave centers in Chamberry and Challes-les-Eaux were established for the 20,000 black troops who chose to spend their furloughs in a resort town.

American soldiers developed a complicated relationship with Y secretaries during the war. While appreciative of the services the YMCA offered, the sight of able-bodied men in civilian dress safely out of harm's way bred resentment against Y secretaries. Alternatively perceived as slackers or even worse, do-gooders, the image of the Y man suffered despite the many good works that he performed during the war.

The YWCA's Role in World War I

The Young Women's Christian Association (YWCA) emerged in the nineteenth century with a parallel mission to protect the morals of young rural women headed to industrial jobs in metropolitan areas. As in the case of the YMCA, the war effort only amplified these concerns and the YWCA worked closely with the CTCA and WCCS to develop programs (including sex education classes) and inexpensive housing to safe-guard local girls from the immoral forces swirling around training camps. In the camps, 124 YWCA hostess huts staffed with 306 Y secretaries offered comfortable places for soldiers to receive visitors, including 17 segregated Hostess Houses set aside to receive black visitors. "Everywhere I found bitter comment on account of the failure of the gov-ernment to provide for colored women at the camps while every possible comfort was provided for white women," a field investigator noted during the war.[65] These huts normally contained a cafeteria, a nursery, and a traveler's aid station to provide basic services to relatives who had often undertaken a long and tiring journey to see their loved one before he departed overseas. Perhaps most importantly, the YWCA provided chaperones who guided visitors from the camps gates to the hostess huts, ensuring that no unauthorized visitors decided to take a private tour of the camp under the pretext of visiting a relative. These services helped families and friends visit their loved ones, usu-ally on Sundays, without disrupting the normal camp routine. YWCA chaperones also allowed unmarried couples to visit without any aura of impropriety surrounding their meeting far away from the watchful eyes of concerned parents.

Encouraging soldiers to keep their families and sweethearts utmost in their minds, both by facilitating the exchange of letters and providing meeting facilities in the camp, increased the risk of fostering home sickness among the troops. CTCA and YMCA officials willingly took that risk, certain that constant contact between a soldier and his family improved morale by reassuring each of their respective well-being. Remembering those at home also gave soldiers a concrete reason to lead a morally upright life while in the service.

In France, the YWCA established 80 hostess houses where soldiers could relax in the company of American women. The organization also ran twenty-four nurses' clubs that offered these women lodging and social programs to give them some respite from the overwhelmingly male environment in which they worked. By the end of the war, the YWCA also found itself offering social services to many of the 10,000 French war brides who married American soldiers and the children they had conceived. Because French women lost their French citizenship as soon as they married an American soldier, the U.S. government reluctantly had to assume responsibility for supporting and transporting these war brides to the United States. The government provided free transport on a naval vessel, but charged each woman one dollar a day for meals and railroad transport to her new home. These women often departed for the United States separately from their husbands, who sailed home with their units, and the YWCA helped them prepare for their new lives by offering courses in English and American history and culture. The YWCA established hostess houses near the ports of embarkation to house these women and their children as they waited for their departure orders. Some YWCA branches even offered housing in the United States for women waiting for their soldier-husbands to receive their discharges from the service.

Religion

Morale officers, CTCA reformers, and YMCA men all hoped to boost a soldier's usefulness to the army by keeping his morals pure, his morale high, and his spirit willing. Army chaplains also played an important role in building battlefront morale, freely enlisting religion to further the cause. By the end of the war, the military had commissioned 2,300 chaplains to serve with troops.

Two schools for chaplains were established in the United States at Fort Monroe in Virginia and Camp Zachary Taylor in Kentucky. Setting an interdenominational tone, the curriculum eschewed theology and instead focused on military and international law, hygiene and first aid. One school for chaplains was also created overseas where candidates followed a ten-week course in meeting soldiers' religious needs at the front and identifying and burying the dead. Chaplains were instructed to offer spiritual guidance, foster morale, conduct religious and burial services, and sometimes inform relatives of a soldier's death.

Over the course of the war, the American Bible Society and the YWCA distributed nearly 4.5 million pocket bibles, New Testaments, and prayer books to soldiers, making the bible the most widely read book in the trenches. Nervous that the war might provide an opportunity for Protestant proselytizing, the Roman Catholic Church forbad its followers from participating in Protestant services. Wartime surveys indicated that religious convictions were high in the American wartime military. In one census of 31,079 troops, only 81 identified themselves as atheists or infidels. A survey of the 82nd Division yielded similar results: out of 32,468 respondents, only 24 proclaimed themselves atheists. This same survey revealed the wide array of religions being practiced in the AEF. Of those responding, 41.9 percent were Catholic, 14.2 percent Methodist, 11.1percent Baptist, 7.3 percent Jewish, 5.5 percent Presbyterian, 4.4 percent Lutheran, 4.7 percent Protestant Episcopalian, 1.4 percent Congregational, 1.2 percent Greek Orthodox, and 1 percent Christian Church.

"Every chaplain was responsible for the religion of every man," noted one Jewish chaplain.[66] Jewish chaplains carried crosses with them in case they were called upon to administer the last rites, and Catholic and Protestant chaplains learned Hebrew prayers. With only six Jewish chaplains available to minister the religious needs of approximately 100,000 Jewish soldiers in the AEF, Catholic and Protestant chaplains often found themselves caring for men of both Christian and Judaic faiths on the battlefield. On the front lines with the 77th Division, one Presbyterian chaplain performed separate funeral services for three men, a Catholic, a Jew, and a Protestant, killed together in a foxhole. In tending to the spiritual needs of the severely wounded, chaplains sometimes erred in determining a soldier's faith. When this same chaplain helped a severely wounded man recite a prayer, the man stopped him midway through the recitation. "When I said 'O Christ who died for me,' he interrupted. 'I'm of Jewish faith, sir.'"[67] All right, the chaplain responded, "we won't put it just that way." The chaplain completed the prayer and then went on to tend others. He learned later that the wounded Jewish soldier died while waiting for an ambulance to take him to the hospital. In the heat of combat, Jewish soldiers who died in battle were often hastily buried without any specific care given to their religion. After one battle, Private Samuel Kaplan was appalled to learn that that in burying a Jewish friend his platoon had "made a nice wooden cross and put it on his grave." A dismayed Kaplan appreciated that "they meant well for they did not know."[68] As one of only three Jews in the entire company, his fallen friend's religion remained unknown to most members of his unit. Hoping to prevent such mistakes from becoming permanent, Jewish organizations convinced Congress to replace the traditional cross with a Star of David to mark the gravesites of Jewish soldiers in official cemeteries. Errors persisted, however. When the Red Cross took photographs of soldiers' headstones after the war and sent them as keepsakes to grieving families, a few Jewish households were stunned to discover crosses on their loved ones' graves. Jewish organizations subsequently sent representatives to France to ensure that the proper markers were in place.

Effectively gaining the trust of the living was as challenging as properly handling soldiers' deaths and burials. One soldier's poem, printed in *The Stars and Stripes*, succinctly summed up the attributes of the ideal chaplain in the eyes of the troops.

> He doesn't wear a Sunday suit nor yet a Sunday face;
> He wears khaki the same as we, and goes from place to place
> A-visitin' the hospitals and cheerin' up each lad
> That for any sort o' reason is laid up and feelin' bad.
> He doesn't pull no highbrow stuff, or talk of Kingdom Come,
> But any "cits' clothes" parson he can sure make out a bum;
> He doesn't mind mild cussin', and he'll smoke a cigarette,
> And doesn't say you'll go to hell for swiggin' somethin' wet.
> Still, if you *ask* him for it, he will tell you, 'bout the Lord,

The First and bravest Christian, Who would never sheathe the sword
Until all wrongs were righted; how He set His people free
Although the Romans nailed Him to the Cross o' Calvary.[69]

Pre-battle services and prayers or talks with chaplains were an important part of a unit's preparation for battle. The general absolution given to those who attended field masses as well as confessions "heard by French priests who didn't understand a word" was an obvious sign to one soldier that "time was running out and . . . we'd be leaving for the front soon."[70] Besides helping soldiers prepare for battle, religion also helped soldiers endure the endless bombardments. "The first shell that I saw hit near me was the greatest sermon I ever heard," an American private serving along the Western Front acknowledged.[71] "It's the funniest thing in the world how religious a fellow can get when he hears the machine gun bullets flying around him. I said my prayers on an average of three times a day," Jack Schofield admitted.[72] Charles Minder found it amusing that the most foul-mouthed and tough members of his unit were now the ones openly falling to their knees in prayer during bombardments. "What a change comes over a man when death is all around him!," Minder observed.[73] Battlefield conversions also occurred, with soldiers promising to lead morally upright lives if God spared them. As the future Commandant of the U.S. Marines Corps, Lieutenant Clifton B. Cates noted, "a few months of active service over here will make a man and a Christian out of most anyone."[74]

Frank R. Dill saw his comrades dig out their New Testaments from their packs during one barrage and the act of simply holding it in their hands helped them retain their composure. "If it was not for the help from the New Testament, I believe I would be a nervous wreck," Harold Pierce admitted.[75] A superstition soon developed within the ranks that bullets would not pierce the New Testament, a conviction reinforced by several true-life incidents. J. Walter Strauss, for instance, discovered a German bullet embedded in the copy that he carried in his breast pocket. If the bible did not physically save them from gunshots, many fatally wounded soldiers nonetheless sought spiritual solace in the words of their favorite passages. "The wounded, who could not be brought in, had crawled into shell holes, wrapped their waterproof sheets around them, taken out their Bibles, and died like that," Gerald Brenan recalled.[76] One American soldier recalled coming across a deceased comrade who "had managed to drag himself to a tree; he was sitting up reading the Testament when he died, for he still had it in his hand."[77]

While numerous soldiers reported praying or turning to God during bombardments, fewer admitted having religious thoughts while in the midst of an assault against German lines. Concerned with fighting and surviving, and acutely aware of the killing underway by both sides, in combat soldiers appeared to accept the dictum that "if you live by the sword, you shall perish by the sword." In the aftermath of battle, some soldiers experienced waves of remorse for having killed, while others felt pangs of guilt for surviving when so many others had perished. Often, troops appeared eager for religious confirmation that they had acted in accordance with God's will. After undergoing the trauma of having his comrade's body explode and splatter all over him during a severe shelling, Duncun Kemerer reflected in a poem why his life was spared. "Death," he asked, "why did not thou take I?" Kemerer answered by writing, "Because also God walked with me, and it is he who decides when Death/shall be."[78] Joseph Lawrence was waiting with his unit to receive their first rations in two days when news came that a mass was about to start in a nearby valley. Despite their evident hunger, a majority of men left the line and rushed to the service, "so thankful were the men for being spared."[79] First Sergeant Norman J. Summers also gave thanks for the protection that his faith offered, noting that "I knew God was with us because if he hadn't been we would never have suffered as light as we did."[80]

The assignment of chaplains to each unit offered soldiers many opportunities to attend formal religious services, often held in unusual settings that made a strong impression upon American troops. Throughout the war, soldiers worshipped in the ruins of shell-damaged churches and makeshift chapels behind the lines. Soldiers often took the lead in constructing small chapels in the woods. Most commonly, however, services were held in open fields. A "field mass was beautiful to witness," wrote Albert M. Etinger, "several hundred men under the open sky in reverent prayer to Almighty God."[81] The experience of receiving communion in a cave or listening to a service while shells exploded in the distance made a distinct impression on many troops, often reinforcing their conviction that they were Christian soldiers fighting on the side of good and right.

Sergeant Alvin York's journey from conscientious objector to decorated war hero crystallized the image of the American soldier as a Christian crusader. Like countless others who at first expressed religious objections to the war, York eventually became convinced that he was fulfilling God's will by fighting. York had grown up in the Tennessee Appalachian Mountains where he experienced a profound religious conversion in 1915 after leading a raucous life filled with gambling, drinking, and fighting. He became an elder in the Church of Christ in Christian Union, and confronted a crisis of conscience when the United States entered the war. "I loved and trusted Uncle Sam and I have always believed he did the right thing. But I was worried clean through. I didn't want to go and kill. I believed in my bible. And it distinctly said, 'THOU SHALT NOT KILL.'"[82] York's application for conscientious objector status was denied, and he entered the military still doubting his ability to fight. After a long theological conversation with York, his battalion commander sent York home to reflect on reconciling his patriotism with his Christian faith. York sought solitude in the mountains, where he became convinced that God sanctioned his participation in the war. York shot into the public spotlight on 8 October 1918, when he single-handedly silenced thirty-five German machine guns, killed at least twenty Germans, and took 132 prisoners before leading his ambushed patrol back to safety. "I am a witness to the fact that God did help me out of that battle; for the bushes were shot off all around me and I never got a scratch," York said by way of explaining his amazing survival.[83] In another postwar interview, York put it this way: "We know that there are miracles, don't we? Well this was one."[84] York returned home amid public acclaim, but refused all monetary offers to capitalize on his feat. Instead, he returned to Tennessee and spent his life working to bring public services such as schools to his neighbors.

As York demonstrated, soldiers freely interwove their religious convictions into their daily lives. Praying became an individual ritual for many soldiers, a way for them to express their own particular fears, concerns, or worries. Soldiers constructed private prayers to serve a variety of individual needs, praying for courage, for guidance, and forgiveness. Some prayed for peace, while others behind the lines prayed for the chance to have an active role in the fighting. Harold Joyce prayed to "help me keep my faith strong," while Sergeant Harry House prayed that "if I was to get hit–Please God kill me immediately." [85]

Their steady exposure to religious doctrine encouraged many soldiers to reflect on the existence of heaven and hell, the possibility of an afterlife, and the nature of God's

Will. "There were many times that I would close my eyes and wonder just what it would be like to be either in heaven or in Hell. Hell could not be any worse than we got," recalled Ernie Hilton when reminiscing about his military service.[86] The horrors of combat along the Western Front caused some to doubt and challenge their faith. For most, these questions of faith centered on questioning how God could allow such suffering to continue. Charles F. Minder had his doubts from the beginning of the war, asking questions such as "if there is a God, why doesn't he put a stop to this?" and "is this evil force, War, more powerful than God?"[87] By the time he met an avowed atheist in his unit, Minder was ready to ponder the argument this soldier made. "Don't you think that the men who have been killed already in this war for the past four years prayed? . . . What the hell good did it do them?," his companion argued.[88] Minder consider the possibility that prayer was fruitless, but in the end found a way to keep his faith by concluding that God was using the war to punish mankind for its sins.

Despite the prominent place that religion played in the institutional and private lives of soldiers, no great sweep of religious revivalism occurred within the army. During the Civil War, religious revival meetings became commonplace behind the lines. In 1917, the American military sought to foster religious sentiment to improve morale and dedication to the cause, while simultaneously avoiding the sectarian strife and overt emotionalism that might accompany evangelical revivals. The college-educated clergy recruited to oversee religious activities within the ranks were also by temperament distrustful of emotional conversions on the eve of battle. In the rough and tumble world of soldier culture, the overtly devout "came in for lots of kidding because they read their pocket Testaments for hours on end. We called them hypocrites and pitied them," Marine Elton Mackin recalled.[89] Some soldier-preachers led revivals within their units, but these were the exception rather than the rule. One notable example was Alvin York, who agreed to visit units in France to bolster morale during the demobilization period and then turned his appearances into de-facto revival meetings.

CONCLUSION

The army adopted an array of methods to gauge and improve morale during the First World War. In stateside training camps, the Morale Division and CTCA oversaw programs devoted to creating a sense of purpose and a commitment to clean living among the troops. Overseas, *The Stars and Stripes*, YMCA, and army chaplains provided ways for soldiers to express their views about military life and spiritual matters, while subtly fostering pride and faith in the nation's war effort. These activities revealed much about soldiers' daily lives including the banal and profound aspects of military service. The traditional pursuit of women and liquor, and the irreverent humor that filled the pages of *The Stars and Stripes* was balanced with the worries and concerns that men facing imminent death in battle confronted as they read their bibles or confessed to army chaplains. Maintaining morale was a public exercise that in many respects revealed the most private thoughts of individual men.

NOTES

1. Ronald Schaffer, *America in the Great War: The Rise of the War Welfare State* (New York: Oxford University Press, 1991), 186.

2. Schaffer, *America in the Great War*, 183.

3. Schaffer, *America in the Great War*, 193–4.

4. Schaffer, *America in the Great War*, 179.

5. Schaffer, *America in the Great War*, 190.

6. Jennifer D. Keene, *Doughboys, the Great War and the Remaking of America* (Baltimore, Md.: Johns Hopkins University Press, 2001), 77.

7. Keene, *Doughboys, the Great War and the Remaking of America*, 77.

8. Keene, *Doughboys, the Great War and the Remaking of America*, 76.

9. Schaffer, *America in the Great War*, 183.

10. Schaffer, *America in the Great War*, 190.

11. Keene, *Doughboys, the Great War and the Remaking of America*, 76.

12. Schaffer, *America in the Great War*, 192.

13. Alfred E. Cornebise, *The Stars and Stripes: Doughboy Journalism in World War I*. (Westport, Conn.: Greenwood Press, 1984), 155.

14. Cornebise, *The Stars and Stripes*, 156.

15. Cornebise, *The Stars and Stripes*, 156.

16. Cornebise, *The Stars and Stripes*, 43.

17. Cornebise, *The Stars and Stripes*, 25.

18. Cornebise, *The Stars and Stripes*, 10.

19. John T. Winterich, (ed.), *Squads Write! A Selection of the Best Things in Prose, Verse & Cartoon from The Stars and Stripes* (New York: Harper & Brothers, 1931), 19–20.

20. Cornebise, *The Stars and Stripes*, 129.

21. Winterich, *Squads Write!*, 39.

22. Winterich, *Squads Write!*, 22.

23. Cornebise, *The Stars and Stripes*, 140.

24. Winterich, *Squads Write!*, 17.

25. Cornebise, *The Stars and Stripes*, 61.

26. Cornebise, *The Stars and Stripes*, 79.

27. Cornebise, *The Stars and Stripes*, 83.

28. Winterich, *Squads Write!*, 73.

29. Cornebise, *The Stars and Stripes*, 10–11.

30. Winterich, *Squads Write!*, 28.

31. Winterich, *Squads Write!*, 32.

32. Cornebise, *The Stars and Stripes*, 113.

33. Cornebise, *The Stars and Stripes*, 115.

34. Cornebise, *The Stars and Stripes*, 114.

35. Cornebise, *The Stars and Stripes*, 115.

36. Winterich, *Squads Write!*, 58.

37. Winterich, *Squads Write!*, 74.

38. Cornebise, *The Stars and Stripes*, 88.

39. Cornebise, *The Stars and Stripes*, 95–96.

40. Cornebise, *The Stars and Stripes*, 98.

41. Cornebise, *The Stars and Stripes*, 99.

42. Cornebise, *The Stars and Stripes*, 45.

43. Cornebise, *The Stars and Stripes*, 43.

44. Winterich, *Squads Write!*, 67

45. Cornebise, *The Stars and Stripes*, 125.

46. Nancy Gentile Ford, *Americans All! Foreign-born Soldiers in World War I* (College Station, Tx.: Texas A & M University Press, 2001), 89.

47. Nancy K. Bristow, *Making Men Moral: Social Engineering During the Great War* (New York: New York University Press, 1996), 69.

48. Bristow, *Making Men Moral*, 70.

49. Bristow, *Making Men Moral*, 43.

50. Ford, *Americans All! Foreign-born Soldiers in World War I*, 110.

51. Lyrics to "Over There," http://memory.loc.gov/learn/features/songs_times/flash.html.

52. *James Reese Europe's 369th U.S. Infantry "Hellfighters" Band*, The Complete Recordings, Memphis Archives, 1996.

53. Fred Baldwin, "The Enlisted Man During World War I," Ph.D. diss., Princeton University, 1964, 138.

54. Bristow, *Making Men Moral*, 20.

55. Ford, *Americans All! Foreign-born Soldiers in World War I* , 101.

56. Jennifer D. Keene, "Intelligence and Morale in the Army of a Democracy: the Genesis of Military Psychology during the First World War," *Military Psychology* 6 (1994): 238.

57. The venereal disease instructional lantern slide lecture is located in World War I Lantern Slide Training Sets, Set F-C3, Otis Historical Archives, National Museum of Health and Medicine, Walter Reed Army Medical Center, Washington, D.C.

58. Bristow, *Making Men Moral*, 92.

59. Bristow, *Making Men Moral*, 15.

60. Bristow, *Making Men Moral*, 51.

61. Meirion and Susie Harries, *The Last Days of Innocence, America at War, 1917–1918*. (New York: Vintage Books, 1997), 139.

62. Baldwin, "The Enlisted Man During World War I," 117.

63. J. Stuart Richards (ed.), *Pennsylvanian Voices of the Great War: Letters, Stories and Oral Histories of World War I* (Jefferson, North Carolina: McFarland & Co., 2002), 18.

64. Mark Meigs, *Optimism at Armageddon: Voices of American Participants in the First World War* (New York: New York University Press, 1997), 87.

65. Bristow, *Making Men Moral*, 148.

66. Christopher M. Sterba, *Good Americans: Italian and Jewish Immigrants during the First World War* (New York: Oxford University Press, 2003), 192.

67. Sterba, *Good Americans*, 193.

68. Sterba, *Good Americans*, 194.

69. Cornebise, *The Stars and Stripes*, 91.

70. Richard Schweitzer, *The Cross and the Trenches: Religious Faith and Doubt Among British and American Great War Soldiers* (Westport, Conn.: Praeger, 2003), 131.

71. Dixon Wecter, *When Johnny Comes Marching Home* (Cambridge, Mass.: Houghton Mifflin, 1944), 407.

72. Schweitzer, *The Cross and the Trenches*, 42.

73. Schweitzer, *The Cross and the Trenches*, 42.

74. Schweitzer, *The Cross and the Trenches*, 43.

75. Schweitzer, *The Cross and the Trenches*, 31.

76. Schweitzer, *The Cross and the Trenches*, 32.

77. Schweitzer, *The Cross and the Trenches*, 32.

78. Schweitzer, *The Cross and the Trenches*, 39.

79. Schweitzer, *The Cross and the Trenches*, 135.

80. Schweitzer, *The Cross and the Trenches*, 43.

81. Schweitzer, *The Cross and the Trenches*, 23.

82. David D. Lee, *Sergeant York: An American Hero* (Lexington: University Press of Kentucky, 1985), 17.

83. Tony Skeyhill Alvin Cullum York, *Sergeant York, His Own Life Story and War Diary,* ed. Thomas John Skeyhill (Garden City, N.Y.: Doubleday, Doran and Company, 1928), 276

84. Lee, *Sergeant York: An American Hero*, 47.

85. Schweitzer, *The Cross and the Trenches*, 36–37.

86. Schweitzer, *The Cross and the Trenches*, 30.

87. Schweitzer, *The Cross and the Trenches*, 218–219.

88. Schweitzer, *The Cross and the Trenches*, 220.

89. Schweitzer, *The Cross and the Trenches*, 196.

4 AMERICANS ALL: THE EXPERIENCES OF MINORITIES AND WOMEN IN THE MILITARY

The composition of the wartime military reflected the diversity of the American population in 1917. One out of every five soldiers was foreign-born, and one out of every ten was black. In addition, 30,000 women voluntarily joined the services to help fill its pressing need for clerks, telephone operators, and nurses. These minority groups each encountered a unique set of challenges during the war. African Americans and women faced difficulties asserting their equality, while foreign-born soldiers found themselves thrust into the great melting pot of military service that hastened their assimilation of American ways. The daily experiences of blacks, foreign-born, and women reveal that the struggle for democracy took place within the confines of the American military as well as on the battlefield.

AFRICAN AMERICAN SOLDIERS

For many African American men the nation's professed wartime goal of saving the world for democracy had a dual meaning. Besides sharing their white compatriots' desire to defeat the Kaiser, black troops also hoped to use their wartime participation as a lever that opened the door to greater recognition of their civil rights at home. From the opening days of the war, black soldiers faced an uphill battle in using honorable wartime service to accomplish these two goals.

Over 96 percent of the 367,710 blacks who served during the war were conscripted. African Americans formed 13 percent of the wartime army, even though they only represented 10 percent of the civilian population. There were several reasons why the army over-drafted African Americans to serve in the wartime military. During the limited time that the army accepted volunteers, it reserved only 4,000 slots for African Americans, therefore there were many able-bodied black men available to draft. Southern draft boards proved notoriously unsympathetic to black claims for deferments as fears circulated that the draft would drain southern communities of all their white men. Finally, in a striking commentary on the disadvantaged economic position that blacks held, the $30 a month that servicemen received actually represented a significant raise for many black workers and farmers. It was therefore harder for black men to receive deferments as the sole providers of their families when entering the military would make it easier, rather than harder, to support their families.

Besides being disproportionately drafted, black men also formed a greater proportion of those who evaded the draft. Nearly 100,000 African American men either failed to register for the draft or neglected to report when called. Sometimes this was by choice, sometimes it was not. For some men, illiteracy prevented them from complying with draft board regulations. Others invoked their religious beliefs to question the purpose of the war. In Lexington, Mississippi, for instance, over two thirds of the men who belonged to the same Church of God in Christ congregation refused to register. In many rural southern regions, the control that white landowners maintained over their black workforce influenced the workings of local draft boards. Some landowners withheld draft notices that arrived in the mail or refused to read them to their workers. When these workers failed to report, the government listed them as deserters. White planters subsequently gained both the advantage of their continued labor and the chance to collect a $50 reward from the government whenever they felt inclined to turn in these so-called deserters. Other planters negotiated with local draft boards to obtain agricultural furloughs for their workers that delayed their induction into the military. In Leon County, Texas, members of a local draft board went as far as to demand that black men go to work for them in return for receiving a draft exemption. Other planters tried to send less desirable workers in the place of valued workers called before draft boards. In these negotiations with local boards, white elites acted as if they owned these men and could freely barter one for another. Whites also used the conscription process to undermine the economic independence of blacks who had successfully created their own businesses or careers. A Little Rock attorney, Milton Wayman Guy, complained in July 1918 that "if a Negro is a tenant or works for some influential white man, he can 'get by the board' as they put it. The Negro who…has his own farm or business, is the one who is hard hit. White men in the same class are placed in Class IV, while Negroes are placed in (Class) 1."[1]

Ironically, their relative isolation in many parts of the rural South provided African American men with some tools to effectively evade the draft. With no form of government identification such as a birth certificate, driver's license or passport to establish their age, African American men could successfully claim to be either too young or too old to register for the draft. Federal investigators spent an inordinate amount of time during the war attempting to establish the age of African American southern men whom they suspected of unlawfully evading the draft. Interviewing white citizens about the probable age of African American men produced no reliable information about the army of migrant workers who moved frequently between jobs at sawmills and lumber camps throughout the South.

In 1917, the army's priority was to induct men headed for the trenches, and consequently few black soldiers were drafted. These delays soon led to wild claims throughout the South that communities were being emptied of their young white men. The draft board in Franklin County, Tennessee, noting the dissatisfaction this caused, reported that "all whites so far have been sent to Camp and no negroes which has created bitter unrest and dissatisfaction among our people."[2] Congressman R.Y. Thomas seconded this concern, writing to President Woodrow Wilson in February 1918 to complain that "people in Kentucky are not liking it very well, that the negroes are permitted to stay at home and hang around the towns and steal, while the white boys are taken from the farms and sent into the army."[3] Responding once again to outside political pressure, the army began inducting large numbers of black troops in the winter and spring of 1918.

African American Soldiers Assigned to Noncombatant Work

African American men who entered the army expecting to serve in the front lines were mostly disappointed. Both white and black soldiers had difficulty reconciling their personal desire to serve honorably at the front with the reality that the army needed vast numbers of support troops to maintain its field forces. Noncombatant work was essential in a modern army that assigned over 60 percent of its total force to positions that helped train, transport, and supply front-line troops. Despite the importance of noncombatant work to the overall war effort, American soldiers still viewed these as low-status assignments given to troops who did not have the physical or mental ability to fight in the trenches along the Western Front.

For black soldiers, noncombatant assignments were particularly hard to accept. Many white soldiers served as noncombatants during the war. None, however, were expressly put in these positions because they were white. The opposite was true for black troops. Within a few months of wrangling within the General Staff over the best way to utilize black manpower, army officials decided to place the vast majority of black men in noncombatant units. African Americans made up approximately one third of the army's laboring units and one thirtieth of its combat force. For the army, this policy addressed white southerners' demand that black men receive minimal training in firearms, yet serve in the military. Fearful that black soldiers would subsequently use knowledge obtained in the army to initiate a racial war in the United States after they returned home, the South exerted considerable pressure on the War Department to fashion a policy that met both military and domestic needs. The army's answer was to place the majority of black inductees in Quartermaster and Engineer units. Such units, one official contended, needed "a minimum of training under arms" and could be quickly shipped out of the country if racial rioting broke out in army training camps.[4]

As chance would have it, the General Staff's final version of the policy to restrict blacks to noncombatant work reached Secretary Baker's desk the morning of the Houston riot. The violent racial conflagration between black Regular Army troops and white police and civilians lent credence to southern concerns about the dangers of training black men to operate guns, and Baker, who had hesitated to endorse such a clearly discriminatory policy, authorized its implementation.

Violence in Houston, 1917

The clash in Houston between members of the 24th Infantry Regiment, local police, and white civilians foreshadowed critical elements of the black soldier's experience during the war. After a stint along the Mexican-American border, the regiment's 3rd battalion arrived on the outskirts of Houston to secure the construction site of Camp Logan in July 1917. A daily war of words soon erupted between the white workmen hired to build the National Guard training camp and the black soldiers guarding it. When confronted with comments like "those niggers would look good with coils around their necks" or "in Texas it costs $25 to kill a buzzard and $5 to kill a nigger," black troops responded in kind with verbal abuse and threats of retaliation.[5] Similar exchanges occurred whenever these soldiers ventured into town. As anger at local whites grew, the unit suffered a major loss of leadership when twenty-five of its best noncommissioned officers left to attend a special training camp underway at Fort Des Moines for black officer candidates and its colonel received a new assignment. The lack of seasoned leadership and the indifference of many white officers to mounting racial tensions soon proved catastrophic. Lack of sympathy between black troops and their white officers was a reoccurring problem throughout the war, with many white officers more than willing to attribute any shortcomings in the performance of black units to the racial limitations of the men rather than their own conduct as leaders.

Soldiers from the 24th Infantry Regiment particularly resented the segregation of streetcars in Houston, and often challenged this city ordinance by sitting where they liked, removing the screens that separated the white and black seating area, and on occasion threatening to derail trains that enforced the policy. Their mounting anger finally exploded on the evening on 23 August 1917, when word reached the battalion that Houston police had arrested and beaten several members of the unit. That morning, a soldier in town tried to stop a Houston policeman from beating a black woman as he arrested her. Infuriated, the policeman hit and arrested the soldier. Corporal Charles W. Baltimore, a member of a military police unit that routinely patrolled the city to keep black troops from clashing with Houston police and civilians, saw the soldier being taken away. When he asked the policeman where he was taking the soldier, he found himself assaulted and arrested as well. Military officials immediately arranged for the soldiers' release, but, as word of the incident reached the 3rd Battalion's encampment, soldiers resolved to take matters into their own hands. Without their officers' knowledge, the men broke into the supply room and began arming themselves and planning their march into town. The calm demeanor of Corporal Baltimore when he returned to camp fooled his white officers into believing that the incident could be quickly laid to rest. In reality, Baltimore was seething with resentment and eagerly marched with a hundred other black soldiers to avenge both this humiliation and the countless others that they had suffered since arriving in Houston. Once they reached the city, the troops began a 2-hour killing spree in which they killed fifteen whites and wounded twelve, some accidentally, some intentionally. The police station where the two men had been taken was put under siege, with four police officers killed outright and another fatally wounded. Four black soldiers died during the melee.

The sight of black soldiers fighting back against segregation and physical abuse shocked the nation. The army's swift and questionable treatment of the mutineers made it abundantly clear that black soldiers could expect little sympathy from army officials over matters of racial injustice. Without a systematic way to determine who had participated in the rampage or had been responsible for the actual killing, the army court-martialed all 156 men who had missed roll call that evening. Through grants of immunity and witness testimony, investigators eventually had enough evidence to charge sixty-three men with premeditated murder and mutiny in time of war. Fifty-four were found guilty, with thirteen being sentenced to die and the rest confined for life at hard labor. On 22 December 1917, the army hanged these thirteen, including Corporal Baltimore, causing consternation in the black community and jubilation among southern whites. Widespread protests from the black community over the swiftness of the executions resulted in a new regulation that required the president to review all sentences of death for wartime convictions.

Two subsequent courts-martial resulted in death sentences for another sixteen men. Letters from concerned black citizens poured into the War Department, causing Secretary Baker to advise clemency for all but six men convicted of killing a specific individual. With the black community demonstrating widespread patriotic devotion "both by their service in the Army and their purchase of Liberty bonds," Baker advised against reopening old wounds more than necessary.[6] Wilson followed Baker's advice, and these six were the last mutineers executed. The NAACP continued to lobby for clemency, and this campaign led to the early release of some prisoners and a sentence reduction to twenty years in prison for the others.

Although the level of violence committed by both black soldiers and the government in this incident remained unmatched during the war, the Houston riot brought into sharp relief some key features of black soldiers' wartime experience. The wave of denunciation from the black press and community over the Houston courts-martial revealed that whites were not the only ones mobilizing politically to plead their case during the war. Civil rights leaders strove throughout the war to protect the rights of black soldiers and open as many doors as possible for them. Their agitation resulted in a minor alteration to the General Staff's original plan to assign all black conscripts to noncombatant positions. In its initial formulation, only the handful of black men who filled the limited number of slots available in black National Guard units would receive training as combatants. Civil rights groups demanded more opportunities for black soldiers to prove their worth in battle. In response, the War Department agreed to form one black combatant division out of conscripts. Assistant Chief of Staff Tasker Bliss hoped that "the colored race, knowing that a combatant division is being formed, will realize, that in the noncombatant service, they are doing no more than their share along with similar white troops, and there can be no reasonable cause for ill feeling."[7] In the end, nearly 40,000 African Americans served overseas in the two combatant divisions, the 92nd and 93rd Divisions, reserved for them. These opportunities were not enough, however, to end complaints about the menial work given to most black troops during the war.

Black Officers and Investigators

Besides prodding the War Department to form another black combatant division, civil rights activists also lobbied hard for the black officers training camp that took place in Fort Des Moines. The decision to support a segregated camp for black officer candidates provoked a bit of soul searching within the ranks of a civil rights elite dedicated to integration. In the end, most accepted the segregated camp as the only way to ensure that blacks entering the army from civilian life had a chance to become officers. Overall, only 1,200 (less than 1 percent) of the 200,000 officers who held commissions during the war were black. Black officers only served in combatant units, where they faced constant charges of cowardice and ineptness. Review boards gradually purged black officers from both the 92nd and 93rd Division. The 92nd Division began the war with 82 percent of its officer corps filled by blacks, it ended with just 58 percent.

Pressure to improve internal racial relations came from within the army as well as from without. To oversee racial matters within the wartime army, Secretary Baker appointed Emmett J. Scott, a former assistant to Booker T. Washington, as a special assistant. During the war, Scott fielded numerous complaints from black soldiers about the racial prejudice that they encountered. He consistently urged the War Department to investigate these complaints and improve its treatment of black soldiers. Midway through the war, two

This privately produced poster underscored the willingness of black men to serve their country in a time of war, portraying them as strong, virile, and patriotic. (*Courtesy of Jennifer D. Keene*)

other investigators, Charles Williams, who investigated camp conditions for the Federal Council of Churches, and Major William Loving, who did the same for the Military Intelligence Division, began documenting the difficult conditions that black soldiers faced.

The portrait that these investigators painted was uniformly bleak. The equipment and housing needs of white troops always took precedence, consequently many black troops suffered through the bitterly cold winter of 1918 living in tents with few blankets and often no change of clothes. These units experienced high rates of illness, yet army doctors often turned ill black soldiers away, seeing them as malingers simply attempting to avoid another day of manual labor. A study of Camps Grant, Dodge and Funston, all located in the Midwest, discovered that over a 4-month period the 366th Infantry Regiment received less protein and fewer calories than white units, an experience likely replicated in other camps as well.

The failure to receive adequate medical care, lodging, and rations bothered black soldiers. Other complaints to Scott focused on the verbal and physical abuse inflicted by racist white commanders. African American soldiers noted that their superior officers sometimes struck or cursed them, and generally made their lives miserable. Other soldiers denounced the army's decision to not even issue uniforms to noncombatant troops working in the vicinity of training camps. "Each southern state has negroes in blue overalls working throughout the state with a pick and shovel," reasoned one General Staff officer, so sending black troops out to work in similar attire would be unlikely to elicit much complaint from neighboring white communities.[8] The effort to diminish these men's status as soldiers in the eyes of white civilians went even further. "We were drafted and given an understanding from our Local Boards that we were to be soldiers to help win the war," wrote Private George Canada from Waco, Texas. Instead, they were "taken out to work under the gun just like we are convicts."[9] Were they slaves or soldiers, many black troops wondered. In some combatant units, anger against white Americans was so strong, that "when black officers taught black men bayonet practice they usually substituted the picture of the rabid white southerner for that of the Hun" on the targets, a radical black newspaper, *The Messenger* claimed after the war.[10]

The act of sending an investigator into the field to investigate these complaints gave the War Department a way to claim that it took black soldiers' concerns seriously and intended to correct abuses. In reality, the reports filed by investigators were mostly scanned by intelligence officials to determine whether unrest among black soldiers was reaching mutinous proportions or if German propaganda was triggering their complaints. Interestingly, investigators often found it more comforting to conclude that enemy propagandists were stirring up trouble because then the actual solution required little change in the behavior or attitudes of white Americans. To better insulate black soldiers from enemy propaganda, intelligence officials usually advised camp commanders to improve the material living conditions of black troops and afford them more recreation if possible.

Racist Attacks against Black Troops

The General Staff, however, had no interest in turning the war into one to advance civil rights. Instead, the War Department urged camp commanders to minimize the potential for racial rioting within the training camps by enforcing a strict policy of segregation, often going against the advice of its own investigators in doing so. The War Department's reaction to a race riot in Camp Merritt offered a striking example of how firmly the General Staff adhered to the belief that segregation was the best way to ensure racial harmony. Located in Tenafly, New Jersey, Camp Merritt was an embarkation camp where troops waited to receive their departure orders for France. In this northern camp, the camp commander stationed black and white troops in close proximity and allowed them to share all recreational facilities. Many southern troops passing through the camp protested this arrangement, but to no avail. In August 1918, however, a group of recruits from Mississippi arrived in the camp and resolved to put an end to the integration of camp recreational facilities. On the night of 18 August 1918, a white YMCA secretary discovered a note on the stamp counter of one of the huts that read:

> You YMCA men are paying entirely too much attention to the niggers, and white men are neglected. Because of this, if it is not corrected by sundown, we are coming to clean this place out. (Signed), Southern Volunteers.[11]

That night these men made good on their threat. They searched all public buildings near their camp quarters and threw any black soldier that they found onto the street. Word filtered back to the barracks where both black and white soldiers buzzed with nervous anticipation over a larger fight to come. Within moments, military police arrived on the scene and seeing black troops assembled outside their barracks immediately jumped to the assumption that they had begun the trouble. Although no orders had been given, the military police fired shots into the crowd of black troops, wounding three men within the barracks and killing one. "Greatest credit must be given [to] the colored officers of a contingent of men from Camp Sherman, who were just across the road from the Camp Taylor men, into whom the guards had fired and who held their men in restraint from attacking the guards from the rear," noted a black YMCA secretary in his report of the incident.[12] The military police quickly confined all men to quarters, and, in the next few days, camp authorities moved all white troops to the opposite end of the camp and quarantined all black troops until they sailed for France. In the ensuing investigation, external investigators sent to the camp put the blame for this incident squarely on the troops from Mississippi and suggested that any white soldiers who refused to abide by camp policies be firmly disciplined. The General Staff, however, opted to fault the camp commander for abandoning a strategy of strict segregation to keep racial friction to a minimum.

Black Soldiers Strike Back

White soldiers' anger over living and working near black troops was only one half of the problem faced by army officials. The willingness of black soldiers to strike back against racial oppression remained a constant worry for army authorities who found themselves struggling to keep racial tensions within the training camps and their environs from spiraling out of control. In the South, local police forces and white civilians continued to physically and verbally abuse black soldiers in an effort to preserve the racial status quo. Many black soldiers, perceiving their strength in numbers, were equally willing to strike back whenever possible to assert their civil rights and maintain their dignity as men.

Sent to South Carolina to train, members of the New York–based 369th Infantry Regiment encountered immediate opposition and suspicion from the townspeople. As one chamber of commerce official noted, "I can tell you for certain that if any of those colored soldiers go in any of our soda stores and the like and ask to be served they'll be knocked down. Somebody will throw a bottle. We don't allow negroes to use the same glass that a white man may later have to drink out of. We have our customs down here and we aren't going to alter them."[13] The regiment's white commander entreated his troops to refrain from retaliation. Colonel William Hayward acknowledged that they were "camped in a region hostile to colored people" but still asked them "to act like the good soldiers you have always been and break the ice in this country for your entire race."[14] Reflecting the strong bond created in this unit between black troops and their white officers, the men did their best to adhere to Haywood's request even when white civilians threw them off streetcars and passing cars knocked them into gutters. Despite their overall restraint, the unit did come close to exchanging blows with white townsfolk. In the first incident, forty men armed themselves and headed to town after hearing rumors that the police had lynched two black soldiers. Upon learning that his men were about to replicate the Houston debacle, Hayward rushed into town and intercepted the group while two envoys visited the police station to discover the truth behind the incident. After winning the men's promise to allow him to investigate before proceeding, Hayward went to the police station where the police vowed that no black soldiers had been arrested or executed. Satisfied, the men marched back to camp. "Those men never drilled better in their lives," Hayward exclaimed in relief.[15] The incident convinced Hayward that keeping his unit in the south would lead to trouble. He secretly departed for Washington, D.C. the next day to meet with Secretary Baker and convinced him to redeploy the men.

The potential for racially motivated assaults continued to plague the 369th Infantry Regiment even when they returned to train in Camp Whitman, New York after twelve tension-filled days in Camp Spartansburg, South Carolina. An Alabama regiment assigned to the camp soon chafed at the presence of black combatant troops in their midst. When the Alabama unit threatened the 369th, its white officers this time supported their troops' desire to fight back. "Early one afternoon, I learned that the Alabamians intended to attack us during the night," Captain Hamilton Fish Jr. recalled in his memoirs. "For our defense, I had to borrow ammunition from another New York regiment, as we had none. After arming our soldiers, I and my fellow officers told them that if they were attacked, they were to fight back; if they were fired on, they were to fire back."[16] When a bugle sounded at midnight to alert the men that the Alabama regiment was approaching, Fish ran out to warn them that his men were armed. The Alabamians called off the attack.

Overseas African American Combat Forces

Over 40,000 black troops served in the two combatant Divisions reserved for African Americans. Because they were only 3 percent of American combat forces, African Americans suffered substantially fewer deaths and wounds than white soldiers. Overall, black soldiers from the 92nd and 93rd Divisions accounted for 773 of the 52,947 battlefield deaths in the AEF, less than 2 percent of its casualties. Of American soldiers wounded, 4,408 out of the 202,628 men wounded were black. If these figures reflected the overall safety that time behind the lines afforded black troops, the figures on disease are less reassuring that assignment to a noncombatant position guaranteed surviving the war. In 1917, the rates for death by disease were 4.92 per thousand for white soldiers and 11.13 per 1000 for black troops. The inferior medical care often given to black soldiers contributed to these disparities. Figures from October 1918 at the height of the influenza epidemic on hospital admission and death rates in the United States support this conclusion. That month, average figures for hospital admissions stateside were 198 percent for whites and 158 percent for blacks, meaning that on average white soldiers were admitted twice to the hospital and black soldiers 1.5 times. Less time in the hospital did not mean that black soldiers were healthier. The death rates for white and black soldiers in October were 9.5 percent and 11.1 percent, respectively. During that same month black and white soldiers overseas had the same rates of admission to the hospital, but still black soldiers were more likely to die, with a 5 percent mortality rate as compared to 3.3 percent for white troops.

The 92nd saw limited combat in France. After one of its regiments performed poorly at the beginning of the Meuse-Argonne offensive in September 1918, the Division spent the rest of the war trying to redeem its reputation. The 92nd Division arrived in France with serious deficits in its training. The fear of assembling 20,000 black combatants in any one camp had resulted in the dispersal of the Division's units throughout the United States for its initial training. Poor weather, a heavy influx of recruits just before the Division left the United States, lack of equipment, and the desire of many white officers to transfer out of the Division all hampered the preparation for combat that these men received stateside. Conditions improved slightly in France, but not enough to turn the Division into a well-trained unit. Despite its inexperience, the 368th Infantry Regiment was assigned the particularly difficult task of closing a gap between the French and

African American soldiers advance into battle under a camouflaged road. (*Courtesy of the Library of Congress*)

American armies at the opening of the Meuse-Argonne offensive. Their first exposure to combat revealed their faulty preparation, but AEF commanders immediately interpreted their failure to complete this mission as evidence that black soldiers could not master complex battlefield tactics. The subsequent controversy over whether the men received orders to withdraw or fled in panic provided an opening for white officers in the division to fully vent their frustration and anger at being associated with black troops. "I wish to go on record," wrote Colonel Fred Brown, the commanding officer of the 368th Infantry regiment, "as expressing my opinion that colored officers as a class are unfit to command troops in present day warfare."[17] A white officer in the regiment attempted to exonerate his performance by labeling the men "rank cowards."

The men of the 368th understood that the army was looking for any excuse to belittle the leadership of black officers and the bravery of black troops. When General Charles C. Ballou, the commander of the 92nd Division, visited the regiment shortly after this incident, he "found himself surrounded on getting out of his car by enlisted men asking him not to judge them on what had happened, telling him that they didn't want to discuss their differences with him, that they wanted to be given another chance to show that they knew how to behave and, if not advance, at least to hold their ground. Then came Colonel Moss, commander of the 367th regiment, bringing a petition from the officers and NCOs of his regiment asking not to be judged on what their neighbors had done, but to have their own chance."[18] In the courts-martial that followed, five black officers were found guilty of cowardice and sentenced to death, sentences that Secretary of War Baker commuted after concluding there was evidence that the men had received orders to withdraw.

The entire 92nd Division was pulled from the front lines, and did not see much active fighting until the final days of the war. Finally, on 10 November the last full day of fighting, the division participated in another organized offensive against German lines. In the wake of this final assault, Major Warner Ross reported, "I have heard of officers and of men and of units–large and small ones, white and also colored, that became panic stricken and useless under fire . . . but I am ready to testify that twelve hundred fifty officers and men [colored] did advance and that the command did hold *without showing the faintest symptoms of panic or retreat.*"[19] In the postwar years, however, reports like Ross's were quickly forgotten by white Regular Army officers who intended to believe the worst about black soldiers. Instead, a relatively minor incident during the Meuse-Argonne offensive took on dramatic historical significance when it became the evidence used repeatedly by army officials after the war to justify their conclusion that black officers were incompetent and black soldiers unreliable in battle.

African American Troops Welcomed in France

The provisional 93rd Division existed only on paper, composed of four independent infantry regiments that spent the war fighting with the French army. Many American Divisions and regiments trained with the French, and, in the spring and summer of 1918, thousands of white Americans went into battle under French command. Only these four black regiments, however, became permanent components of French Divisions. The decision to give these four regiments to the French helped Pershing reduce two pressing problems for his command: the steady French insistence that the Americans funnel soldiers into the Allied armies and the doubts that many American white officers had about the fighting abilities of black troops. With France's successful record placing soldiers from its North and West African colonies in the front lines, Pershing gave these soldiers to an ally that had both the experience and willingness to use black men in combat. If they stayed under American command, the chances of these elite troops actually fighting appeared dim. Since arriving in France, the 369th Infantry Regiment had spent its time loading and unloading boxes rather than completing its infantry training. No complaints from black troops, therefore, greeted the news that they were headed to French lines. The white commander of the 369th Infantry Regiment, William Hayward summed up the situation this way, "we are *les enfants perdus* [the lost children] and glad of it. Our great American general simply put the black orphan in a basket, set it on the doorstep of the French, pulled the bell and went away. I said this to a French colonel with an 'English spoken here' sign on him, and he said 'weelcome leetle black babie.'"[20]

When they received their permanent assignments to French Divisions, these four regiments had to turn in their American equipment and arms, including their Springfield model 1903 rifles. In return they received French Lebel rifles, which the men regarded as an inferior weapon. They were, however, glad to get French gas masks that did not include the nose clip featured in the American model. The men kept their American uniforms, but wore French helmets. It took some soldiers time to adjust to French rations that included large amounts of soup and bread rather than the hefty portions of meat and vegetables the American Army provided. At first, the men received the normal French allowance of a liter of wine each day, which French troops tended to drink throughout the day or dilute with water. This was soon discontinued, when American troops, unused to drinking wine on a daily basis, drank their undiluted wine immediately. After a few incidents of drunken wild shooting, the wine rations stopped.

The 369th Infantry Regiment boasted an illustrious war record. It served for 191 days at the front, the longest of any American regiment. The 369th, 371th, and 372st Infantry Regiments of the 93rd Division all received the *croix de guerre* from the French in recognition of their bravery under fire.

The Germans attempted to exploit racial divisions within the American army by encouraging black soldiers to abandon their white comrades. "Can you go to a restaurant where white people dine, can you get a seat in a theatre where white people sit, can you get a Pullman seat or berth in a railroad car?. . . there is nothing in the whole game for you but broken bones, horrible wounds, broken health or death" read propaganda leaflets dropped into lines held by black troops.[21] Although these pamphlets offered an accurate description of the Jim Crow South, such obvious propaganda had little effect on African American soldiers who were well versed in the atrocities committed by German troops in Belgium and France, and whose close ties to the French gave them even greater motivation to defeat Germany.

The positive experiences of the 200,000 black troops who went to France during the war extended beyond the French willingness to use them as combatant troops and decorate deserving units with military medals. Behind the lines, black troops found the white French population eager to make contact with American troops who had come to help drive the Germans out of their country. The warm reception that they received quickly established France as a model egalitarian and democratic society in the minds of most black soldiers. The image of France as a color-blind culture came from the daily interactions between African American soldiers and French civilians who welcomed black troops into their homes, cafes, and restaurants without any hesitation. "These French people don't bother with no color line business," wrote one soldier to his mother. "They treat us so good that the only time I ever know I'm colored is when I look in the glass."[22] The willingness of young French women to date black soldiers or establish friendships with them also provided a striking contrast with the social segregation practiced in the United States. The civil rights activist W. E. B. Du Bois summed up the feelings of many black troops when he noted at the conclusion of the war that "for bleeding France and what she means and has meant and will mean to us . . . we gladly fought."[23] Their fondness for France prompted African American soldiers to contribute over 300,000 francs to *The Stars and Stripes* fund for French war orphans.

As an imperial power with colonies in Africa, France had its own particular history of discrimination and racism that escaped the notice of most African American troops. Accustomed to welcoming colonial troops who had come to protect the motherland, French civilians were more than willing to accept another group of visiting black men rendering a valuable service to their country. The French did not treat all black men similarly. Instead, they demonstrated a marked preference for "civilized" American soldiers who brought plenty of ready cash with them and represented the power and strength of the U.S. Army. Troops from West Africa, while lauded for their fearlessness in battle, were often kept far from civilian communities to prevent too much interaction with the local population.

Angered by the hospitality the French bestowed on American black troops, American white soldiers tried to transport American-style racism to foreign soil by warning the French that blacks had tails and criminal tendencies. One black sailor had a ready response when he encountered such rumors among the French population. He simply reached into his pocket for a picture that he carried around of a lynching to offer ample evidence of white savagery. The eagerness of French women to date African

American soldiers was a particular point of controversy between white and black troops. French civilians were often shocked to see visceral racial hatreds expressed so openly, and the extreme racism of some white Americans often provoked even more affection for black soldiers among the French. One young French woman demonstrated this reaction in a letter she composed to an African American soldier in which she accepted his offer of friendship "because I know now what is your hard condition. I have spoken to white men, and always I have seen the same flash [lightening] in their angry eyes, when I have spoken them of colored men. But I do not fear them for myself; I am afraid of them for you, because they have said me the horrible punishment of colored men in America."[24] Army officials tried to stop racial confrontations between white and black soldiers by assigning each race different French villages to visit in their off-duty hours or prohibiting black soldiers from appearing in public with respectable French women. These latter measures only slightly curtailed contact between African American soldiers and the French civilian population. Instead, these orders mostly served to underscore the racist character of the American Army to its black troops.

The African American presence in France did more than expose the French to American-style racism and race relations. The renowned band leader James Europe headed the regimental band of the 369th Infantry Regiment, a group that performed concerts throughout France and introduced many Europeans to American-style ragtime and jazz. Noble Sissle, a well-known musician in the troupe, recorded the reaction of one group of French civilians when they heard this music for the first time. As the band hit its stride halfway through the concert, "the audience could stand it no longer, the 'jazz germ' hit them and it seemed to find the vital spot loosening all muscles and causing what is known in America as an 'eagle rocking fit' . . . when the band had finished and people were roaring with laughter, their faces wreathed in smiles, I was forced to say that this is just what France needs at this critical time."[25] When Europe and his band played in Paris, nearly every audience responded joyfully to the kinetic and vibrant syncopated rhythms coming from their instruments. The band, one reporter noted, "filled France full of Jazz."[26] Europe's band was the most famous, but by no means the only African American military band that played ragtime and jazz for French audiences during the war. Parisians' enthusiasm for big band jazz soon developed into a fascination with African American music, art, and literature that fueled the creation of a vibrant expatriate community of black artists and intellectuals who took up residence in the French capital after the war.

FOREIGN-BORN U.S. SOLDIERS

When the American Army arrived in France, many French soldiers were amazed by what they saw. "You could not imagine a more extraordinary gathering than this American army," one French soldier wrote to his family,

> There is a bit of everything, some Greeks, some Italians, some Turks, some Chinese, some Indians, some Spanish, and also a reasonable number of Huns. Truthfully, almost half of the officers have German origins. This doesn't seem to bother them. But doesn't this seem to you a strange outlook? As for me, I could hardly see myself fighting against my country, even if I had left it a long time ago. They don't seem to remember it. . . . There are among the Americans the sons of French emigrates and the sons of Hun emigrates. I asked one son of a Frenchman if the Germans could be trusted to fight against their brothers and cousins, he said without hesitation "yes!"[27]

Official wartime propaganda contained a special appeal to immigrants, reminding them that they had a duty to support their adopted nation. (*Courtesy of the Library of Congress*)

Foreign-born men accounted for nearly one fifth of the American wartime army, approximately half a million of the four million man force, reflecting the waves of heavy immigration to the United States in the years immediately leading up to the war. The thousands of second-generation immigrants raised in ethnic enclaves entering the army pushed the numbers of foreign-speaking troops even higher. Overall, these troops introduced forty-six different languages into the training camps.

Many foreign-speaking troops entered the army as conscripts. Draft boards were instructed to induct foreign-born men from friendly nations who had become American citizens or were in the midst of the naturalization process. Selective Service regulations allowed draft boards to conscript immigrants from nonenemy nations who had completed the necessary paperwork, but were still in the 5-year waiting period. The draft law exempted foreign-born men who did not intend to become citizens, but nearly 200,000 men relinquished this exemption and were conscripted. In May 1918, Congress passed legislation that waived all naturalization requirements for soldiers serving in the wartime army who received honorable discharges. Nearly 280,000 men took advantage of this opportunity to gain immediate citizenship. When the war drew to a close, army officials throughout the nation held naturalization ceremonies where immigrant soldiers took their oath as American citizens. "I earned my right to citizenship by being willing to die for my country," observed Knud J. Olsen, a Danish-American who served with the 82nd Division.[28]

By the war's mid-point, some native-born Americans began to complain that exemptions for nondeclarant aliens had created a subclass of "alien slackers," a term used to describe immigrants who lingered in the safety of their own homes while native-born American men fought and died overseas. Reflecting the rising resentment against immigrants, the *New York Sun* remarked, "The apparent injustices of stripping the land of American youths to furnish a fighting force in Europe while leaving millions of aliens at home to enjoy the rewards of peaceful industry has undoubtedly got on the people's nerves."[29] In their zeal to ensure that all eligible aliens served, local boards ended up over-drafting the immigrant population. Overall, immigrant soldiers represented 18 percent of the total wartime force, even though the foreign-born were only 14.5 percent of the overall American population. Occasionally, over-eager boards scooped up nondeclarent immigrants as well, leading to protests from a few thousand men who contested their induction. Some of these men went to court or appealed for help from their embassies, leading to the eventual release of 1,842 men from wartime service.

Many foreign-born men, however, were eager to serve the Allied cause and their adopted nation. Their families' own particular experiences in Europe often colored foreign-born and second-generation troops' attitudes about the war. Most American press coverage focused on the Western Front, but immigrants from the Russian, German, and Austro-Hungarian Empires paid close attention to how fighting on the Eastern Front affected their homelands and relatives overseas. Serbian, Croatian, Polish, and Slovenian immigrants from Eastern Europe avidly hoped for a Central Power defeat, believing this would free their nations from German or Austro-Hungarian control. Armenian, English, French, Italian, and Belgian immigrants had other reasons to pray that their homelands prevailed against Central Power aggression. Overt enthusiasm for the war within many of the nation's immigrant communities, therefore, revealed a broader sense of purpose than the one embraced by Americans farther removed from their immigrant roots. For many recent immigrants, service in the American military became a way to both honor their adopted country and ensure the well-being of their homelands.

Duel Allegiances for Foreign-Born U.S. Soldiers

The dual loyalties of first- and second-generation immigrants did not always provoke enthusiasm over America's entry into the war. Irish-Americans harbored longstanding resentments against Great Britain, which flared anew after the British brutally suppressed the Irish independence movement during the Easter Rebellion in 1916. The German-American community tended to support Germany during the period of neutrality, and, once the United States declared war on Germany, all first-generation immigrants became enemy aliens ineligible for service. Some German immigrants were already serving in the American military when the war began. These men were allowed to stay in the service and some even fought in France if their commanding officers attested to their loyalty. Second-generation Germans were eligible for the draft, but faced immediate suspicions about their loyalty. Military intelligence officials used a large cadre of soldier informants to investigate their comrades and ascertain their trustworthiness.

Despite the willingness of most foreign-speaking soldiers to comply with the draft, Army officials worried that foreign-speaking troops remained too far outside the mainstream culture to understand why they had been called to fight Germany. To ensure that the message of fighting "to make the world safe for democracy" reached these troops, camp commanders organized a host of patriotic celebrations intended to bridge the gap between Old and New Worlds. Many of these festivities featured traditional ethnic entertainment and music, as well as patriotic American songs. Besides lecturing soldiers on America's purpose in the war, invited speakers regaled foreign-speaking troops in their own language about the feats of their homelands and emphasized the important contribution that their nationality made to the American army. Extolling the efforts of Italy became particularly important to Italian-born and Italian-American soldiers in the wake of Italy's disastrous defeat in the battle of Caporetto in November 1917. Many Italian soldiers often felt slighted with so much press attention focused on the sacrifices of France and Britain. After receiving protests from Italian organizations and soldiers, the War Department instructed camp commanders to prominently display the Italian flag alongside the flags of other Allied nations throughout the camp, and to include mention of Italy's feats in all addresses to the soldiers that highlighted the Allied war effort.

At the War Department's urging, the ethnic press printed letters from foreign-speaking soldiers serving in the American army evincing enthusiasm for military service and the cause. Finding such letters to print was not difficult. As one army translator noted, most soldiers "spoke highly of the treatment extended to [them], and manifested an eagerness to get at the Kaiser. Some of the letters made it evident that the writers were urged by a double motive, that of loyalty to his adopted country and full zeal for the liberation of his native country; but in most cases the tone of the letters was like that of the American soldiers, anxious to do his full duty."[30]

The dual loyalties of Czech, Slovak, Polish, and Jewish immigrants created distinct wartime experiences for each group of soldiers that digressed somewhat from the typical service records compiled by foreign-speaking troops. When the United States declared war on Austria-Hungary in November 1917 after Italy's defeat at Caporetto, the government designated first-generation immigrants from any part of the Austro-Hungarian Empire as enemy aliens ineligible for service in the American army. In response, Czech and Slovak immigrants lobbied for permission to form an independent legion that would fight with the French army overseas. Momentum for creating the Czechoslovakian Legion puttered out in September 1918 when the United States recognized Czechoslovakia as an independent nation and removed Czechs and Slovaks from the enemy alien list. Over 138,000 Poles served with the American Army, but the Polish community also created a Polish Legion for Polish immigrants who did not intend to become American citizens or Polish-Americans not subject to the draft. Nearly 20,000 Polish volunteers from the United States fought with the Polish Army in France through service in the Polish Legion. Attempts to create Russian and Armenian Legions never went beyond the planning stages.

Many Russian Jews retained painful memories of their lives under tsarist oppression. Avoiding conscription into the Tsar's army, where Jews faced abuse and were forced to abandon all their religious practices, motivated many to leave Russia and immigrate to the United States. Jewish immigrants read alarming wartime reports of retreating tsarist troops who forced nearly 600,000 Jews to relocate eastward as the army adopted a scorched earth strategy to stymie the German invasion. These refugees lost their homes and livelihoods, suffered epidemics of cholera and typhoid, and faced starvation when packed into new communities unable to handle this sudden influx. These concerns initially put many Jews in conflict with two critical features of the American war effort: joining an Allied force that included Russia and using a draft to raise the wartime army. By 1917, however, the Russian Tsar had abdicated and a new parliamentary government had formed. Jewish immigrants had high hopes that this new government would curb the Anti-Semitic abuses of the past. Perhaps more importantly, many Jewish immigrants did not intend to return to Russia and tended to view conscription into the American army quite differently from forced induction into the Russian army. "When my turn to be drafted came, it didn't bother me at all. As a matter of fact, if I hadn't been drafted, I think I would have gone anyway. Both my parents had been Jewish immigrants from Europe, and this country had been good to our family," one soldier noted after the war.[31] When Wilson endorsed the Balfour Declaration, which announced British support for the creation of a Jewish homeland in Palestine, Jewish immigrants in the United States gained an additional reason to support the Allied side. Like the Czechs, Slovaks, and Poles, the Jewish community organized a Jewish Legion to pursue the dual goals of securing an Allied victory and obtaining an independent state for its people. The United States never declared war on the Ottoman Empire, which controlled Palestine, so the Jewish Legion fought with the British Army. Over 5,000 Jews from the United States who were ineligible to serve in the American army joined the Jewish Legion.

Although unique circumstances shaped the service records of Czech, Slovak, Polish, and Jewish soldiers, they also shared many of the expectations and challenges generally faced by foreign-speaking soldiers in the wartime army. Foreign-born men who initially enlisted in local National Guard units often hoped to fight alongside men with the same ethnic background and language competencies. This was the promise, for instance, used to recruit Italians into a National Guard machine gun unit organized in New Haven, Connecticut. The Italian community sent this unit off to war expecting their sons, husbands, and brothers to fight side by side for the duration. A local committee solicited donations from neighborhood businesses and fraternal societies, and then used the funds to purchase small, gold crucifixes for each man and a large American flag for the unit to carry into battle. These gifts were presented to the men in a ceremony at Yale Field attended by friends and families as well as the mayor of New Haven. The crosses around their necks, the committee's secretary hoped, would give the men "on the battlefield, where the fight is raging, the memory, the encouragement, the concern and the heartbeat of the entire [Italian] Colony."[32] Immediately upon their induction into federal service, however, these men discovered that the army was quickly absorbing local units like theirs to create a national, mass army. This particular unit became part of the 102nd Infantry, 26th Division, where the 75 Italians did not even form the majority of the 178 men in their company.

In regular units assigned a large proportion of immigrant soldiers, some comical situations often arose. The 77th Infantry Division drew in a large number of drafted men from New York City, boasting recruits from over forty different nationalities who often had only elementary English skills. "Imagine the difficulties of teaching the rudiments of military art to men, however willing, who couldn't understand; officers have had sometimes to get right down on their hands and knees to show by actual physical persuasion how to 'advance and plant the left foot,'" one officer noted with exasperation.[33] In one company, men arranged themselves by linguistic groups, so that when an English command was given, each corporal could quickly translate it for their squad in time for the men to perform the required maneuver. When a new captain arrived in the company and decided to re-group the men by height, chaos reigned on the drill field until he realized his mistake.

Religious and Cultural Concerns of Foreign-Born Soldiers

Serving alongside friends and neighbors had other benefits besides providing a common language and a comforting link to the home front. Serving with men who shared the same ethnic background sometimes meant a better chance of having specific religious needs met. At Camp Upton, a camp located on Long Island, the mayor of New York arranged for special trains to bring Jewish soldiers into the city to observe Yom Kippur where synagogues provided lodging for troops without homes in the city. The camp commander brought rabbis to camp to conduct services in the YMCA auditorium for those Jewish soldiers too ill to travel to New York City. Similarly, members of the Greek Orthodox Church within the 27th Division were excused from drill for the Feast of St. Nicholas after church officials requested that troops be allowed to follow the tradition of renewing their vows to the church on this holiday. Polish troops in Camp Gordon preferred to hear Catholic mass in their own language and successfully lobbied for a Polish priest to hear their confessions. Throughout the United States, the Knights of Columbus searched for foreign-speaking clergy who could visit the training camps to give mass in the native languages of foreign-speaking troops. Jewish civilians also created the Jewish Welfare Board to provide religious services for Jewish soldiers, but the under-funded organization only managed to get a handful of workers in the training camps and overseas during the war. The Jewish Welfare Board did, however, successfully distribute 145,000 prayer books and 80,000 bibles in Yiddish and Hebrew.

Before January 1918, individual camp commanders decided when and how they would honor special requests concerning religious practices. With the start of the new year, however, the newly formed Foreign-speaking Soldier bureau created uniform policies to handle the special religious needs of the diverse soldier population. The army still made no provisions for kosher meals, a deficiency that some Jewish families tried to remedy by sending their sons regular kosher meals throughout their stateside stay in the training camps. The War Department did, however, order all camp commanders to provide Jewish soldiers with one pound of matzos or unleavened bread during Passover and to grant Jewish soldiers furloughs on major Jewish holidays such as Passover, Yom Kippur, and Rosh Hashanah. The order even extended to the war zone, where divisional commanders were advised to excuse men from duty "where deemed practicable" to allow them to observe Jewish religious holidays.[34]

The Foreign-speaking Soldier bureau also helped troops resolve unnerving and complex bureaucratic tangles. Foreign-born soldiers often had trouble getting allotment checks sent to their relatives, either because clerks misspelled long and unfamiliar names, or because of the difficulty in sending mail to remote areas of Europe during the war. To ease comprehension problems in the camps, the Foreign-speaking Soldier bureau translated information about the allotment procedure and War Risk Insurance into multiple languages. Italian-born soldiers faced a unique bureaucratic challenge because the Italian government considered them deserters from the Italian army and exacted heavy fines from any family member living in Italy as a penalty for their alleged desertion. After receiving several complaints, the War Department compiled a list of all Italian-born men serving in the American army and secured a formal exemption for them from the Italian government.

The efforts to respect the religious and cultural customs of foreign-born troops reflected the army's tolerance for diversity as it strove to turn these men into English-speaking American soldiers. This approach to assimilation was noticeably at odds with the harsh 100 percent Americanism advocated by ultrapatriot civilian groups that viewed assimilation as a complete jettisoning of any foreign ways. In marked contrast to this approach, an array of Progressive reformers and ethnic community leaders worked with the army to introduce a more moderated approach that did not force foreign-born troops to choose between the Old and the New Worlds as they assimilated. Instead, foreign-born soldiers were able to retain their ethnic identities, but were still expected to demonstrate their loyalty to the new country and learn American ways.

Preserving the cultural traditions of foreign-speaking soldiers became the responsibility of the social welfare organizations that structured camp recreational activities. The YMCA organized Greek, Italian, and Polish evenings to celebrate the food, music, and dances of these cultures and to give men from these nationalities a way to socialize with one another outside the barracks. Living outside of their ethnic communities for the first time, military service also exposed many foreign-born troops to American customs and culture. Italian immigrants serving in the 26th Division, for example, took part in their first Thanksgiving dinner while serving overseas.

To ensure that foreign-speaking soldiers received the language skills that they needed to fight effectively, the Assistant Secretary of War Frederick Keppel eventually instructed training camp commanders to give all foreign-speaking soldiers 3 hours of English instruction a day for 4 months. Men learned critical military vocabulary such as "rifle," "tent," "guard," "tank," "march," "aeroplane," "howitzer," and "Red Cross." Civics, history, science, conversational French, and instruction in geography, especially showing recruits the war zones, became part of these training camp curriculums as well.

In the spring of 1918, the army began assigning incoming foreign-speaking troops to developmental units before transferring them to national army units. Developmental units were created to rehabilitate men initially considered unfit either physically or mentally for service. Illiterate or foreign-speaking soldiers fell into this classification. "Instead of distributing the non-English speaking men among the English speaking and thus creating confusion and misunderstanding, they can be grouped, handled and controlled together, and the wastage which has existed of time, money and foreign human material can be brought to an end," one army bulletin predicted in outlining the new program.[35] After a successful experiment in Camp Gordon, Georgia that grouped men who spoke the same language together for intensive English-language tutoring while providing a normal schedule of drilling, the War Department ordered thirty-five training camps to institute the same system to prepare foreign-speaking soldiers for service abroad. Development battalions, led by bilingual officers and noncommissioned officers, sprang up across the country in the summer of 1918 to offer 6-week courses of specialized instruction before breaking the men into platoons that eventually went overseas as replacements for men lost in battle. Grouping the men into platoons, the War Department believed, would give these men a support network overseas, yet the small size of a platoon would allow them to continue improving their English language skills as they interacted with others in their companies or regiments.

Prejudice against Foreign-Born U.S. Soldiers

Overall, very little ethnic strife divided the wartime army, although instances of ethnically motivated violence did occur. On 13 October 1917, Gentile soldiers pulled a Jewish soldier named Otto Gottschalk from his bed in a North Carolinian training

This Americans All! poster celebrated the loyalty and achievements of immigrant soldiers. (*Courtesy of the Library of Congress*)

camp. The men stripped Gottschalk naked, threw him into a muddy trench, then dragged him behind a building and beat him with clubs. Rather than simply acting on their own anti-Semitic impulses, the men in this case were obeying explicit orders from their captain to attack Gottschalk. The captain went through two courts-martial, but was acquitted each time. This level of anti-Semitic violence was rare in the wartime army, but many Jewish soldiers still faced overt discrimination that barred their entry into desirable units and hampered promotions. In the barracks, isolated Jews assigned to primarily Gentile units often endured daily slurs and jibes from their comrades, which sometimes led to blows. "Even in the fighting divisions right on the lines the Jewish boys had trouble," asserted Lieutenant Jacob Rader Marcus. Anti-Semitism, he concluded, "exists at all times and under all circumstances."[36] Trying to pass as a Gentile almost never worked as a strategy to avoid abuse, Marcus claimed. After speaking with other Jewish soldiers, he concluded that the Jews who fared the best were those who stuck up for themselves when challenged openly by Gentile bigots.

Throughout 1918, the War Department tried to purge derogatory terms like "wop," "dagoes," "hunkies" and "guineas" from soldiers' vocabulary. Revealing the pervasiveness of ethnic slurs, one soldier recollected that his unit drilled to a song that included the line "the Jews and the wops and the dirty Irish cops," without anyone giving these words a second thought.[37] Although regulating the speech of soldiers proved mostly fruitless, watching military authorities publicly reprimand men for employing ethnic slurs did boost the morale of many immigrant soldiers. After seeing his captain discipline a group of men for name-calling, an Italian soldier exclaimed, "I felt like hugging and kissing the Captain as he was telling the company that we Italians were as good men as they were, and that we should be respected as brothers."[38] These efforts to create an inclusive and more tolerant environment within the military clearly affected how some native-born soldiers viewed their foreign-born comrades. "American All!" read the slogan emblazoned on a popular wartime propaganda poster, a message that Lieutenant Samuel Nash repeated in a letter that he wrote to his family. "The real man of the whole crowd is the ordinary garden variety of enlisted man, sgt.[sergeant], cpl.[corporal] or private, the fellow who really does the work and the suffering. And in the American Army it didn't seem to make any difference whether he spoke Polish, Italian, Yiddish, Irish, or plain American, he was a wonderful soldier," decided Nash.[39]

Many foreign-born troops expressed less shock than native-born Americans over the often primitive living conditions that existed in rural France. Overseas, Americans entered villages dominated by a centuries-old Catholic church whose inhabitants still received their daily news from a town crier. The reality of European peasant life where people wore wooden shoes as protection against the mud, cooked over fireplaces rather than stoves, and lived with their livestock under one roof reminded foreign-born soldiers how far they had come from their childhood days spent in similar circumstances. Their language abilities often complimented this cultural familiarity with European ways. Italian-speaking soldiers, for instance, often found it easier than their English-speaking comrades to understand and learn French.

In their postwar recollections, many foreign-born soldiers felt satisfied with the service they rendered to their adopted country in time of war. Louis Van Iersel from the Netherlands summed up the significance of serving in such a polygot force by noting that "I learned to get along and respect all people."[40] When Van Iersel entered the military, he did not speak English. His fluent German and French, however, proved quite valuable for the American Army in France. Van Iersel received the *croix de guerre* for infiltrating German lines and convincing a German officer to surrender his force of sixty men. He was also awarded the Medal of Honor for going behind enemy lines to gather information and then successfully warning his battalion that the Germans planned a heavy artillery bombardment on their position. The thousands of lives that Van Iersel saved due to both his bravery and his distinct linguistic skills offer just one example of how the American army benefited from the unique abilities and dedication of its foreign-speaking soldiers.

WOMEN IN THE U.S. MILITARY

When the United States entered the war, most Americans assumed that women would make their primary contribution to the war effort on the homefront. Mothers and wives fulfilled an important patriotic obligation when they made sure that their menfolk conformed to Selective Service regulations. Every woman needed to "inspire, encourage and urge the men of her family to perform their patriotic duty," declared Dr. Anna Howard Shaw, president of the National American Women's Suffrage Association. "This is the service of sacrifice and loyalty which the Government asks of the women of the nation at the present critical hour."[41] Besides sending family members off to war with smiles and encouraging words, multitudes of women also volunteered their labor to aid the war effort. Under the auspices of the Women's Committee of the Council of National Defense, the government mobilized women to conserve food, plant victory gardens, knit socks, roll bandages, and sell war bonds. The shortage of civilian laborers created additional economic opportunities for women to work in factories or for one of the new federal agencies created to oversee the massive economic and military mobilization.

As reflected by these numerous activities, women's primary contribution to the war effort came on the home front. Yet, the wartime ethos that placed heavy emphasis on voluntary service coupled with strong economic incentive to seek war-related employment also motivated thousands of female workers to join the American Expeditionary Forces or one of the social welfare agencies working with troops in France. At least 16,500 women traveled overseas during the war to work as nurses, canteen hostesses, ambulance and truck drivers, clerical workers, telephone operators, dietitians, bacteriologists, and librarians. At home, 12,000 women worked for the Navy and Marine Corps, while army hospitals and offices employed thousands of women as nurses and clerks.

The women who served tended to be white, Christian, native-born, thirty-something, single, and nearly all had previous work experience. These traits were not accidental, but instead reflected the careful screening given to applicants. Only three African American women served as YWCA hostesses overseas, and no black nurses traveled to France. Because the YWCA dominated the recreational life of soldiers and Military Intelligence officials gave applications from Jews especially close scrutiny to uncover any possible connections to radical political movements, Jewish women had limited opportunities to serve overseas as well. The Jewish Welfare Board eventually managed to send one hundred female welfare workers to France, but most did not arrive until after the armistice. Until the final months of the war, the army prohibited the sisters and wives of soldiers from enlisting in an effort to screen out those who might have ulterior motives for joining. Officials also tried to discourage enlistments by "camp followers," a term used to describe single-women actively seeking either a husband or sexual liaisons, by heavily circumscribing female army workers' social lives. The YWCA and Red Cross rejected many younger applicants out of concern that they were too immature to handle the responsibilities of wartime work and worried that older women lacked the physical stamina for overseas service. Officials screening applications considered women in their thirties in their "zenith" with enough maturity, common sense, and good judgment to handle the challenges of working at the front.[42]

The white, Christian women who traveled overseas mostly came from the lower middle class and had lived independent lives before the war. Many volunteers had already spent substantial time living in cities where they created careers centered on work outside the home. These women had their own reasons for volunteering. Some did so out of a patriotic desire to serve their country; others were swept along like their male counterparts with the romantic notion of taking part in a great adventure that allowed one to break out of the humdrum rhythms of daily life. "I wanted to travel, see some of the world and experience new adventures," recalled Oleda Joure, who worked as a telephone operator overseas.[43] Still others believed that wartime work provided an opportunity for educational or occupational advancement. Some had more personal reasons for seeking service overseas. "My grandfather lost a leg in the Civil War," noted one Red Cross nurse, "Clara Barton...took him from the battlefield in a dumpcart and saved his life. Small wonder, then that I was brought up on grandfather's wooden leg, and tales of Clara Barton, and that I just naturally gravitated to the Red Cross service."[44]

Although most did not join to explicitly further the cause of female equality, some women initiated internal campaigns for equal treatment once they came face to face with officers who trivialized their contributions, undermined their authority, and exercised excessive control over their social lives.

Women's Jobs in the Military

When bringing women into the military, the army went to great lengths to ensure that their presence disrupted the status quo as little as possible. The positions that women assumed in the military as nurses, clerks, telephone operators, and typists were jobs that civilian society had already accepted as appropriate for women. Women who had ventured into more controversial careers had a tougher time gaining a foothold in the army. Women were welcomed as nurses in the U.S. Army Nurse Corps, but not as doctors. Female physicians accounted for almost 3 percent of all physicians in the United States (totaling nearly 6,000), but Wilson refused to allow female doctors to serve in the army because as commissioned medical officers they would be in a position to command men. The official decision to reject applications from female doctors did not completely prevent them from treating ill soldiers, however. Some worked as contract surgeons on army bases, others as researchers in army laboratories, and a few even went overseas with the Red Cross. Because they were not formally inducted into the military, these female physicians never held an officer's rank.

Nurses

The Civil War established the precedent of using female nurses in time of war, and, in 1901, the War Department created the U.S. Army Nurse Corps. Army nurses accompanied troops to the Mexican border in 1916 when fighting broke out between the United States and Mexico where they gained practical experience in the field that later proved invaluable when they got the France. Nurses faced little overt opposition over enlisting because the public and army viewed caring for wounded men as a legitimate female avocation.

The Red Cross Nursing Service served as the official reserve for the Army Nurse Corps and spearheaded the recruitment of female nurses. The Army Nurse Corps grew from 400 to over 21,000 by the time of the armistice. Only half of these women traveled to France. Before they headed overseas, the Red Cross outfitted each nurse with a kit that included a hat, outdoor uniform, rubber boots, a raincoat, three pairs of shoes, woolen underwear, pajamas, a sleeping bag, and a blanket roll.

Once overseas, most nurses worked in base hospitals that consisted of forty officers, one hundred nurses, and two hundred enlisted sanitation troops. A colonel usually oversaw management of the entire hospital. The chiefs of medicine and surgery held the rank of major and managed the male staff of physicians and also commissioned officers. Next in the chain of command was a chief nurse who supervised the nursing staff, followed by enlisted sanitary troops who worked in the hospital kitchen, laundry, and wards, sometimes with the help of local French civilians employed by the hospital.

Nurses provided critical care to wounded and sick soldiers. Without antibiotics to fight infections, the kind of nursing that soldiers received often meant the difference between life and death. Dirt from the trenches could contain human and animal fecal matter or the residue of a poisonous gas, creating the risk of serious infections for wounded men. Cleansing wounds properly was critical to a soldier's survival. After the

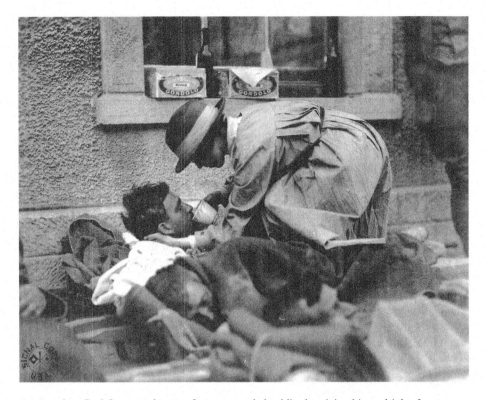

An American Red Cross worker comforts a wounded soldier by giving him a drink of water as other wounded men sleep on stretchers placed outside as they await transport to an army hospital. (*Courtesy of the National Museum of Health and Medicine, Armed Forces Institute of Pathology, Washington, D.C., Reeve 012200*)

doctor removed all the damaged or infected tissue, the wound was left open and irrigated daily by nurses who then applied a fresh dressing. This put nurses, one orderly realized, in "constant contact with dreadful agony, which expressed itself in irrepressible moans and shrieks" from the wounded men.

Good nursing was also critical for soldiers stricken with influenza or pneumonia whose recovery depended on warmth, good food, and bed rest. Recognizing the vital contribution that nurses made at the height of the influenza epidemic, in October 1918 Pershing canceled a previous request for replacement doctors and instead urgently asked the War Department to send 1,500 more nurses. With nurses in short supply and army hospitals overrun with wounded and ill men, nurses juggled as many as fifty patients at a time while working 14- to 18-hour shifts that month.

Most nurses worked in hospitals behind the lines, but some traveled to the front to assist surgeons operating on patients deemed too critical to transport behind the lines for treatment. In range of enemy shells, these nurses worked under difficult and trying conditions. One nurse noted that her front-line hospital had no electric lights, was without water for days, and under intermittent enemy attack yet continued to receive a steady influx of patients. "Imagine having 280 medical patients and six medicine glasses, no cups or bowls available . . . ," she wrote. "I *never* want to see another case of pneumonia following influenza, it is a dreaded disease that is filling our AEF cemetery fast."[45] The rush of wounded and dying men often meant that nurses worked 20-hour shifts, with barely a moment to think or eat. The horrific scenes that many witnessed never left them. Years later, army nurses vividly recalled peeling off bandages to reveal wounds filled with maggots, seeing a man's lungs pumping in an open chest wound, holding severed hands and feet, trying to cut the clothes off burned men who screamed in agony, and watching men take their final breaths. Some nurses felt close to hysteria themselves at moments as they watched shellshocked men writhe on the floor. "[I] still get a lump in my throat when I think of their suffering," one nurse remembered.[46] Despite the danger and chaos of front-line duty, the sense of accomplishment they felt after working at the front gave many nurses tremendous satisfaction. Over 200 American nurses were decorated for bravery under fire, and several nurses were wounded during the war. Two hundred and thirty-five nurses died during the course of the conflict, including 134 in the United States, all from disease.

Although a critical nursing shortage arose during the war, the army only allowed a handful of black nurses to enlist. A total of nine black nurses cared for black troops stationed at Camp Sherman, Ohio, and Camp Grant, Illinois. At first, nurse Aileen Cole Stewart recalled, the War Department systematically rejected all applications from black nurses, but "in 1918 the Red Cross called us up because of the flu epidemic." People, she recalled, "were dying everywhere. It was dreadful."[47]

Army nurses were considered officers without rank, an undefined military status that created numerous problems for these women. As officers, they were expressly forbidden from socializing with enlisted men. Yet, as officers without rank, they could not give orders. Their lack of rank made it impossible for many army nurses to do their jobs. Patients often refused to follow their directions and orderlies ignored their commands. Nurses and enlisted sanitary troops worked side by side in the wards on a daily basis. Yet, "in the hospital where I was stationed, the head nurse of our operating room had to go to the officer in charge before the men . . . would do any work whatsoever or even report for duty. . . . They absolutely refused to take orders from the nurse," reported one nurse, echoing a common complaint voiced by army nurses.[48] Ward orderlies already felt they were performing tasks considered women's work in civilian life such as peeling potatoes, scrubbing floors, washing linen, and cleaning corpses. Many men simply refused to compound their sense of emasculation by taking orders from female nurses. "The fact is that we were a little on the defensive," acknowledged one male orderly.[49] Besides confronting insubordinate male orderlies, female nurses also resented having to secure permission from the male officer supervising each ward (who usually had no medical training) to retrieve supplies or medicine ordered by doctors for their patients. Angered, army nurses enlisted the help of their professional association to lobby Congress for redress. Nothing came of these wartime protests, although after the war, in the wake of women gaining the right to vote, Congress agreed to grant army nurses "relative rank." This reform limited their authority to the vicinity of medical hospitals and left nurses under the command of all male medical officers.

Female nurses also encountered problems with male doctors, who clearly outranked them and sometimes took advantage of the power that they wielded. Some doctors treated nurses as personal assistants, whereas others were simply discourteous. Nurses were forbidden from attending enlisted men's dances, yet expected to provide the female companionship for officers' social events. For exhausted nurses, attending these festivities became yet another obligation to fulfill. Almost every nurse could relate a troubling tale of sexual harassment concerning officers who kissed and groped their female dance partners or badgered them relentlessly for dates.

Women's Support Staff Roles

Nurses were not the only American women working in the AEF. Another 6,000 women provided key staff support overseas. Female clerical workers were allowed to enlist directly as yeomen or marines in the Naval or Marine Corps Reserve. These women received the same pay as male yeomen, could advance to noncommissioned officer status, and were eligible for veterans' benefits. The enlightened views of Secretary of the Navy Josephus Daniels were not mirrored by Secretary of War Newton Baker who refused to create an American version of the British women's auxiliary corps. The American women who went to work for the army did so as civilian employees or as volunteers in one of the official social welfare agencies authorized to provide services to the troops. These women filled positions as telephone operators (affectionately nicknamed "Hello Girls"), translators, typists, and as hostesses in base recreation huts run overseas by the YWCA and stateside by the Commission on Training Camp Activities. They wore uniforms, had to abide by military regulations, and were supervised directly by male army officers. Yet, because they never held any official rank in the American Army, they were not eligible for veterans' benefits after the war. Finally, in 1979, Congress retroactively recognized AEF telephone operators as official members of the military. In a collective ceremony, thirty or so women in their eighties and nineties gathered to receive honorable discharges from the U.S. Army.

Women working as hostesses performed a wide variety of tasks that included baking and serving doughnuts, sewing buttons, running the canteen or library, writing letters for troops, organizing entertainment, or providing female companionship during dances. Female hostesses strove to create a homelike environment that reminded troops of the mothers and sisters they had left behind. Underscoring the platonic intent of the hostess mission, the *Ladies' Home Journal* assured its readers that female war workers "are the 'little mothers of the battlefields' whom you read about as cooking, mending, singing, praying . . . serving hot coffee to sentinels in the dead of night, and doing what you mothers of fighters would do for your boys if YOU were over there."[50] On large bases, hostesses usually worked under the supervision of male war workers. Others were assigned to specific Divisions, and, when the Division moved, they followed. Working alone, these hostesses put up mobile huts, built furniture, and secured needed supplies to open a canteen near the Division's staging area.

The most valued hostesses had pleasing personalities that exuded care and concern and enough organizational talent to provide wholesome recreational diversions for the troops. By comparison, 500 telephone operators and clerical workers worked alongside men in jobs that put a high premium on their language and secretarial skills. The modern army was a large bureaucratic organization that required thousands of workers who could type, file, take shorthand, and operate telephones. Civilian industries had already begun defining clerical work as a primarily female occupation, and few soldiers entered the army trained to type or operate switchboards. The military status of female army clerks varied tremendously. In some cases, women were sworn into military service and actually given rudimentary drill instruction before embarking overseas. Others signed contracts as civilian employees. Besides employing American women to perform clerical and communication tasks, the AEF also hired English-speaking French and Belgian women and borrowed female workers from the British Women's Auxiliary Corps.

American women took great pride in the skilled work that they performed. "For days I was on duty from eight in the morning until ten at night," recalled telephone operator Grace Banker, handling calls that transmitted status reports from the front and commands from headquarters. "But it seemed worth while when we gazed at the prison pen filling up with German soldiers," she admitted.[51] The press, however, cultivated an image of the "hello girls" that highlighted their female attributes rather than their mastery of machines or contribution to the army's advance in battle. "I reckon," one male journalist wrote, "the well-modulated, courteous and very American accents of a hello girl dripping in at the left ear have much the same effect on a homesick American as the soothing hand of a nurse on a sick soldier."[52]

Female telephone operators and clerical workers lived in special houses established by the YWCA where strict rules and regulations governed their off-duty hours. The women needed passes to stay out after dark, had to travel in groups of two or more, and could not fraternize with enlisted men. Some women chafed under these restrictions, but others appreciated the efforts of the YWCA to protect their virtue. Modeled after female college dormitories or working-class women's boarding houses, living in YWCA quarters safeguarded the reputations of women working in a highly masculinized and sexually charged environment. Most female army workers were older than the troops, which also apparently discouraged many romances from developing with male soldiers.

Besides providing valuable services to the troops, female workers were also instructed to be charming and friendly. After a long day's work, they were still expected to attend base dances that were, one war worker admitted, "far more work than pleasure to us."[53] Both military officials and social welfare workers hoped that the presence of virginal American women in France would discourage men from seeking out French lovers or prostitutes. Marguerite Cockett advised groups of YWCA hostesses headed overseas not to take soldiers' interest in them too seriously, explaining "they look straight in our eyes but they don't see us. They see mother, wife, or the girl back home."[54] Not all soldiers' attention was so innocent, and, in some canteens, women took care to walk back to their lodgings together to lessen the chance of an attack from drunken soldiers returning to their quarters. After days and days of attending male-dominated social events, many female war workers sought out the relative tranquility of female-only companionship and recreational facilities to relax.

When President Woodrow Wilson recommended that the Congress finally pass the Nineteenth Amendment to allow women to vote, he noted that the nation owed women the vote as a reward for the vital contributions that they had made to the war effort, "not merely in the fields of effort in which we have been accustomed to see them work but wherever men have worked and upon the very skirts and edges of the battle itself."[55] Female military service, therefore, helped strengthen the case for suffrage after the war. Besides advancing the campaign to grant women the vote, women's military service had several other lasting effects. After the war, nurses were granted relative rank and the work of female war workers paved the way for the creation of an official female army corps in World War II.

Gender Roles Remained Unchanged

Overall, however, the wartime work of women in the military failed to herald in any immediate change in postwar gender roles. Traditionalists saw military service as a way to restore virility to a generation of men made soft by the conveniences of modern life, while many prominent female peace activists argued that a mother's love could become a powerful force for peace in the world. Women who served their country in uniform during the war challenged these prevailing gender stereotypes. The key roles that women willingly assumed in the AEF undermined the generally held belief that military service was incompatible with the female temperament. The army's dependence on their labor belied the notion that wartime military service remained the exclusive domain of the nation's male citizens. Yet, the recruitment of female war workers, unlike the domestic campaign for female suffrage, engendered little controversy during the war. The army and press often trivialized the importance of female labor to the war effort while mainstream female activists tended to ignore rather than herald the achievements of female war workers.

Ultimately, the inclusion of women into the wartime military had little impact on prevailing attitudes about the limits and contours of women's economic role in American society or their suitability for military service. Yet, as individuals, the women who served overseas went on to lead professionally successful, independent lives and enjoyed a modicum of social mobility. Veteran nurses found themselves in especially high demand, and telephone operators returned home to find their industry booming.

CONCLUSION

Women war workers, foreign-born soldiers, and African American troops all had distinct experiences in the wartime military. Each faced enough discrimination to turn the war into a crusade to both defeat Germany and protect their civil rights. In achieving these overall goals, foreign-born soldiers fared the best, entering the army at a time when Progressive reformers had already embraced a more inclusive and tolerant notion of assimilation. African Americans advanced the least, encountering a hostile and oppressive racial climate within the military that was only alleviated by their experiences in French society. Women struggled to establish their authority in a mostly male institution, settling for individual gains rather than a wholesale overhaul in the proscribed roles for women in American society. Reflecting the tremendous diversity of the American population in 1917–1918, the wartime army did not escape the racial, ethnic, and gender tensions of the day.

NOTES

1. Jeanette Keith, *Rich Man's War, Poor Man's Fight: Race, Class and Power in the Rural South during the First World War* (Chapel Hill: University of North Carolina Press, 2004), 129.

2. Keith, *Rich Man's War, Poor Man's Fight*, 123.

3. Keith, *Rich Man's War, Poor Man's Fight*, 123.

4. Jennifer D. Keene, "Raising the American Expeditionary Forces: Early Decision Making in 1917," in *Battles Near and Far: A Century of Overseas Deployment*, ed. Peter Dennis and Jeffrey Grey (Canberra, Australia: Army History Unit, Department of Defence, 2005), 58.

5. Stephen L. Harris, *Harlem's Hell Fighters: The African American 369th Infantry in World War I* (Washington, D.C.: Brassey's, 2003), 108.

6. Bernard C. Nalty, *Strength for the Fight: A History of Black Americans in the Military* (New York: The Free Press, 1986), 105.

7. Keene, "Raising the American Expeditionary Forces," 59–60.

8. Jennifer D. Keene, *Doughboys, the Great War and the Remaking of America* (Baltimore, Md.: Johns Hopkins University Press, 2001), 40.

9. Jennifer D. Keene, "Protest and Disability: A New Look at African American Soldiers During the First World War," in *Warfare and Belligerence: Perspectives in First World War Studies*, ed. Pierre Purseigle (Boston: Brill, 2005), 224.

10. Keene, "Protest and Disability," 221.

11. Keene, *Doughboys, the Great War and the Remaking of America*, 95.

12. Keene, *Doughboys, the Great War and the Remaking of America*, 96.

13. Harris, *Harlem's Hell Fighters*, 116.

14. Harris, *Harlem's Hell Fighters*, 122.

15. Harris, *Harlem's Hell Fighters*, 126.

16. Hamilton Fish, *Memoir of an American Patriot* (Washington, D.C.: Regnery Gateway, 1991), 26–27.

17. Arthur E. Barbeau and Florette Henri, *The Unknown Soldiers: Black American Troops in World War I* (Philadelphia: Temple University Press, 1974), 153–4.

18. Meirion and Susie Harries, *The Last Days of Innocence, America at War, 1917–1918* (New York: Vintage Books, 1997), 374.

19. Barbeau and Henri, *The Unknown Soldiers*, 161.

20. Frank E. Roberts, *The American Foreign Legion: Black Soldiers of the 93rd in World War I* (Annapolis, Md.: Naval Institute Press, 2004), 55.

21. Keene, *Doughboys, the Great War and the Remaking of America*, 99.

22. Tyler Stovall, *Paris Noir: African Americans in the City of Light* (Boston: Houghton Mifflin, 1996), 18.

23. Jennifer D. Keene, "French and American Racial Stereotypes during the First World War," in *National Stereotypes in Perspective: Americans in France, Frenchmen in America*, ed. William L. Chew (Atlanta: Rodopi, 2001), 261.

24. Stovall, *Paris Noir*, 18.

25. Reid Badger, *A Life in Ragtime: A Biography of James Reese Europe* (New York: Oxford University Press, 1995), 167.

26. Badger, *A Life in Ragtime*, 196.

27. Keene, *Doughboys, the Great War and the Remaking of America*, 109.

28. Ronald Schaffer, *America in the Great War: The Rise of the War Welfare State* (New York: Oxford University Press, 1991), 185.

29. Nancy Gentile Ford, *Americans All! Foreign-born Soldiers in World War I* (College Station, Tx.: Texas A & M University Press, 2001), 53.

30. Ford, *Americans All!*, 142.

31. Christopher M. Sterba, *Good Americans: Italian and Jewish Immigrants during the First World War* (New York: Oxford University Press, 2003), 70.

32. Sterba, *Good Americans*, 48.

33. Sterba, *Good Americans*, 115.

34. Ford, *Americans All!*, 122.

35. Ford, *Americans All!*, 86.

36. Sterba, *Good Americans*, 195.

37. Ford, *Americans All!*, 141.

38. Ford, *Americans All!*, 123.

39. Sterba, *Good Americans*, 188.

40. Ford, *Americans All!*, 140.

41. Susan Zeiger, *In Uncle Sam's Service: Women Workers with the American Expeditionary Force, 1917–1919* (Philadelphia: University of Pennsylvania Press, 2004), 12.

42. Zeiger, *In Uncle Sam's Service*, 36.

43. Zeiger, *In Uncle Sam's Service*, 37.

44. Zeiger, *In Uncle Sam's Service*, 48.

45. Carol R. Byerly, *Fever of War: The Influenza Epidemic in the U.S. Army during World War I* (New York: New York University Press, 2005), 116–7.

46. Zeiger, *In Uncle Sam's Service*, 134.

47. Byerly, *Fever of War*, 145.

48. Zeiger, *In Uncle Sam's Service*, 119.

49. Zeiger, *In Uncle Sam's Service*, 122.

50. Zeiger, *In Uncle Sam's Service*, 57.

51. Zeiger, *In Uncle Sam's Service*, 100.

52. Zeiger, In Uncle Sam's Service, 91.

53. Zeiger, *In Uncle Sam's Service*, 72.

54. Zeiger, *In Uncle Sam's Service*, 64.

55. Zeiger, *In Uncle Sam's Service*, 137.

5   FIGHTING OVERSEAS

Because of the late entry of the United States into the war, American soldiers only fought in 1918. This final year of the war saw both the continuation of static trench warfare and the emergence of a war of movement in which both the Allied and German armies alternately succeeding in putting their foes on the run. American soldiers, therefore, had a wide variety of combat experiences that included enduring the ghastliness of trench warfare, advancing over heavy wooded and densely defended terrain, suffering gas attacks, and initiating rudimentary strategic bombing.

For all the horror that American soldiers witnessed in combat, the American army never suffered any crisis of morale that caused soldiers to uniformly question the purpose of the war. American soldiers took solace in the feeling that they were participating in a great historic event. "I wouldn't have missed it for anything," exclaimed one soldier to his wife, content that he and his comrades had passed the test of courage in their first sustained encounter with the Germans.[1] At the front, soldiers proved capable of absorbing the personal trauma of participating in combat without losing faith in their leaders or the justness of the war. As Donald Kyler recalled, "I had seen mercy killings, both of our hopelessly wounded and those of the enemy. I had seen the murder of prisoners of war, singly and as many as several at one time. I had seen men rob the dead of money and valuables, and had seen men cut off the fingers of corpses to get rings. Those things I had seen, but they did not affect me much. I was too numb, [but nonetheless] I had the determination to go on performing as I had been trained to do, to be a good soldier."[2]

American soldiers' enthusiasm about the war was particularly striking to Allied troops, especially the French who often remarked that the Americans reminded them of themselves in 1914. Indeed, the truly disgruntled soldiers within the AEF were not men at the front, but those assigned at laboring or specialist tasks behind the line. The crisis of morale in the American army war took place in the training camps and dock facilities where noncombatants labored to unload boxes, build roads, or transport supplies. More than seeking a chance to die for their country, these troops craved the recognition and respect that naturally went to combatants.

Soldiers fought and worked in a variety of circumstances, creating tremendous diversity in the overseas soldiers' experiences. The organization of combatant units, the material supplied to them, the various functions performed by different branches of the military, and the realities of trench warfare all shaped the experiences of combatant troops. The wide array of services provided by noncombatant troops supported the army in the field, embracing both highly skilled and unskilled tasks, some of which kept troops in relative safety behind the lines and others that put them in as much danger as combatant troops. The harrowing experience of sailing overseas was shared by all troops, regardless of their eventual destination in France. While a unique episode in the soldier's military record, the dangers encountered on the high seas were a routine part of daily life for American sailors who transported troops, protected convoys, mined the North Sea, and searched for German U-boats, the term for German submarines, taken from the German name for the ship: *unterseeboot*.

THE WAR AT SEA

There's about two million fellows from the North, South, East and West
Who scurried up the gang plank of a ship;
They have felt the guy ropes paying and the troopship gently swaying
As it started on its journey from the country of the blest.
They have washed in hard salt water, bucked the Army transport grub,
Had a hitch of crow's nest duty on the way;
Strained their eyes mistaking white caps for a humpback Prussian sub
Just at twilight when 'the danger's great, they say'
When their ship had lost the convoy they were worried just a bit,
And kinda thought the skipper should be canned;
And the sigh of heartfelt feeling almost set the boat to reeling
When each of those two million sighted land.
—*The first stanza of a poem entitled* "There's About Two Million Fellows"
by Sergeant Albert J. Cook.[3]

All American soldiers began their overseas experience by walking up a gangplank to board a ship headed for Europe. Only half of these troops embarked aboard American ships. In January 1918, facing a dearth of American ships to transport men and material, Pershing entered into negotiations with the British to secure their assistance in getting Americans across the Atlantic as quickly as possible. After a month of tense discussion, Pershing emerged with a major victory—an agreement from the British to provide shipping for six Divisions. In return for this help, Pershing agreed to send the infantry and auxiliaries of those Divisions to complete their training with the British rather than the French. This agreement opened the door to substantial British help in transporting the AEF overseas. Ultimately, over one million men traveled to France on British ships.

By 1918, the Allies had abandoned the earlier practice of letting single ships take their chances in the U-boat infested waters around Britain and Ireland. Instead, troop ships and merchant vessels now traveled together under the protection of cruisers and destroyers. An earlier debate within British and American naval circles over whether convoys discouraged or encouraged U-boat attacks was quickly put to rest by the dramatic reduction in the numbers of ships sunk by German submarines. Using naval vessels to protect ships from U-boat attacks, both near ports and on the high seas, was hugely successful. Not a single U.S. troop ship was sunk during the war. There were some accidents, however. Sailing as part of a convoy demanded rigid discipline from crews and captains. Every ship had to maintain a strict distance from nearby vessels while following a uniform zigzag pattern through the water. Conducting these maneuvers was particularly difficult at night when the ships sailed with lights. Cruisers accompanied convoys across the Atlantic, and two days out of port when the threat of a U-boat attack increased, destroyers arrived to guide the ships to Brest. Many sailors enjoyed transport duty. "When we met a troop convoy, the whole atmosphere seemed to be surcharged with joy, emanating from the thousands of men on the ships," one sailor recalled.[4]

Convoys offered defensive protection against U-boat attacks. The Americans also went on the offensive, deploying destroyers and submarine chase vessels to hunt down U-boats in the North Sea. German U-boats found it difficult to hit fast and mobile destroyers. With their shallow draft, destroyers tended to pass over the average path of the torpedo. A fleet of U.S. destroyers arrived in Ireland in May 1917 to help reverse the perilously high shipping losses inflicted by German U-boats that winter and spring. "It is impossible for us to go on with the war if losses like this continue," Britain's Grand Fleet Commander, Sir John Jellicoe, told Admiral William E. Sims, the commander of American naval forces in Europe.[5] In 1917, the Germans sunk more than half of the 12 million tons in Allied shipping lost during the entire war. Working side by side with the British destroyer fleet, the Americans patrolled the English Channel and North Sea. Over the course of the war, the Americans sunk 8 of the 130 U-boats that the Germans lost in the last two years of the war.

"There is no motion on land or sea comparable to that of a destroyer," Ensign Joseph Husband recalled. "Rolling often in five-second jerks at an angle sometimes over 50 [degrees] there is combined with the roll a quick and violent pitching."[6] The extremely stormy winter of 1917–1918 exacerbated the destroyer's normal pitching to and fro, making it impossible to eat off tables or even sleep in bunks. These difficult conditions kept crews alert during the tedious duty of searching for U-boats. Destroyers often patrolled for days without actually seeing any submarines, just the debris of boxes, barrels, and dead horses from ships they had sunk. "You'd almost be glad to see a ship sunk, anything to cheer up the monotony of the patrolling," one veteran recalled.[7] Still, for all the boredom and danger that sailors faced, few wanted to trade places with the infantrymen headed for dry land. After his stint escorting one transport into harbor, a sailor recorded his thoughts in his diary. "You look at them and pity them having to go in the trenches. Suppose they look at us and wonder why anyone is damn fool enough to roll and jump around on a destroyer," he wrote.[8] Overall, the United States lost three warships during the war to enemy attack, including the *Jacob Jones*, a destroyer sunk by a German torpedo on the southeastern tip of England. Sixty-four out of the 110-man crew perished in this attack, including some who died of exposure in life rafts while waiting overnight for rescue.

American subchasers and Q-ships abetted destroyers in tracking down and attacking German submarines. Duty on both ships was perilous. Subchasers were 110-foot wooden vessels outfitted with depth charges to drop on German submarines. Rough seas or bad weather often sidelined these fragile ships. Late in the war, subchasers began using hydrophones (a precursor of sonar) to pick up the sound of a U-boat's underwater engine. An operator listening through headphones heard a signal in each ear that emanated from separate tubes trailing in the water. When the sound was equal in both ears, the operator could determine the direction but not distance of the submarine. Working in a squad with two other chasers, the three could pinpoint the exact location of the submarine through triangulation and launch a depth charge attack. Rough water or too many other vessels in the vicinity could make the signals hard to detect, however. By the end of the war, the Americans had 120 subchasers in European waters.

The Americans also experimented with the Q-ship, a British idea that involved hiding guns behind the bulkheads on a merchant ship manned with a naval crew trained to act like civilian sailors. The idea was to attract U-boats and then fire on them before they had time to launch a machine gun attack, a tactic U-boat captains used against unarmed targets to conserve increasingly scarce torpedoes. The Americans only launched one Q-ship, the *Santee*, which the Germans sunk on its first mission.

Yet another group of sailors tried to contain the threat of U-boats by working with the British to lay a huge field of mines between Scotland and Norway in the North Sea. In the last year of the war, the two navies laid a band of mines that stretched 230 miles long and as much as 35 miles wide in some places. The tension and danger for these crews never abated for a moment. Working fifty-hour shifts, minelaying ships worked two or three ships abreast to lay mines at 500 yard intervals. Each mine was one yard in diameter and contained 300 pounds of TNT. Heading out to sea with a ship packed with high explosives meant "living on the edge of eternity," one naval officer noted.[9] American crews laid 56,571 of the 70,117 mines that formed the mine barrage.

Overall, 81,000 sailors and 370 American ships served overseas, offering troop-ships and merchant ships varying degrees of protection from the German U-boat menace. The trip across the Atlantic, although certainly not as dangerous as laying mines or deliberately seeking out a submarine, was still so perilous and event-filled that many men believed they deserved a medal simply for enduring the journey overseas. For a short time, every soldier headed overseas got a taste of the nail-biting anxiety that sailors confronted on a daily basis.

The experiences of the New York 15th Infantry (an African American unit re-designated as the 369th Infantry Regiment after its arrival in France) reflected how aging ships, congested waterways, and sheer bad luck could turn the thirteen-day cruise into a nightmare that men never forgot. For many soldiers, this was their first ocean voyage and rumors of German submarines patrolling the Atlantic coast added to their nervousness about the trip. The men were scheduled to sail on the *Pocahontas*, a renamed German ship that the U.S. government had seized in 1914 and put in storage for three years before recalling the ship into service as a troop transport vessel. Before surrendering the ship, its German crew had destroyed as much equipment as possible. The quick refitting that the vessel received in 1917 barely made it sea worthy. Nonetheless, on 8 November 1917, members from the New York 15th Infantry Regiment boarded the ship and, following standard protocol, waited until night to begin their journey. As evening fell, workers extinguished all lights around the pier and tugboats pulled the darkened ship into the shipping lanes. The men stood on deck as the ship sailed past the island of Manhattan to join the waiting convoy. All went well for a few hours as the convoy steamed through calm seas, then suddenly the ship began to lurch and slow. The piston rods had snapped, slowing the *Pocahontas* so much that keeping up with the convoy became impossible. As the other ships chugged on steadily to France, the *Pocahontas* turned and limped back to New York a mere twenty-four hours after departing.

It took two weeks to repair the ship, during which time the troops waited in Camp Merritt, New Jersey, where the men took advantage of their proximity to their friends and family in New York City to slip away for clandestine visits. The tempting delights that Gotham offered young men proved hard for soldiers to resist, whether or not they had families in the city. Men frequently went AWOL, or absent without leave, while awaiting their embarkation orders, creating constant headaches for commanders. For the army, the pull of the city created several problems. First, the secrecy of shipping orders meant that men were subject to deployment at a moment's notice. A unit that sailed below strength because some men had gone AWOL played havoc with shipping schedules designed to move as many men as quickly as possible to France. Soldiers took a calculated risk that their unit would not sail without them because few wanted to face the consequences if it did. The likely outcome for these solders was some time in the brig and reassignment to another unit headed overseas. For those who had developed loyalties and friends in a particular unit, reassignment was often a bitter pill to accept. Even more troubling from the military standpoint, however, was that men on the verge of deployment overseas were placed in quarantine after they had undergone their final medical screening for venereal disease and other illnesses such as influenza. Soldiers who subsequently snuck away for some final female companionship before heading to France risked contracting a sexually transmitted disease. Transporting ill or infected men to France where they would require medical treatment reduced the effective strength of the overseas army, and enraged Pershing who issued strict instructions to keep men with venereal disease at home.

After their second stint in the embarkation camps, the men of the 15th Infantry Regiment finally re-boarded the repaired *Pocahontas*. This time the ship did not even make it out of the harbor. A fire in the coal-filled bunkers created so much heat that all the coal had to be removed until the bunkers cooled. Taking no chances that some men might disappear into the city for another quick visit, the troops were ordered to stay on the ship during the ten days it took to re-paint and re-load the bunkers. Frustrated and bored, the men noted with amusement that their families and friends thought they were on their way to France when in reality they were just a few miles from their homes. They finally set sail for a third time two weeks later in a blinding snowstorm. "That night was such a one as a writer of fantastic sea tales would describe in choosing an appropriate setting for running a blockade," one officer recalled, "pitch dark, and snowing, with a gale of wind, and very cold."[10] As the raging sea tossed the ship relentlessly, crashing waves and pelting snow covered the deck with ice. In the darkness, the ship passed too close to a British oil tanker anchored in the harbor and a line from the *Pocahontas* got caught in the tanker's anchor line. For several hours, the two ships tossed side by side without hitting each other, giving the crew hope that they could wait out the storm and then untangle the lines. At three o'clock in the morning, a terrific bolt sent half-dressed men scurrying from their bunks in a panic. The tanker had begun crashing into the side of the *Pocahontas*. "I never knew that lifejackets could be worn in so many different ways," quipped one soldier.[11] While the men waited anxiously for the abandon ship signal, the crew got to work putting bumpers between the ships and disentangling the lines. When dawn broke the crew surveyed the damage, which included torn away metal plates above the waterline and crushed lifeboats. The ship's commander now had twenty-four hours to make the necessary repairs before the waiting convoy left. Enlisting help from skilled infantrymen aboard, soldiers and sailors lowered themselves in slings over the side of the ship in the numbing cold to fix the holes. By evening the *Pocahontas* joined the convoy.

After three tries, the *Pocahontas* was finally on its way. It was unusual for one ship to encounter so many different problems in one journey, but these types of mechanical problems and accidents plagued numerous voyages throughout the war. At sea, the men aboard the *Pocahontas* faced the more typical challenges of seasickness and boredom. The rolling pitch of the ship created agony below for men crowded into bunk beds stacked four high who often failed to make it to the latrine or deck to vomit. "The smell from the engine room, the kitchen, the crowded hatches, the good and bad cigarettes on all sides kept a sick one in a constant state of squeamishness," one soldier recalled.[12] For men unaffected by seasickness, the shortened workday gave them many hours to study or write. The men ate and worked on a compressed schedule. "By four o'clock we had supper because all the kitchen mess tables and everything had to be done during daylight as not a light was allowed on the ship after dark, not even a cigarette could be smoked on deck," one soldier recalled.[13] Besides lifeboat drills, the men also passed the time picking lice off their clothes during informal "cootie drills." Medical officers inspected soldiers' heads regularly for head lice, which they treated by shaving the heads of the afflicted and giving them bars of antilice soap. By the time the men saw land, they were ready to kiss the ground and never leave, one soldier recalled. In his diary, the commander of the New York 15th succinctly summed up the obstacles his unit had overcome on the journey: "27 December landed at Brest. Right side up."[14]

Despite all the mishaps that beset the *Pocohontas*, the men had the good fortune of sailing for France before the influenza epidemic hit. The military estimated that over the course of the war the flu struck 8.8 percent of troops while en route overseas, killing 5.9 percent (or 789 men) of those infected. Many men who fell ill on the high seas survived the voyage only to die within a few days of landing in base hospitals. If the numbers of deaths within five days of landing are taken into account, then the death toll from influenza contracted during the ocean crossing rises to 4,000. The *Pocahontas* became infamous for the accidental mishaps that it endured, but the USS *Leviathan* gained renown for the far-more tragic calamity of landing in France with two thousand flu victims. On its arrival, soldiers working in the port in Brest began unloading ill men, walking four miles with each stretcher to carry the patients to the base hospital. The disaster was an example of how the exigencies of war created circumstances that helped the flu epidemic flourish. The *Leviathan* carried 6,700 as a passenger ship, but refitted as a troop transport ship it was authorized to carry 11,000. Overcrowding and poor ventilation below deck created nearly perfect conditions for the airborne flu virus to flourish.

Soldiers' efforts to hide their illness also increased the chances of infection spreading in the enclosed ship environment. Ivan Farnworth recalled how he rolled the thermometer on top of his tongue and convinced the medical officer that he had a naturally red face to pass the medical exam. His buddies then wrapped him in an overcoat and carried his belongings onto the ship. Farnworth recovered from his bout with the flu on the journey overseas, but probably infected others who may not have been so lucky. Farnworth did not sail on the *Leviathan*, but his story reflected similar efforts made by ill men on this ship to stay with their unit and avoid reassignment after their recovery. Some made it by medical examiners only to fall out of ranks, unable to keep up as their units marched up the gangplank. Alerted to the ruse, medical officers boarded the ship and removed a hundred men before the *Leviathan* left. Despite these precautions, within one day at sea, over 700 men fell ill. Two days later an inferno raged aboard, according to one navy report. "Conditions during the night cannot be visualized by anyone who has not seen them," the report noted. Sick men vomited where they lay and "pools of blood from severe nasal hemorrhages of many patients were scattered throughout the compartments, and attendants were powerless to escape tracking through the mess." Medical attendants tried to nourish patients by giving them water and fruit, which the ill men often threw up immediately. "The decks became wet and slippery, groans and cries of the terrified added to the confusion of the applicants clamoring for treatment," the report continued.[15] Seventy died during the voyage, and hundreds of the two thousand ill men unloaded in Brest died within days of the landing. The tragic crossing did not interfere with the ongoing war effort, however. For five days after the *Leviathan* landed, overworked black stevedores replenished its coal supplies, often sleeping in the same bunks that flu victims had just evacuated. Although the experience of the *Leviathan* was unusually severe, during the fall of 1918 deaths at sea from influenza became a normal part of the journey to France.

Once troops left the ship, their journey in many respects had just begun. Now soldiers had to travel to their training camps, and then eventually to their battle positions. Moving around was constant in the lives of soldiers, and one enduring memory for soldiers was traveling in French boxcars, called Forty and Eights, because they could hold either forty men or eight horses. Trains transported soldiers traveling long distances. More commonly, units changed their posting on foot. "I would say [France] was the largest country in the world," wrote Private Christian Blumenstein, "due to the fact that it seemed so, in all of the hiking that we did when I was there."[16]

HEADING TO THE FRONT: THE ORGANIZATION OF
THE AMERICAN ARMY

Early decisions reached by General John J. Pershing about the organization of combatant divisions reflected his assumptions about how soldiers would fight. The American "square division" contained four infantry regiments and three artillery regiments. Each American division contained 979 officers and 27,082 men, and enough support troops to bring the total near 40,000 troops, making them twice the size of European Divisions. Pershing's doctrine of open warfare privileged the firepower of the infantry over the artillery, a preference apparent when Pershing rejected an early suggestion by Colonel Charles P. Summerall to double the size of both the infantry and artillery. As a result, these supersized American divisions went into combat with the same number of artillery troops and guns as smaller European divisions. Each division contained two infantry brigades (made up of two regiments) and one field artillery brigade (including two artillery regiments that carried a total of forty-eight 75mm guns and a third that employed twenty-four 155mm howitzers).

Although the artillery support within American divisions paled in comparison to the Allies, these units were amply supplied with machine guns. Each American division carried 224 heavy machines guns into battle, compared to German divisions that employed closer to 100. Every American division also contained a heavy weapons company that brought six mortars and four 37mm guns, as well as sixteen heavy machine guns, into battle.

Pershing created large divisions in the hopes of increasing the Americans' staying power in the field. Each regiment contained 112 officers and 3,720 men, who formed three battalions and one machine gun company. Each battalion had four companies, who were in turn divided into four platoons. Within each platoon, four groups of specialists were each given a distinct battlefield task. The first squad contained riflemen, while the second had riflemen equipped with French VB tromblons (rifle grenade dischargers). The third platoon functioned as the maneuver element of the squad with 17 riflemen, and the final platoon contained four Chauchat automatic rifles, which along with the riflemen, provided a base of fire for the platoon's advancement.

Uniforms and Kit

Soldiers arrived in France outfitted for combat and long stretches of outdoor living. They often changed or discarded some of the items in their uniforms and kit (equipment) along the way. Men jettisoned the khaki leggings and broad-brimmed campaign hat that shaded one's face in the hot sun favored in the training camps, replacing these items with wool leggings and a rectangular-shaped overseas cap that could be easily folded and carried in a pack when a steel helmet was worn. American soldiers spent much of their time battling the cold and wet weather in northern France. A double-breasted overcoat with an adjustable belt and a raincoat or poncho protected soldiers from the elements. Many soldiers preferred ponchos because they kept a man and his pack dry, and could serve double-duty as the roof on a makeshift shelter or dugout. The disadvantage of wearing a poncho was the difficulty that men had reaching their gas masks in cases of sudden or unanticipated attacks. A raincoat made it easier to reach the mask, but the treated canvas was not as waterproof or versatile as the poncho.

Most soldiers entered the active zone carrying a standard pack and cartridge belt. How much they kept during the long marches and grueling advances was another story. The roads leading to the front were littered with discarded items that soldiers were too weary to carry any further. Each soldier ideally carried 100 rounds of rifle ammunition on a cartridge belt around his waist that also had eyelets to hang a bayonet, entrenching tool, first aid kit, or canteen. The cartridge belt also made it possible for a soldier to carry his backpack. A soldier's haversack had no straps, but was attached with

American soldiers, fully uniformed and equipped, greet a French couple after liberating areas occupied by Germany for years. Note the knapsack, canvas canteens, and entrenching tools carried by each soldier. (*Courtesy of the National Archives*)

suspenders over the shoulders and around the waist to the cartridge belt. Soldiers carried their rations and washing kit in their haversacks, and sometimes attached a smaller pack to the bottom of the haversack that contained a poncho, a blanket, and additional clothing. Troops placed their mess kits in external pockets, and some chose to attach their bayonet or shovel to the haversack rather than the cartridge belt. During major advances, soldiers often needed to carry more than 100 rounds of ammunition into battle. On those occasions soldiers received cloth bandoliers that contained additional rounds and could be discarded when depleted. In addition, soldiers might wear vests with hand grenades placed in individual pockets. Wrapping the vest tightly to their bodies with cloth straps prevented excessive rubbing from inadvertently detonating a grenade. Finally, all soldiers went into battle with gas masks, which they carried in a leather pouch around their necks or on the hip. To prevent the bag from flopping around, many soldiers tied the bag to their chests.

Once in the active zone, medals and chevrons gave each individual's uniform special distinction. American soldiers received honors from the French army, most commonly the *croix de guerre*. The American military awarded the Distinguished Service Medal (DSM) to recognize meritorious service to the government in a position of great responsibility or during military operations and the Distinguished Service Cross (DSC) to reward extraordinary acts of heroism on the battlefield. The Medal of Honor (commonly called "The Congressional Medal of Honor") recognized exceptional acts of heroism. The criteria for each of these citations were quite high; therefore few soldiers received them. Chevrons that indicated time overseas and divisional insignia were the most common adornments worn by soldiers overseas. Soldiers received a gold V-shaped bar after six months service overseas that they wore on the lower left sleeve above the cuff. At first, the AEF only awarded these service chevrons to soldiers who served in the "Zone of the Advance," but an ensuing controversy over how to define this geographical area caused AEF Headquarters to relent in July 1918 and award the chevron to all troops who served in the theatre of operations under Pershing's command. Men with less than six months service overseas wore a blue chevron, while wounded men wore a gold stripe. Soldiers who never made it overseas were eventually given silver chevrons, which many saw as a badge of shame. In a poem published by *The Stars and Stripes*, one soldier imagined the ideal homecoming for a soldier with a silver chevron:

> But, my darling, don't you bleat.
> No one thinks you had cold feet;
> You had to do as you were told;
> Silver stripes instead of gold.[17]

At the end of the war, American soldiers also received a victory medal and campaign ribbons to denote the various battles in which they fought.

Besides service chevrons and medals, each division adopted a special insignia during the war to help soldiers identify members of their own units in battle, keep track of their equipment, and develop a sense of *esprit de corps*. Each insignia usually reflected a distinctive character trait associated with the men of that division. The First Division, for example, adopted an insignia containing a shield with a red number one to illustrate the long, bloody history of the first American unit in battle. The 32nd Division chose an arrow as an emblem to highlight its prowess in battle, because the men "shot through every line the Boche put before them."[18] The 26th Division, nicknamed the Yankee division for the

National Guard units from New England who formed the division, put the monogram "YD" on its vehicles and mules even before the AEF officially asked Divisions to develop insignia. The 42nd Division selected a rainbow to represent the 26 states and various immigrant communities that contributed men to form the division. Other Divisions, like the 77th and 91st Divisions, had more uniformity in the residential origins of their troops. Men from the 77th Division, who mostly hailed from New York City, wore a picture of the Statue of Liberty on their sleeves, while the fir tree became the emblem of the 91st Division, which drew men from the Pacific Northwest.

Weapons

American material and financial support for the Allied side played a major role in the victory over Germany. Since 1915, American manufacturers had been an important source of munitions and raw materials for Britain and France. Nonetheless, many American troops went into battle with foreign-produced or designed munitions. In part, this reflected the earlier conversion that American companies had made to gear their factories to produce weapons for the foreign armies placing orders and the inability of these firms to retool fast enough to produce American-designed weapons in the needed quantities. Similarly, the French and British armies had already stockpiled large numbers of weapons that they parceled out to the under-supplied Americans in return for raw materials. American soldiers, therefore, sometimes went into battle with foreign-designed or manufactured weapons simply because they were available, not because they were better.

Two cases in point were the British Enfield rifle and the French Chauchat light machine gun. In developing his training doctrine, Pershing placed heavy emphasis on the one weapon that the United States possessed in abundance, the Springfield Model 1903 rifle. Yet in 1918 most American troops ended up fighting with modified British Enfield rifles because American factories were already producing these rifles in large quantities for the British when the United States entered the war. The French gave the AEF approximately 16,000 Chauchats in 1917 to ease equipment shortages and provide more transport space for troops. The Chauchat, sometimes considered the worse-designed machine gun ever manufactured, was universally loathed by the French and American soldiers who were forced to use it. The complex recoil system did not allow for a steady aim and because it was largely manufactured from poor quality stamped steel parts it was prone to frequent jamming and failures. To ease supply problems, the Chauchat was designed to use the same ammunition as the French Lebel rifle. Using this ammunition in the Chauchat solved one problem by creating two others. The ammunition was so heavy that it cancelled out the weight advantage of the light machine gun and also required a re-design of the magazine, which increased the likelihood of stoppages. The Americans redesigned the machine gun's magazine to accept the American .30 caliber and renamed it the M1918 Machine Rifle. The .30 caliber round was more powerful than the French 8mm which helped its combat effectiveness but added to the reliability problem by putting additional strain on the mechanism.

American machine gun companies fought mostly with French Hotchiss heavy machine guns that they often transported on carts pulled by mules, providing a glimpse into how modern and premodern technology were employed during the war. The Hotchiss suffered from feeding mechanism problems and had a low rate of fire. The British-designed Browning M1917 was more reliable, but in short supply. The Americans also used the Vickers Machine Gun (designed and produced in the United States and the standard machine gun of the British army and for Allied aircraft). The Lewis machine gun, an American-designed machine gun that the British enthusiastically manufactured, was only used by the American Army for training. The Americans depended primarily on the Hotchiss, Vickers, and Browning M1917 machine guns until September 1918 when enough American-produced Browning machines guns and automatic rifles arrived at the front to replace them.

Mastering the machine gun required nearly two months of steady training within the United States. Crews memorized the name and function of every part, which instructors then put on the ground and had men assemble while blindfolded. Learning to repair the machines also consumed days of instruction, as trainers intentionally rigged the machines to jam and then left it to the crews to determine the problem and fix it. Day after day, machine gun crews performed drills in loading, aiming, and firing their guns. They learned to maneuver the fifty-two-pound Hotchiss over open fields, find cover, and build camouflaged nests. After finishing their course of stateside training, machine gun crews headed to France to complete their course of instruction with French machine gun companies. There, like all American soldiers, machine gunners faced the reality of war. After being complimented for their effective machine gun fire in Company B, 306th Machine Gun Battalion, 77th Division, Charles Schweitzer grimly noted, "We were complimented for our good work. I smiled to myself, being complimented for being murderers. If we were back home and killed a man, we would be electrocuted or hung for it—but over here, it's perfectly all right. I don't see any difference."[19]

The element of surprise from hidden guns ended as soon as the crews opened fire, and machine guns crews came to appreciate that the destructive power they wielded was matched by the determination of the enemy to eliminate them. Machine gun crews referred to themselves as suicide clubs, subject to immediate shelling and attack once they revealed their position by firing their guns. "The reason is obvious," one sergeant recalled, "for when a man sat behind a gun and mowed down a bunch of men, his life was automatically forfeited."[20] Enraged, attacking soldiers rarely took machine gun crews prisoner, opting instead to kill them on the spot. Soldiers may have cursed machine gunners on the other side, but the affection they felt for their own knew no limits. As one soldier-authored ode to the machine gun so eloquently noted,

> Anywhere and everywhere.
>   It's me the soldier's love,
> Underneath a parapet
>   Or periscoped above;
> Backing up the barrage fire,
>   And always wanting more;
> Chewing up a dozen disks
>   To blast an army corps;
> Crackling, spitting, demon-like,
>   Heat-riven through and through–
> Fussy, mussy Lewis gun–
>   Three heroes for a crew![21]

Hand grenades also proved critical in combat. By the time the Americans entered the war, hand grenade technology had evolved considerably to include incendiary and gas grenades as well as offensive and defensive grenades. Soldiers used offensive grenades in the open or during an assault. They created a lethal explosion limited to an eight-yard range that protected the thrower who was usually out in the open. The defensive grenade could be used from the trenches, which offered the thrower protection from the blast, and had a lethal fragmentation of close to one hundred yards.

The United States entered the war without a standard hand grenade, and the first troops to fight overseas adopted the grenade used by the nearest Allied force, either the British Mills Bomb or the French F1. The French grenade had the characteristic "pineapple" pattern casing that helped fragmentation and by 1917 used the reliable and waterproof "*Billant*" fuse system that contained a pin and lever safety. After the soldier pulled the pin and released the lever, a plunger with two hammers struck the primer to begin a five-second time delay fuse. The fuse set off a detonator that ignited the main charge breaking the case along the pineapple pattern into fragments. Besides the French F1, soldiers used other specialized hand grenades to accomplish specific tasks. A thermite grenade dropped down the gun of captured enemy artillery created enough heat to fuse the breech mechanism shut. A gas hand grenade delivered a small amount of gas to dugouts or bunkers without decapacitating the attacker.

If these grenades represented the advancement of military technology during the war, the assortment of trench knives, maces, clubs, and daggers that soldiers sometimes carried illustrated that traditional weaponry had a place along the Western front as well. These weapons were particularly useful during night patrols when the flash of rifle fire could give away a squad's position.

The standard small box respirator gas mask issued to American troops was made of rubber cloth and connected to a filtering canister by a short hose. Each man kept his gas mask in a canvas sack that hung either from his belt or haversack. At a moment's notice when the gas alarm sounded, men had to quickly secure the mask to their faces with rubber straps. The mask pinched the nose closed, forcing men to breathe through a rubber tube that they held in their mouths. Men often had to wear these masks for hours at a stretch, during which time they could not eat or drink. The eerie alien feeling created by groups of masked men was compounded by the need to also secure gas masks to horses and mules. As hard as these masks were to wear while sitting still in the trenches, they became nearly impossible to endure when soldiers were on the move. The nose clip made it impossible for a soldier to get the air needed to sustain prolonged exertion. Heavy breathing increased condensation in the mask, and many troops on the offensive found their vision completely obstructed by fogged-up lenses. An antifogging paste was available, but the film that it left on the mask also distorted a soldier's line of vision. Some soldiers resorted to removing the faceplate while keeping the nose clip and mouthpiece in place, leaving the soldier's eyes unprotected. Despite the continued warnings and efforts of officers to discourage this practice, it continued throughout the war and many soldiers incurred eye damage after exposure to mustard gas.

THE TRENCHES

Because the Germans had built their trenches first along much of the Western Front in 1914, they had the advantage of higher and drier terrain. This gave the Germans an important tactical advantage, and also meant that German soldiers often enjoyed much better living conditions in the trenches than Allied troops. In the mostly flat fields of Flanders, for instance, even the slightest elevation protected the Germans so well that displacing them from these small hills required a tremendous expenditure of British men and machines. In these low lying fields only a few yards above sea level, it became impossible to construct traditional trenches. As soon as the British dug a few feet into the ground, water filled the bottom of the trench. Instead of constructing the trench by digging down, a parapet or command trench was constructed mostly by building up. After digging a foot or so into the ground, the rest of the trench was built by placing sandbags as thickly as possible until the trench measured seven to eight feet deep and six to seven feet wide. Command trenches were also located in the Argonne Forest where the Americans fought because the high water table prevented troops from digging too far into the ground.

Whether trenches were built up or dug into the ground, the vocabulary used to describe various features of the trench was similar. The front of the trench was called the *parapet*, and the back of the trench the *parados*. To look over the parapet, either to peer out onto No Man's Land (the vacant stretch of terrain that separated the trenches) or to prepare for a massive assault over the top, men stepped on a ledge called the *firestep*. To bolster the sides of the trenches and prevent them from collapsing from minor shell bursts, both sides reinforced the trench walls with either sandbags, timber, or bunches of twigs.

The trenches were not simply two straight lines facing each other. Such a design would have put defending troops at great risk. If the enemy broke through a straight line, it would only take one machine gun set up at one end of the trench to mow down all the men within it, a situation that the military termed *enfilading fire*. Instead, French trench design followed a zigzag pattern, while the British and Germans created patchworks of small L-shaped corridors linked by traverses. Most trench systems consisted of three lines: a front-line trench, the support trench, and the reserve trench, all connected by smaller trench lines called traverses. The labyrinth of trenches added a tremendous amount of mileage to the terrain that troops actually occupied. If considered as a straight line, the trenches that extended from the North Sea to Switzerland ran for nearly 550 miles. By 1915, the Allies estimated that on their side alone, they were maintaining 15,000 miles of trenches along the Western Front.

No soldier spent the entire war in the trenches. Instead, troops rotated between the trenches and reserve or rest areas in the rear. The normal rotation put troops in the line for three weeks and behind the line for one. The exact duration of a stint in the trenches could vary, dependent on whether a unit was in training, in an active or quiet sector, and the availability of replacement troops.

Just before heading to the trenches for the first time, each man received a set of two aluminum disks stamped with their name, rank, and serial number to hang around their neck with a cotton string. They marched into battle knowing that the army had already taken steps to ease identification of the casualties certain to befall the unit. Troops rarely occupied the same stretch of trenches more than a few times. For most soldiers, therefore, the news that they were headed to the trenches usually meant a long march, often fifteen to twenty miles, from their rest area to a new part of the sector. Men received ten minutes rest for every hour of marching, and those who could not keep up fell out along the way. Trucks sometimes picked up the stragglers, but others became separated from their units and wandered for days before rejoining them. Once the men were in position, they began the exhausting exercise of moving into the front lines. Troops both left and entered the trenches at night to minimize the chances of directed enemy shellfire hitting them. Men moved forward one platoon at a time with a hundred

Soldiers leaving a trench during World War I. (*Courtesy of the Library of Congress*)

yards separating each one, maintaining strict silence as they stumbled forward in complete darkness. A guide with excellent map-reading skills led troops into their new position before dawn broke. Moving through the maze of trenches, men had no idea where they were going and could only follow the man in front of them through mud and water as they trudged onward. The strain of carrying heavy backpacks and feeling their way in darkness while enemy flares exploded overhead exhausted troops before they had even reached their position. Once soldiers finally made it to the frontlines, the unit that they were relieving followed the same procedure to withdraw from the line. Some units found an unexpected welcome awaiting them when they finally reached the frontlines that made the ordeal of reaching the trenches seem pointless. "Goodbye 42nd, Hello Seventy-seventh" read a banner attached to a German observation balloon when men from this division arrived at the front for the first time.[22]

Trench Warfare

At the beginning of the war, both sides tended to place most of their men in the frontline trenches, to be ready at a moment's notice for an attack. Soon, however, commanders learned the importance of reserving enough men to launch a successful counter-attack. Throughout 1916, Allied commanders opened up offensive operations by launching massive artillery barrages intended to soften up the opposing side before waves of men headed over the top. Commanders originally expected extensive artillery barrages to dramatically reduce the opposition that troops faced in crossing No Man's Land. In reality, although terrified, many enemy troops survived the bombardments in underground dugouts or reserve trenches. Using bombs to destroy the barbed wire entanglements on No Man's Land created even more craters for troops to traverse before reaching enemy lines. Although they were often only going a few hundred yards, making their way through the mounds of earth and debris that littered this moon-like landscape, all while carrying 70 pounds of equipment, exhausted troops before they even encountered an enemy soldier. Having enough troops in reserve to launch a counterattack and push the enemy back to his own trenches became critical and eventually changed the way that commanders apportioned their men in the trenches. The French moved to a defense in depth approach early in the war, while the Germans waited until 1917 to abandon its earlier preference for one heavily manned trench line supported by concrete machine gun bunkers every thousand yards. The British adopted a hodge-podge of tactics, and finally embraced thinly held frontlines as an official policy in 1918. The American Army, which trained with the French and British, followed suit.

Trench warfare put all men in danger, but some had jobs that exposed them to even more risk than the average soldier living in the trenches. The most advanced position of the line was not the front-line trench but the listening post. Listening posts were a way to reclaim as much territory as possible in No Man's Land. As often as possible, armies appropriated large shell craters near their trench lines as listening posts, sometimes connecting these to the main lines through communication trenches and sometimes sending men over the top to reach them. Men assigned to listening posts were exposed to grave danger. A handful of men sat isolated from the bulk of the army, listening for the sounds of an enemy attack. If one came, these posts turned into suicide positions. Even if the soldiers succeeded in sending up a flare to warn their units that an attack was coming, there was little chance of escaping back to the relative safety of the main trench lines. Men in listening posts were also frequently targeted for abduction by enemy patrols seeking prisoners who could provide useful intelligence. Two African American soldiers, Henry Johnson and Needham Roberts, gained acclaim in the United States, particularly in the black community, for successfully fighting off a German patrol trying to take them prisoner. Roberts and Johnson were part of a party of five sitting in an isolated listening post on the night of 14 May 1918. Detecting some movement outside their post, the two gave the alert when they discovered an enemy patrol bearing down on them. "The Germans cut us off from retreating and we had to fight. It was 25 against us 2," Roberts wrote in a letter home. "Having thrown all my grenades, I was wounded and put out of the fight. But my comrade Johnson resisted and drove them away all alone."[23] The "Battle of Henry Johnson," as the press soon dubbed this heroic struggle between one lone American soldier and twenty-five Germans, had begun. When two Germans attempted to enter their shelter, Johnson emptied his rifle into one and clubbed down the other with his rifle butt. As Johnson battled with these two enemy soldiers, another two began carrying the wounded Roberts away as the desired prisoner. To free his comrade, Johnson jumped onto the soldier holding Roberts's shoulders. "As Johnson sprang, he unsheathed his bolo knife, and as his knees landed upon the shoulders of that ill-fated Boche, the blade of the knife was buried to the hilt through the crown of the German's head," his commanding officer, Captain Arthur Little attested.[24] The men holding Roberts dropped him and scattered, but Johnson's battle was not quite finished. The soldier that Johnson had clubbed with his rifle had recovered enough to draw his pistol and shoot Johnson. Now severely wounded himself, Johnston nonetheless managed to plunge his knife into his assailant's abdomen. "The enemy patrol was in a panic. The dead and wounded were piled upon stretchers and carried away," Little reported.[25] Critically injured and losing blood, Johnson continued to harass the retreating Germans with grenades. An official investigation concluded that Roberts and Johnson had killed four of the Germans who attacked them that night.

Snipers performed another highly specialized function in the trenches, ever on the alert for a careless enemy soldier who exposed himself during the day. As a general rule, snipers never fired more than two or three shots from the same position to avoid detection. Although some operated from the trenches, most headed out to No Man's Land during the day where they moved between shell holes wearing camouflaged clothing and in some cases sought cover in hollowed trees.

During the First World War, radio was in its infancy. Telephone communication, while more reliable than radio, was vulnerable to artillery attacks that cut the lines. Faced with constant delays in repairing broken wires or running new lines to freshly taken positions, commanders relied on trench runners to carry messages between the front and rear and to make contact with the units on their flanks. Runners also provided reconnaissance by scouting ahead to bring back valuable intelligence about the enemy position. Trench runners needed good knowledge of the terrain in their area of operations and excellent map-reading skills. Because trench runners were often alone and in exposed positions, their losses were high.

Although not particularly dangerous work, sanitary troops in each unit had the unpleasant task of handling the human waste created by hundreds of thousands of men. Lavatories were often dug at the end of designated saps, which were simply filled in when they became full. Metal buckets that could be emptied behind the lines or over the top were sometimes placed at the end of specially constructed saps.

Life in the Trenches

Outside of moments when troops were engaged in a major attack, trench life soon developed a predictable routine. A typical day in the trenches began just before dawn when the men assembled and went on alert in case the enemy was planning to attack that day. If dawn passed with no attack, then the men prepared breakfast. Along most of the Western Front, tacit truces protected the men from enemy shelling as they ate. Such "live and let live" arrangements were informal agreements to refrain from needless shelling unless preparations for an attack were underway. In some quiet sectors of the front, troops even went so far as to shell at predictable times so that opposing troops knew when to take cover or purposefully shot shells high so that they mostly missed the opposing side. Every "live and let live" arrangement was subject to upheaval when a fresh unit arrived. If one side broke the pattern, the other would follow suit until another truce could be informally arranged through either verbal exchanges across No Man's Land or the establishment of predictable behavior patterns. When American troops first entered the lines to train with French divisions along quiet sectors of the front, French soldiers complained that by shooting at anything and everything the Americans unnecessarily disturbed the "live and let live" truce that made life bearable in the sector. During their time in the trenches, Americans soon learned to mimic their Allies and follow at least the ritual of taking a break from the war during mealtimes.

During the day soldiers mostly stayed hidden, out of sight from the snipers ready to shoot them, the airplanes looking for troops to strafe with machine gun fire, and observation balloons on the lookout for targets to relay to artillery crews. Troops passed the time cleaning their rifles to keep them in working order and trying to combat the rats and lice that infested the trenches. Steady artillery shelling by the enemy meant constant repairs to restore trench walls and defenses, work that assigned groups of soldiers undertook throughout the day. Maintaining the trenches by pumping out water or digging new latrines occupied the daylight hours of others.

At some point during the day, soldiers would also try to sleep for a bit. Dugouts provided some shelter from the elements and enemy fire, and were found in various sizes and styles. The smallest and most common were called "cubby holes," "bolt holes," or "funk holes," and were individual shelters dug about half way up the trench wall. These rudimentary shelters offered soldiers minimal protection from shell splinters, but perhaps more importantly gave men a place to lie down that was relatively dry and off the trench floor. Formal dugouts were underground shelters with reinforced walls of scavenged timber, corrugated iron sheets, and sandbags. Standard dugouts shielded a squad of men from the rain and cold, and offered more protection from shell fragments than cubby holes. Because the trenches ran through the remains of many destroyed villages, the Allies readily converted cellars and church crypts into dugouts for troops. Nearly every Allied dugout had water in it, and the constant moisture in these dark and cramped spaces created a damp and pungent environment. Dugouts in the front lines tended to be shallower than those found in the support and reserve trenches, which had to withstand heavier enemy shelling. The Germans tended to direct artillery fire at the rear to maximize the chances of hitting a large concentration of Allied soldiers and to minimize the risk of shellfire falling short and landing on their own troops stationed in the frontlines. Dugouts in the reserve and rear areas, therefore, could run as deep as thirty to forty feet.

Deeper dugouts behind the lines also served as command posts where regimental and divisional officers conferred during battles. Dugouts designed specifically for officers tended to have more amenities. This was particularly true on the German side, where the discovery of comfortable and cozy dugouts astounded the Allied soldiers who captured them in 1918. Accustomed to much more primitive accommodations, Allied troops marveled at the electric lights, ventilation, sitting rooms with wallpaper, painted ceilings, telephones, and proper beds that the Germans installed in their officers' dugouts. Even dugouts reserved for German enlisted men boasted paneled walls and proper ventilation, in sharp contrast to Allied troops who lived in darkness with mud and water in theirs throughout the war.

Even the protection of dugouts, however, did not eliminate the sheer terror of enduring an artillery barrage. Light barrages sent over half a dozen shells every ten minutes or so. Heavier ones fired twenty to thirty shells on a unit every minute. In the prelude to an attack, heavy barrages went on for hours. "To be shelled is the worse thing in the world," noted one American soldier. "It is impossible to adequately imagine it. In absolute darkness we simply lay and trembled from sheer nervous tension."[26] Clayton Slack privately concluded, "Those that weren't scared, weren't there."[27] Deafening noise and pulverizing artillery were regular features of every doughboy's stint in the trenches. Artillery fire caused nearly 70 percent of all wartime casualties in the AEF, so troops soon learned to tell the difference between incoming shells. Corporal Elmer Roden recalled that "in combat we named the different shells by their sounds, they were whiz-bangs, 75s, and the large ones from heavy artillery we called GI cans."[28] Other nicknames for high explosive shells included "ash cans," "trolley cars," and "Jack Johnsons," named after the famed African American boxer.[29] Properly identifying incoming shells helped soldiers predict how much imminent danger a particular barrage posed.

"Whenever the sound is as if crying the danger is slight, as the shell will pass over your head" explained Private Ernie Hilton.[30]

To combat the constant terror of enduring regular artillery shelling, troops developed an array of superstitions and coping mechanisms. Some soldiers accepted that sheer luck determined who lived and who died. "I don't think I survived because of talent or know-how . . . It was a matter of luck, I think I can safely say," Corporal Meyer Siegel concluded after the war.[31] Other soldiers embraced the belief that the shell that killed a man "had his number on it." Bernard Eubanks became obsessed with this idea while in the trenches. One night, "I had a strange dream or nightmare really. My company number was 84. During an intense bombardment I saw a huge missile coming my way with my number, 84, on it . . . but it passed over and never touched me."[32] After this reassuring dream, Eubanks gained a sense of calm and confidence that helped him cope with the daily bombardments. Other soldiers put less stock in this common superstition. "They claim that a man's shell has his name on it, if it's for him," wagged Sergeant Harry Weisburg, "but it is the part of a wise man to keep his nose out of the way of another man's shell."[33]

Nights were not a time to sleep along the Western Front. About one third of most units went "over the top" each night to perform maintenance and reconnaissance, while another third headed to the rear to collect supplies and rations or to carry wounded men to the rear. No Man's Land was the strip of land that separated the Allied and German trench systems. The actual distance between the two lines depended on the sector, with some trenches as close as 7–8 yards and others as far as 500. Regardless of the distance between the two lines, some ubiquitous features of No Man's Land existed. Scores of barbed wire covered this barren strip of pockmarked land to hamper the progress of attacking enemy troops. At night, this moonlike landscape came alive as small patrols scrambled out of the trenches to repair damaged wire or lay even more. Teams of troops threaded the barbed wire through metal stakes with a corkscrew tip that entered the ground noiselessly. Nightly patrols also conducted small raids to capture enemy prisoners who might reveal valuable military information.

The constant work that soldiers performed in the trenches day and night meant that men had little time to sleep during their tour in the frontlines. Unrelenting fatigue became a hallmark of trench duty for both soldiers and officers alike. While the men performed the physical labor, officers had the responsibility of organizing daily work parties and patrols, inspecting the men, and determining what supplies they needed from the rear. In addition, officers wrote reports on nearly every action undertaken in the trenches and had to decipher a steady stream of orders from the rear.

Enemy fire was an expected part of trench warfare. Depending on the season, freezing temperatures and steady rain added to soldiers' misery while mud, lice, and rats were a constant regardless of the weather. The wet winter and spring in northern France created a thick, gooey mud that made even the shortest journey through the trench system extraordinarily difficult. Every army had accounts of men drowning in the mud out in No Man's Land, sucked under before rescue parties could reach them. Exposed to the bitter winter cold in northern France, soldiers struggled to keep warm. The Allied armies experimented with various heating systems in the dugouts but the stench created by packs of dirty, sweating men was often unbearable. Heaters that burned smokeless coke or dry chips were placed outside in the trenches, but proved difficult to keep alight during periods of rain or heavy winds.

Standing water in the trenches that was an annoyance during the summer became life threatening in the winter. Days upon days of wet socks and boots created the perfect conditions for trench foot to take hold, a condition similar to frostbite that turned feet blue or red. If gangrene set in, a soldier risked losing a toe or sometimes the entire foot to amputation. To combat trench foot, men carried several changes of socks with them to the front. Every evening, re-provisioning parties brought dry socks up from the rear to replenish frontline stores, socks usually supplied by droves of female volunteers at home who knitted this essential item for the Red Cross. Soldiers ideally changed their socks twice a day, taking care to dry their feet and then coat them with grease before putting on a clean pair of socks. Ensuring that men changed their socks and inspecting for trench foot became yet another daily duty for already overtaxed officers.

Decomposing corpses posed another serious health risk for troops. Corpses attracted rats. "We soon became tired of killing them," noted one combat veteran. "I have often wondered why there were so few rat bites. Probably the rats felt that it was not worthwhile fooling with live humans when there were so many dead ones around."[34] Rats also found ample nourishment from the food remnants that troops discarded on the floor of the trenches. Living amidst thousands of rats became one of the most repulsive parts of daily life in the trenches. Feasting on human flesh, rats grew to gigantic proportions and multiplied by the thousands. They had little fear of living humans, roaming freely over the bodies of sleeping men and unit food supplies.

Rats were at least easily visible to the naked eye. The tiny vermin that bit human flesh from morning to night were harder to detect but just as vile. Men developed inventive names for the hated louse, including "cooties," "grayback," "seam squirrel," or "Bolshevik flea." In the trenches, soldiers spent what little free time they had on "cootie hunts," running a finger along the seams of their clothing to flush out the lice that they then burned. Letters to *The Stars and Stripes* suggested other effective ways to eradicate these pests such as running a heated wire along the seams of clothing or using "Sag," a salve that counteracted poison gas, to kill lice. Besides being a nuisance, lice also carried trench fever, which caused shooting pains in the shins and a high fever, as well as typhus. Although rarely fatal, the recovery was prolonged with soldiers often requiring months of rest before they could return to active duty. Delousing became a standard part of leaving the trenches, a process that involved sterilizing troops' clothing to kill the vermin and dunking soldiers in huge vats of hot water. Unfortunately, the delousing treatment only killed the living lice, not the eggs laid in the threads of the fabric. Once these eggs hatched, the supposedly deloused soldier would suffer anew.

Unburied corpses also attracted armies of flies, which along with other vermin such as head lice and mites, could adversely affect a soldier's general health. Constant scratching from bug bites created open wounds in the skin susceptible to infection in the unhealthy trench environment. The armies spread creosol to kill the flies, chloride of lime to reduce the spread of infection from corpses and polluted trench water, and shaved troops' heads to stamp out head lice to little avail. In the war against vermin, the army clearly lost.

Gas

The stench of death filled the trenches. The combination of decomposing corpses, the unbathed bodies of the living, overflowing latrines, and smoke assaulted the senses on a daily basis. By far the scariest smell, however, suggested the presence of gas. The most recognizable photograph from the First World War depicts a line of blindfolded men, each with a hand on the shoulder of the man in front, shuffling slowly along. Gas

An example of a massive gas and flame attack along the Western Front launched by the French. If the wind changed direction, the gas would drift back into Allied lines. (*Courtesy of the National Archives*)

became synonymous with the war in the spring of 1915, when the Germans exploded the first chlorine gas canisters into Allied lines in Belgium. This initial gas attack helped the Germans advance as French, Algerian, and Canadian troops withdrew in panic. Chemical weapons did not deliver on their initial promise to end trench deadlock. Instead, gas became another defensive weapon used to hold the line that worsened an already miserable situation even more so. Before long, both sides employed gas regularly and took precautions to defend their armies by equipping soldiers with box respirators to withstand gas attacks. Gas was a fickle weapon capable of turning back on the attacker if the winds changed. Despite its ability to hurt friend as well as foe, by 1918 one out of every four shells fired along the Western Front contained gas.

By 1917, the Allies and Germans had stockpiled a large and diverse arsenal of chemical weapons. In the training camps American soldiers heard lectures that vividly described the workings of each particular gas. Troops also spent time in simulated gas chambers where they learned to put on and breathe through gas masks while sitting in the midst of smoke standing in for chlorine and phosgene gas. These drills continued when soldiers entered the trenches. Officers repeatedly warned their men that there were only two types of soldiers in a gas attack: the quick and the dead.

Chlorine and phosgene gas attacked the respiratory system, causing a gradual buildup of fluid in the lungs that prevented men from breathing properly. Eventually, chlorine and phosgene gas victims literally drowned to death in their own bodily fluids. Death from exposure to chlorine gas could take an excruciating amount of time, as men remained conscious for days as they gradually suffocated. Men soon learned to identify these gases by their smell and color. Chlorine gas had a greenish-yellow tint and a strong, distinctive odor that recalled a mixture of pineapple and pepper, while phosgene was a clear gas that smelled like rotten fish. Easy to detect, each of these gases dissipated fairly quickly and gas masks offered good protection against them.

Mustard gas provoked the most fear among soldiers because it did not have a color or smell, and it remained hidden in crevices and dugouts for weeks after its initial dispersal. By stripping the mucous membrane of the bronchial tubes, mustard gas made every breath an exercise in torture. Out of an estimated 70,000 gas casualties in the American Army, 39 percent were from mustard gas. Noble Sissle vividly remembered walking through the gas ward of the hospital to visit a wounded comrade. "As you walked down the aisle by the rows of cots," Sissle recalled over twenty years later, "you could see how the different ones were suffering. Some of them in places where their eyes were, were just large bleeding scabs; others, their mouths were just one mass of sores; others had their hands up, and there were terrible burns beneath their arms, where the gas had attacked the moisture there. I had often heard of the horribleness of the torture, but these scenes are generally kept from the soldier in order to keep from lowering his morale."[35] Gas masks offered only minimal protection from mustard gas, which could seep through the skin, clothes, and even heavy trench boots. The army distributed an ointment called Sag paste for soldiers to spread on their exposed skin to prevent blisters, which was effective if used ahead of time. It was unrealistic, however, to expect soldiers to apply this paste continuously to their bodies, especially since it tended to cake once a soldier began to sweat. In addition, if a soldier left the ointment on too long after exposure to mustard gas, the gel eventually became saturated and the poison made its way to the skin.

The army provided protective cotton suits treated with linseed oil to artillerymen, medics, and decontaminating units likely to undergo sustained exposure to mustard gas. Artillerymen could not easily relocate their guns during a battle, while medics needed extra protection to help wounded and gassed men. The airtight fit of these protective suits, replete with hoods, mittens, and special boots, made men so stifling hot that few could stand to wear them for more than fifteen or twenty minutes. Instead, artillerymen made heavy use of Sag paste, and shaved their heads, underarms, and pubic areas to apply the ointment directly to their skin. They also often used French Tissot gas masks that did not contain a nose clip or mouthpiece. Besides being a more comfortable gas mask to wear, the Tissot did not fog up like the American box respirator.

The difference between life and death often depended on a soldier's ability to detect the initial symptoms of exposure to gas. Sometimes, a soldier did not know that he had been exposed to mustard gas until it was too late and he became vomiting, lost his sight, or developed severe blisters on his skin. Immediate immersion in hot, soapy water was the most effective treatment for skin exposure to mustard gas. A few units went into battle with mobile degassing units that consisted of eleven men, a five-ton truck with a 1,200-gallon capacity, and a heater that fed hot water to portable showers. The decision to organize degassing units came too late to help the vast majority of gas casualties.

After a gas attack, troops tried to remove low-lying gas with a trench fan. Swishing a long pole with a strip of canvas attached to it created an upward air current that usually did little except exhaust the fanners. Setting strategic fires in the trenches proved a better method for removing low-lying gas, as did requiring men to step in buckets of lime before entering a dugout to neutralize any mustard gas on their shoes. Decontaminating units also attempted to cleanse the ground that troops occupied, entering the trenches after a gas attack to fill shells holes with lime and new earth and taking away exposed equipment and clothing. They also located and removed unexploded gas shells from the front.

Both men and horses wore gas masks along the Western Front for protection during a poison gas attack. The horse's skin and soldier's hands remained exposed, however. (*Courtesy of the National Archives*)

Constructing gas-proof dugouts was another way to reduce gas casualties. To prevent gas from entering a dugout, troops hung a fitted blanket treated with glycerin over a wooden frame entranceway and kept the blanket damp. The blanket barrier was useless, however, if a gas shell exploded near the dugout entrance and blew the blankets open.

The gas learning curve for many units was quite steep, especially in places where mustard gas had permeated the ground, air, and water. When a platoon of the 28th Division was on its way into the line for the first time, the men inadvertently spent the night in shallow shell holes recently created by mustard gas shells. The next morning, they awoke to find their backs severely burned and blistered. Thirsty troops desperate for water who took a drink from a stagnant pool of water in a shellhole also sometimes found themselves in the hospital with mustard gas poisoning.

In the field, officers rarely second-guessed a soldier who claimed he was a gas victim. In the hospitals, however, medical personnel soon developed some checks to weed out malingers from the truly afflicted. One test was to offer a gas victim a large meal. Those who retained a hearty appetite and willingly consumed the food were promptly returned to the line.

Gas sentries gave the alert for men to don their gas masks after hearing the hiss of gas leaving a canister, seeing a cloud of gas, or smelling a suspicious odor. Some gas sentries simply shouted "Gas!" Others used air horns, steel triangles, or police rattles. Gas officers organized a unit's defense against gas attacks and gave troops instruction. Teaching proper gas discipline to novice replacement troops and complacent veteran troops was an ongoing challenge. Late in the war, gas officers also advised commanders who wanted to utilize gas as an offensive weapon.

By 1918 the U.S. Army was producing large quantities of various gases in the Edgewood Arsenal that American troops could pour into French or British artillery shells. Few American commanders employed chemical weapons in their attacks, however, concerned that gas shells would inevitably misfire and explode into their own ranks or increase the likelihood of retaliatory gas attacks from the Germans. American chemical warfare doctrine therefore centered primarily on protecting troops from a gas attack.

AMERICAN AIR SERVICE

The excitement and heroism of the air war captivated well-to-do American men even before the United States formally entered the conflict. These men flocked to join the *Escadrille Lafayette*, an American unit in the *French Service Aeronautique* created in 1916. Far fewer enlisted in the French Foreign Legion or served as ambulance drivers with the American Field Service, other ways to aid the French before the United States declared war. As one American volunteer with the French Foreign Legion noted, "there is no romance or anything to the infantry."[36]

Forming an American air unit in 1916 had obvious propaganda value for the French, certain to give Americans a more personal interest in the Allied cause by providing them with individual Americans to follow into combat. For their feats during the battle of Verdun, American pilots emerged as international celebrities. The group's colorful antics and unique personalities provided perfect press copy for American newspapers eager to publicize their achievements. Appealing to the American ethos of individualism, members of the *Escadrille Lafayette* designed their own uniforms, painted the image of an American Indian wearing a war headdress on their planes, and adopted male and female lion cubs as mascots. "Whiskey" and "Soda" became celebrities in their own right, and curious French civilians and soldiers often gathered to watch squad members wrestle with the lion cubs outside their aerodrome in Bar-le-Duc, a town near Verdun. The group trained the lions to hide in the bushes and pounce on unsuspecting passersby. As the lions stood atop their prey and roared, the airmen, hysterical with laughter, would emerge from hiding to save the terrified victim. By 1917, however, the strain of air combat, the deaths of many comrades, and the relentless media attention began to take its toll on the members of the *Escadrille Lafayette*. Seasoned veterans, the men lost some enthusiasm for war as a great adventure—a transformation that many other American soldiers would undergo in the coming year.

Eugene Bullard, the only African American pilot of the war, found his opportunity to fly by serving with the *Escadrille Lafayette*. Born in Georgia, Bullard ran away from home at the age of eight to begin a nomadic life that included living with gypsies and working as a jockey and live target for ball tosses at carnivals. When he was ten, Bullard stowed away on a ship to England where he learned to box. After touring Europe as a professional lightweight, Bullard settled in France and in 1914 when war erupted, he decided to join the French Foreign Legion. He was soon transferred to the 170th Infantry Regiment, a regular French army unit that contained other Americans. After receiving a disabling wound in the battle of Verdun, Bullard bet a fellow American soldier that he could become the first black pilot of the war. He received his flying certificate from the French army, but waited some time before receiving orders for the front, perhaps indicating that the French had doubts about the abilities of a black pilot. In August 1917, Bullard headed to the front where he decorated the side of his Spad 7 aircraft with the picture of a dagger stuck in a bleeding heart and the phrase "tout sang qui coule est rouge" (all blood that runs is red). Bullard flew with his own mascot, a small monkey that he purchased from a Parisian prostitute. He cut a dashing figure with gleaming tan boots, scarlet breeches, and a chest full of military decorations and medals that he wore on a daily basis. He was, noted a fellow American pilot, "a vision of military splendor such as one does not see twice in a lifetime."[37] In 1917, Bullard tried unsuccessfully to transfer into the American Air Service along with the white pilots of the *Escadrille Lafayette*, but the United States refused to allow men of color to fly. Bullard was subsequently grounded by the French after clashing with a French officer. He returned to the 170th Infantry Regiment and served in a service unit for the rest of the war. After the war, Bullard capitalized on his fame by running a series of successful nightclubs in Paris and married a French countess.

Relegating airplanes to the Signal Corps, the peacetime army had a limited view of their usefulness. Both Congress and Pershing quickly realized that the past two and a half years of combat demonstrated the importance of aircraft to gather intelligence, conduct reconnaissance, and defend frontlines from strafing attacks by enemy pilots. Congress authorized a lavish spending bill to spur the manufacture of needed aircraft, while Pershing created an air service within the army. Turning an obsolete force of 300 planes with fewer than 1,500 officers and men into an effective air corps proved too difficult for both American companies and the military. Supply problems and faulty designs hampered efforts to equip the air service, and the majority of American pilots flew French planes during the war. Overall, American factories produced 11,754 planes, but only 11 American squadrons flew American-produced planes. American-built DeHaviland-4s (DH-4) did not reach the front until the fall of 1918, where pilots quickly dubbed them "Flying Coffins." French planes carried gas tanks coated in rubber that expanded to seal minor holes created by sparks or bullets. A single bullet hole in the unprotected gas tank of the DH-4, however, sent gas pouring all over the fuselage as the pressure-fed gas system continued to pump gas out of the tank. It was often only a matter of moments before a spark or bullet set the gas and plane aflame, created a fiery death for the pilot. "Flyers at the front were generally afraid of this plane," the Inspector General's Office concluded at the end of the war.[38] Establishing a coherent plan for building the air service proved equally problematic, and six different commanders cycled through the agency in its first year. By the end of the war, only 45 squadrons (flying a total of 740 planes) had reached the front out of 190,000 men recruited into the air service.

For a man under thirty interested in learning to fly, training often began at a university authorized to provide basic ground training. After completing this civilian course, successful students could enter an army flying school in the United States where they trained on Curtiss "Jennies." Pilot training was a risky endeavor. Of the 677 American pilots who died during the war, nearly one third or 263 died from accidents in stateside training camps. Since there were no combat planes available in the United States, pilots completed their training in France, usually starting over again with French Nieuports. The largest

Eddie Rickenbacker became the most celebrated American pilot of the war. (*Courtesy of the National Archives*)

American flying school overseas was in Issoudun, a village about 65 miles south of Orleans that began training pilots in October 1918. One recruit summarized the conditions that he discovered there as "a sea of frozen mud. Waiting in (a) shivering line before dawn for the spoonsful [*sic*] of gluey porridge slapped into outstretched mess kits, cold as ice. Wretched flying equipment. Broken necks. The flu. A hell of a place, Issoudun."[39] Overseas, pilots first learned to fly solo, then advanced to acrobatics and finally to formation flying. Acrobatic training simulated actual battle conditions. After practicing stick handling on the ground, a student headed to the skies to try the maneuver himself. Sending out novices to try difficult acrobatic moves inevitably led to crashes when the pilot failed to come out of a tail spin. After mastering the evasive tricks that would save his life in air combat, pilots proceeded to aerial gunnery school where they learned to fire machine guns into observation balloons and handle gun jams. Some pilots became specialists in aerial reconnaissance or headed to the balloon corps, but the rest were now headed to the front.

The first few flights in combat were an important part of a pilot's training, a time when he learned how to keep his eyes unfocussed as he turned his head so he could detect any slight movement that signaled the presence of enemy aircraft. Eddie Rickenbacker, who gained renown as a leading American ace, returned from his first patrol without, he thought, seeing anything in the sky. His instructor, Major Raoul Lufbery, a famous pilot from the *Escadrille Lafayette*, laughingly told him that fifteen friendly and enemy aircraft had crossed their line of sight during the flight. Many "fliers were shot down in the early part of their career before they had really learned how to see," noted one pilot.[40]

Death haunted Great War pilots in combat. Out of every 100 trained pilots who reached the front lines, 33 died. Risk was part of the job, many pilots quickly realized

"[Y]ou played a dangerous game," admitted one flyer, "by becoming too fond of the other pilots—you paid a heavy price when they caught it."[41] In combat, men dueled with enemy pilots sometimes only fifty feet away, and flew without parachutes to save them if their planes caught fire or spun out of control. Besides crashing directly into the ground, pilots often burned to death while strapped to their machines. Lufbery's own fiery death demonstrated that even for experienced pilots, the skies were always forbidding. Lufbury, decorated with the Legion d'Honneur and British Military Cross for his feats, jumped to his death when his plane caught fire as he chased down a German plane taking observation photographs. When he was buried behind Allied lines, American planes flew overhead and dropped roses on his grave.

One American pilot aptly summed up the flyers' ethos: "nobody had any plans for tomorrow."[42] A favorite poem of the *Escadrille Lafayette*, "The Dying Aviator," bespoke the violent death many a pilot suffered:

> Two valve springs you'll find in my stomach,
> Three spark plugs are safe in my lung,
> The prop is in splinters inside me,
> To my fingers the joy-stick has clung.
> Take the cylinders out of my kidneys,
> The connecting rods out of my brain;
> From the small of my back get the crankshaft,
> And assemble the engine again.[43]

The first fully trained American air squadron, the 94th squadron, entered combat in the Toul sector in April 1918, with Rickenbacker as a member of the unit. A professional racecar driver before the war, Rickenbacker knew how to accurately judge speed and distance, and to bide his time before making a move against an opponent. Initially assigned as a chauffeur to Pershing, Rickenbacker soon transferred to the air service where he learned to fly. His impact was felt immediately. As the engineering officer at Issoudun, Rickenbacker designed a wheel fender that kept mud from flinging off an airplane's wheels and onto the propellers during take-off, a design flaw that sometimes caused the propeller to snap. In the air, Rickenbacker scored 26 victories and won the Medal of Honor for downing two German planes while making a solo run over enemy lines.

While Rickenbacker and his colleagues garnered acclaim for their individual feats along the frontlines, General Billy Mitchell experimented with sending pilots to attack supply depots in the rear. Mitchell gleaned much of his faith in aircraft's offensive potential from Major General Hugh Trenchard, the commander of the British Royal Flying Corps, who argued that forcing the Germans to use their pilots to defend key rear bases would help the Allies overcome a better manned and equipped German air force at the front. After much success in employing this approach in the summer of 1918 at Chateau-Thierry and Soissons, Mitchell took command of American aerial combat operations in the fall.

During the battle of St. Mihiel, Mitchell assembled nearly 1,481 French, British, and American aircraft, the largest concentration of airpower in any single wartime operation. Mitchell used the planes to strafe and bomb first one side of the salient, then the other and sent others to harass rear area installations. In the Meuse-Argonne campaign, Mitchell had to limit attacks on rear bases to provide needed intelligence to

The ace pilot Frank Luke gained fame for his skill in shooting down German observation balloons, but eventually suffered a nervous breakdown and lost his life in aerial combat. He is pictured here in front of the wreckage of an enemy observation balloon. (*Courtesy of the National Archives*)

front-line infantry troops. He still managed to assemble 500 planes and mount the largest bombing operation of the war on 8th October, when the Americans and French dropped 32 tons of bombs on a German counter-offensive force forming five miles behind their lines. This bombing campaign gave the Americans a chance to disrupt German battle plans and destroy enemy aircraft dispatched to stop the attack.

There were some embarrassing moments during the Meuse-Argonne campaign, however. One squadron became lost in the fog and was taken prisoner after it mistook Coblenz for Metz and landed behind enemy lines without dropping a single bomb. The stress of combat also took its toll on American pilots. During the battle, the Germans benefited from the clear view of the battleground that their high position and observation balloons provided. To shoot down German aerial balloons, Mitchell relied on airmen like Frank Luke, considered the best pilot in the American air service by many of his peers. Nicknamed the "Arizona balloon buster," Luke was the quintessential pilot: wild, insubordinate, and a loner. By the end of September, however, Luke had become mentally unhinged after watching his best friend die to save his life. On 16 September, the men flew out together to attack two German balloons. Focused on his targets, Luke failed to notice the arrival of six Fokker combat planes, which his friend took on alone to give Luke time to escape. Besieged with grief and guilt over his friend's sacrifice, Luke became reckless and unpredictable, often taking off by himself on unauthorized missions to attack enemy balloons. Three days into the Meuse-Argonne campaign, Luke's erratic behavior led to his grounding. In a gesture of immediate defiance, Luke headed for the skies and dropped a note to his squadron commander telling him to watch the three German balloons in the distance. To the amazement of his squadron, Luke shot down all three and then proceeded to strafe German troops on the ground. When he was finally forced to land his plane behind enemy lines, a wounded Luke refused to surrender, firing his pistol at the surrounding crowd of German soldiers until they shot and killed him.[44]

Many ideas that influenced the future of aerial combat operations came out of the war. Although he did not have the time or means to implement this plan, in October 1918 Mitchell suggested to Pershing that he drop an infantry Division by parachute behind enemy lines. Similarly, in the final months of the war a rudimentary strategic bombing campaign was already taking shape. The Northern Bombing Group, part of the navy's air corps, successfully bombed German submarine bases, while the army air service targeted transportation and communication facilities in the rear. "Our experience demonstrated that aerial bombardment of towns, railroads, bridges, etc, produced little material effect; it has a moral effect, however, if constantly repeated," Second Army commander Hunter Liggett concluded at the war's close, articulating a philosophy that heavily influenced American bombing strategy in World War II.[45]

NONCOMBATANTS

Despite the understandable wartime preoccupation with the fighting man, noncombatants were a large and essential segment of the soldier population. Noncombatants formed sixty percent of the overall wartime force, with roughly thirty percent performing skilled work and another thirty percent serving as laboring and support troops. Using large numbers of noncombatant soldiers to maintain fighting men in the field was a dramatic shift from the past, changing the nature of military service for hundreds of thousands of men. In the Civil War, over 90 percent of troops fought in battle. Civilian workers who followed the Union army offered their services to cook, wash clothes, provide entertainment, and even bury bodies for the military. Facing a shortage of civilian labor in France and the United States, the American Army in World War I relied on soldiers to unload boxes from ships, build needed roads and bridges, and even take photographs. Pershing liked having complete control over the workforce performing essential functions for the military, and readily adopted a new organizational structure that placed both combatants and noncombatants under his command.

Delivering Supplies

The efforts to build a shadow noncombatant army that supported the fighting army in the field got off to a slow start. The Line of Communications (LOC), an umbrella organization that housed a variety of noncombatant services, struggled to find and transport needed supplies. Without enough men or machines to keep up with ships arriving from the United States, cargo sometimes sat in French harbors for over a month before beginning a slow land journey to American Divisions training throughout France. Some American soldiers temporarily wore British uniforms adorned with brass buttons bearing the symbol of the royal crown because the LOC failed to procure enough American uniforms to outfit the field army. While troops went without desperately needed supplies, valuable shipping and railroad transport space occasionally went to waste. One Division, for example, received boxes addressed to a Boston department that contained baby clothes, while another got hundreds of wagon bodies but no wheels to attach to them. By far the greatest supply problem, however, was distributing the mountains of supplies that arrived on a daily basis to widely dispersed troops. Supplies sent to the 42nd Division piled up in a ten-acre field because the Division only had six trucks making deliveries to troops spread out over an eighteen-mile billeting area. Other Division commanders complained that even while training behind the lines their men often went for days without receiving any potatoes, vegetables, or bread as part of their ration—hardships more commonly associated with frontline duty. Describing the breakdown in supply lines "as an eye-sore" and "a disgrace to the United States," Colonel Johnson Hagood informed GHQ in November 1917 that "French and Canadian Officers and troops seeing the men in this pitiable condition have come to their rescue and helped them out."[46] The problems that the United States faced in feeding and supplying its men in the training areas did not bode well, many commanders feared, for maintaining an army in the field.

In February 1918, Pershing reorganized the supply services into the Services of Supply (SOS). The army at first considered naming the Services of Supply, the "Services of the Rear" but jettisoned this title after contemplating the fun that soldiers might have with the name. Only noncombatant troops served in the SOS, but every fighting division also contained some noncombatant units to provide sanitary, transportation, engineering and supply services to the division. At its peak, the SOS oversaw the Quartermaster Corps, the Medical Corps, the Engineer Corps, the Ordnance Department, the Signal Corps, the Air Service, the Motor Transport Corps, the Transportation Corps, the Chemical Warfare Service, Military Police, and the Army Service Corps. As this list reveals, noncombatants' duties varied significantly and often put them in the line of fire. Engineering troops sent to construct bridges or Signal Corps troops laying telegraph or telephone lines in the combat zones came under shellfire, as did truck drivers bringing supplies to the front and ambulance drivers taking wounded men to hospitals.

It took until July 1918, when General James Harbord took over the organization, for Pershing to grant the commander of the SOS the independent powers that he needed to fashion an effective supply service. The SOS resolved earlier procurement problems by developing a reserve depot system that stockpiled supplies throughout France. Improvements in the railway, motor, and animal transport systems also helped carry these materials to field troops more efficiently. The SOS also realized that purchasing some items such as clothing and blankets in Europe was cheaper and more expedient than ordering them from overtaxed American factories and using precious shipping space to bring them to France.

The routine of the trenches allowed for regular mealtimes and relative ease in getting provisions to troops once the SOS made these improvements. Transporting food, clothing, and ammunition to advancing troops proved more difficult. According to official figures, the AEF was the best-supplied army in the world. The reality in the front lines was often something else. "You see a man may be very well equipped, and a day later have lost everything, like hat, overcoat, equipment, and of course, all extras," one sergeant noted in a letter home.[47] The tendency of troops to jettison equipment to lighten their loads in the heat of battle added to the burden of properly equipping men for combat.

A division in the field required an average of twenty-five railway cars filled with supplies to stay in the line for one day. The battalion of men designated to collect the supplies in a wagon train would find all the Division's perishable and nonperishable items in one place when the ration train arrived. Units too far forward to easily reach the standard gauge railroad depot received their supplies by narrow gauge railways or trucks. Because animal transport was so important to the rationing and supply process, the Quartermaster Corps also took charge of providing horses and mules to the army. Over the course of the war, the AEF used 181,983 horses and 61,377 mules, many procured in France.

Food

As the war progressed, the Quartermaster Corps dramatically improved its handling of rations. In the heat of combat, soldiers still had to rely on canned beef and hard tack, but otherwise American soldiers received daily rations of fresh meat and vegetables. Delivering food to the troops was the last step in a complex network created by the Quartermaster Corps to prepare and procure appealing and nutritious food for American troops. Quartermaster troops toiled in a special AEF bakery in Is-sur-Tille to bake 750,000 pounds of bread every day and grew vegetables throughout France in army farms. Within Divisions, quartermaster troops prepared daily meals in "rolling kitchens" where they either served food directly to troops, or put meals in insulated cans that carrying parties took to soldiers at the front so they could enjoy a hot meal in the trenches. Besides feeding troops, the Quartermaster Corps also clothed them and helped preserve troops' health and morale by running laundries, delousing stations, and baths.

Burying the Dead

Soldiers assigned to the Quartermaster Corps did more than provide services to the living. Graves Registration units buried the fallen, undertaking the disagreeable but important task of identifying and registering the dead. At first, the army relied mostly on fighting men to bury their comrades. Combat soldiers understandably avoided this unpleasant task as much as possible, sometimes leaving the corpses of men and horses out in the open for days at a time. As the bodies began decomposing, they attracted flies and maggots by the thousands, and even worse became grisly sights of horror that undermined the resolve of troops. "The effect upon the morale of combatant troops of being compelled to bury their own dead is very bad," the Chief Surgeon of the First Army noted. "During conditions such as they were at Chateau-Thierry when the bodies soon became black, swollen, discolored remnants of humanity, literarily covered with maggots, the effect is of course tremendously bad."[48] In the fall of 1918, pioneer infantry troops followed units into battle to handle the grisly task of burying the dead in temporary graves marked with rough crosses or the man's identification tags and rifle. The truly backbreaking work for these troops was burying the large number of horses killed in battle. Once the fighting ceased in the region, Graves Registration and labor troops (many of whom were black) fanned out across the battlefields to collect these bodies from their temporary graves to rebury them in designated rear area cemeteries. The bodies of the fallen were moved once again at the end of the war, when they were either shipped home for burial or buried overseas in a permanent American military cemetery.

Communications, Photography, and Engineering to Support the War Effort

The Quartermaster Corps focused primarily on the physical wellbeing of troops, while the Signal Corps created the communications infrastructure needed to command a mass army effectively in battle. Signal Corps troops erected nearly 2,000 miles of telephone poles that dotted the landscape behind the lines and lay 44,000 miles of lines that traversed the combat areas. By the end of the war, the Corps had also developed small aircraft radio-telephones, introducing radio as the future of battlefield communications. Soldiers in the Signal Corps also made heavy use of technologies from the past. The U.S. Army first used observation balloons in the Civil War and in France the Signal Corps organized balloon companies to provide intelligence about enemy movements and activities. Other Signal Corps units taught pigeons to carry messages. Carrier pigeons could only be trained to fly between two locations, so officers mostly used them to send one way communications from the front to the rear, unless the front-line unit was in a fixed position. Pigeons could fly much farther and faster than a human messenger walked or ran so they came in handy to send emergency requests to the rear. Sailors and pilots also used carrier pigeons to report accidents or crashes. During the Meuse-Argonne offensive, pigeons carried 402 messages for the AEF. Several pigeons achieved renown for aiding troops in dire straits and were decorated for their service. The most famous carrier pigeon was *Cher Ami* who carried twelve important messages during the Meuse-Argonne campaign, including a message from the "Lost Battalion" of the 77th Division to halt an artillery barrage that was falling on the men trapped behind enemy lines. Though shot through the chest and wounded in the leg *Cher Ami* managed to return to his roost to deliver the message from Major Charles W. Whittlesey. *Cher Ami* was awarded the *croix de guerre* with Palm and the Distinguished Service Cross for his actions. He died in 1919 from his wounds and was inducted into the Racing Pigeon Hall of Fame in 1931.

Monitoring enemy lines from an observation balloon exposed the soldier to enemy fire from artillery and airplanes, but gave a birds-eye view of the action. (*Courtesy of the National Archives*)

Besides facilitating verbal and written communication, the Signal Corps also took photographs that provided aerial intelligence for commanders and created a visual historical record of the American war effort. Signal Corps photographers supplied most of the images that filled newspapers and magazines at home during the war. The government only credentialed twenty civilian photojournalists to take pictures overseas, therefore the bulk of photographs came from official military photographers working for the Army Signal Corps. A cadre of soldier cameramen also compiled film footage for government documentaries. In an effort to provide a full historical accounting, photographs documented virtually every aspect of soldiers' daily lives from induction to demobilization including work, combat, entertainment, transport, parades, and interaction with French civilians.

The government heavily censored all images appearing in the press, prohibiting the publication of any photographs that depicted dead Americans. Published photographs of wounded men usually showed stoic American soldiers receiving satisfactory care by Army doctors. Photographs of ruined French villages and numerous pictures of mutilated German dead were the closest Americans at home got to viewing the actual aftermath of combat during the war. Many soldiers carried clandestine Kodak cameras with them and took numerous unauthorized photographs that eventually found their way into private albums across the nation. Yet few of the images taken by either professional or amateur photographers adequately conveyed the nature of combat along the Western Front. Poor weather and the realities of trench warfare limited photographers' ability to take photographs that adequately conveyed the chaos, emotion, or excitement of battle. Images of men hovering in the trenches revealed horrendous living conditions but not the terror of going over the top into a hail of machine gun fire and artillery shells. Wide panoramic shots showed bursts of smoke and groups of men advancing, but relayed little emotion or the larger strategy devised by commanders. The few photographs that depicted actual fighting were often posed shots intended to satiate public curiosity about the experience of combat.

The U.S. Army Corps of Engineers built the AEF's transportation network by constructing roads, port facilities, and railroads to transport goods and men to the front. Many quartermaster troops worked on construction projects managed by the Corps of Engineers. Each Division also contained a regiment of engineers to facilitate the movement of troops and supplies. In addition, the Army Corps of Engineers took the lead in organizing the army's first tank corps and developing chemical weapons. Eventually, these two services evolved into independent army agencies, the Tanks Corps and the Chemical Warfare Service.

Nearly 240,000 engineers served in France, including 40,000 African Americans. Vividly dramatizing the risky nature of some engineering work, the first American casualties of the war were Sgt. Matthew Calderwood and Pvt. William Branigan from the 11th Engineers, wounded on 5 September 1917 while helping construct railroads for the British Third Army. Engineering units attached to divisions went into combat alongside infantrymen and machine gunners to reconnoiter the terrain ahead, build the pontoon bridges needed to maintain the advance, or repair the trenches. Other engineers drew detailed maps from aerial reconnaissances, which were printed in the thousands at an army facility in Langres.

Besides overseeing and providing the manpower for major construction projects, army engineers gathered the raw materials needed to build bridges, ports, piers, docks, railroads, rail yards, and repair facilities. The 28th Engineers operated a rock quarry that provided crushed stone to build roads. By October 1918, American forestry

American engineering troops built the bridges and roads needed to move troops and supplies to the front. (*Courtesy of the National Archives*)

engineers were operating over a hundred sawmills in France to produce millions of railroad ties and wooden boards from lumber harvested in southern and central France. Engineering troops used these materials to construct nearly 1,000 miles of standard-gauged railroad tracks around American port facilities and to move supplies from ships to warehouses that engineering troops also built. Other engineering units built narrow-gauged railways to transport material to units at the front. To store food, engineers constructed specialized refrigerated and bakery facilities.

Although engineering and quartermaster troops performed tasks crucial to fighting a modern war, men assigned to these branches often complained that their work did not make them feel like soldiers. General Harbord, the commander of the SOS, acknowledged that these men toiled at tasks bearing much resemblance to jobs found in civilian life and were "doomed to spend the rest of their lives explaining why they served in the Services of Supply" to relatives and friends at home who equated military service with fighting.[49] The title that one noncombatant selected for his wartime diary, "The Diary of a Dud," accurately reflected the disappointment that many noncombatants felt about serving behind the lines. Another solder expressed his dissatisfaction with noncombatant work by writing to *The Stars and Stripes*, "I have just received a letter from home saying that my mother is proudly displaying a service flag because 'yours truly' is with the AEF in France. As I happen to be only a field clerk . . . I am wondering if it is right to let her display this flag… I don't like to be masquerading at home as a soldier."[50] Harbord tried to reassure these men that they "did more for their country by living for it than they could possibly have done by dying for it," but many soldiers returned home unconvinced.[51]

The Military Police

Combat soldiers complained immediately about any delay or inconvenience they encountered when receiving supplies, but they rarely blamed individual soldiers working in the Quartermaster Corps or Engineers for these problems. The willingness to hold a fumbling bureaucracy responsible for transgressions evaporated, however, when soldiers came into contact with the most hated branch of the SOS, the Military Police (MPs). Universally despised, the MPs policed French towns where soldiers went to drink and relax; rounded up stragglers as the army advanced into battle; and generally enforced military regulations on base. For African American soldiers, violent encounters with racist MPs intent on preventing any contact between black soldiers and white French women became a defining aspect of their overseas experience. The brutality of MPs who combed Paris after the war in search of soldiers who had gone absent without leave or stayed in the city on expired passes provoked a congressional investigation into the beatings and torture regularly administered in Paris-area military prisons. Few combat soldiers retained lasting memories of the noncombatants who built the roads, provided the food, and transported equipment to the front, but nearly all remembered their encounters overseas with the military police.

FIGHTING IN NORTH RUSSIA AND SIBERIA

During the First World War, several thousand American troops were sent to fight in North Russia and Siberia. Unlike troops submerged in trenches along the Western Front, American soldiers sent to Russia were deployed over a vast amount of territory and fought out in the open on more traditional-style battlefields. The elements, however, proved every bit as challenging in Russia as in France. Rather than rain and mud, these soldiers struggled to survive the snow-drenched and bitterly cold Russian winter. One key difference separated soldiers in France and Russia, however. For American soldiers in Europe, the war ended on 11 November 1918. Those sent to Russia continued to fight well into 1919.

Several factors led to the American intervention in the Russian Civil War. Politically, the Wilson administration wanted to help shape a democratic future for Russia. Militarily, the Allies realized that Germany's victory over Russia in March 1918 freed the German army to transfer millions of men from the Eastern to the Western Front. Sending Allied troops into Russia was one way to force Germany to keep more troops on guard along its eastern border.

Having heralded the emergence of a parliamentary system in Russia during the March 1917 revolution, Wilson vehemently opposed the Bolsheviks' rise to power in the wake of the November revolution. Wilson believed that communists had illegitimately thwarted the Russian peoples' desire to establish a democracy and took solace in the fact that, with twenty different factions struggling for control, the future of the Russian Revolution was still very much in doubt. Hoping to influence the direction of the revolution, Wilson offered American aid to anti-Bolshevik movements. Initially, the United States helped Lenin's opponents covertly. The Wilson administration funneled money through Allied governments and gave the Russian Embassy in Washington funds to purchase military supplies for anti-Bolshevik forces. American diplomats and military attaches in Russia recruited local citizens to conduct sabotage missions and organized an extensive intelligence-gathering operation that provided important information to foes of the Red Army. Wilson initially rejected direct intervention as an option, feeling it would violate his own call in the Fourteen Points to give Russia an unhampered chance to form a new government. He also thought the mission might backfire. The presence of Allied troops on Russian soil, Wilson feared, might help the Bolsheviks draw reluctant Russians to their side by calling for unity to expel the invading forces. In many respects, Wilson accurately forecast the exact scenario that unfolded after the Americans agreed to join the Allied intervention in North Russia and Siberia.

Although Wilson firmly believed that the war would be won or lost on the Western Front, he reluctantly agreed to send a small number of American troops to participate in the Allied mission to North Russia and Siberia. In part, Wilson made this concession as a gesture of goodwill towards his Allies who were still disappointed over the American refusal to amalgamate their troops into the French and British armies. Wilson also convinced himself that the Allied intervention would protect the Russian people from Bolshevik attacks, thus allowing democracy to flourish in Russia. Concern over the plight of the Czech Legion also influenced Wilson's decision to send American troops to Siberia. When Russia abruptly signed a separate peace with Germany, these Czech fighters were stranded along the Eastern Front. As the Czech Legion battled its way out of the interior of Russia, Czech leaders called on the Allies to come to the rescue of troops who were willing to fight on the Western Front. Japan offered to intervene in Siberia on behalf of the Allies, but this offer raised concerns that letting Japan enter Russia alone might inadvertently further Japan's imperialistic ambitions in the East.

Focusing solely on the plight of the Czech Legion, Wilson framed the intervention in humanitarian terms for the American people. Yet, Wilson only authorized the Siberian mission after the Czechs had taken over most of the Trans-Siberian Railway and rallied large numbers of anti-Bolshevik Russians to their side. Instead of leaving Russia when Allied soldiers arrived, the Czech Legion stayed in Russia to form the fighting nucleus of the Allied campaign against the Bolsheviks. The newly formed Czech government agreed to keep these 40,000 troops in Russia, hoping that in return Allied goodwill would benefit Czechoslovakia at the eventual peace conference.

In Siberia, 8,388 Regular Army troops came directly from the Philippines to join an Allied expedition that included Japanese, British, French, Chinese, Canadian, and Italian troops. In keeping with the defensive orientation of their mission, the Americans mainly guarded the city of Vladivostok and the Trans-Siberian Railway to keep supplies flowing to Czech fighters in the field. By taking over guard duties, the Americans freed anti-Bolshevik forces to fight against the Red Army. Major General William S. Graves, the expedition commander, struggled to stay neutral and avoid direct engagement with the various counter-revolutionary factions vying for control of Siberia. When Graves received his instructions from Washington, Secretary of War Baker cautioned him to "watch your step; you will be walking on eggs loaded with dynamite."[52] Overwhelmed by the stench of decaying garbage strewn throughout the streets, the chaos and anarchy in Vladivostok became immediately evident to arriving American troops. Graves came into instant conflict with other Allied commanders over the true mission of American troops in Siberia. When a contingent of 1,500 troops arrived before their commander in August, Allied commanders promptly had them accompany Japanese soldiers on a 1,000 march to rout out German and Austrian prisoners of war and Bolshevik soldiers. When Graves arrived in September 1918, he quickly determined that the joint Japanese-American victories against the retreating Bolshevik force would pull the Americans into the Russian Civil War. Graves recalled his troops to Vladivostok where they spent the winter struggling to avoid frostbite and amputations when temperatures dipped as low as sixty degrees below zero. Bored, far from home, and uncertain of the reason for their

deployment in Siberia, drinking vodka in local bars and purchasing the services of prostitutes became popular pastimes for American soldiers between their stints patrolling
the city. When spring arrived and the snow melted, American soldiers clashed with
Bolshevik partisans and rival White factions as they tried to keep the Trans-Siberian
Railway open. The tracks and telegraph poles were subject to daily sabotage from local
Bolshevik sympathizers, who also occasionally ambushed American patrols. Relations
with local Russians became strained as American soldiers found it impossible to tell
friend from foe. In the aftermath of a Bolshevik partisan attack against Americans on
patrol near Romanaovka, American troops recognized a local man among the enemy
dead who had regularly sold them milk. Anti-Bolshevik forces were often no better,
willing to murder or torture any one who challenged them as they vied for control of
the region. Local peasants often pleaded with American troops to protect them from the
rampages of particularly brutal warlords whose forces freely raped, pillaged, and decapitated residents. The reign of terror unleashed by rival Cossack guerila forces also occasionally victimized American troops. One band of Cossacks poured machine gun fire
into a boxcar of sleeping soldiers; another kidnapped and brutally beat an American
corporal. Complicating matters further, the Americans suspected that their erstwhile
ally Japan was encouraging Cossack terrorism to further its own imperialistic designs
in Siberia.

In June 1919, Wilson finally broke with the neutral stance that had become increasingly impossible to maintain in Siberia by choosing to support strongman Admiral
Aleksandr V. Kolchak. The Allies extracted a promise from Kolchak that he would hold
elections once he took Moscow, but many observers noted Kolchak was a counter-
revolutionary who wanted to either restore the old Tsarist system or form a new military
dictatorship. Foreshadowing the difficult decisions that many future American presidents
would face in opposing communism, Wilson evidently decided that anything was better
than Bolshevism. Many peasants felt otherwise, however, and without their support or an
infusion of more foreign troops, Kolchak's army and government disintegrated in
November 1919. Dismayed by the growing military and political quagmire in Siberia and
facing increased criticism at home over the prolonged presence of American troops in
Russia, Wilson began withdrawing soldiers from Siberia in January 1920. In the end,
rather than saving the Czech Legion, the Americans abandoned it. The Czechs fought
and bargained their own way out of Siberia by turning Kolchak over to the Bolsheviks.

Five thousand miles away in North Russia, 5,710 drafted troops in the 339th Infantry
Regiment, one battalion from the 310th Engineers, 337th Field Hospital and 337th
Ambulance Company of the 85th Division served alongside 11,130 British, French and
locally recruited Russian soldiers. Wilson linked this mission as well to the Czech Legion,
instructing American troops to keep the port city of Archangel open as a possible escape
route for the Czech Legion. But he also authorized the Americans to provide assistance
"to steady any efforts at self-government or self-defense in which the Russians themselves
may be willing to accept assistance."[53] Whether the Americans could offer this broader
assistance by simply defending Archangel from Bolshevik attack or whether it required
going further afield became a point of interpretation that created much conflict between
the British commanders in charge of the Allied mission and American soldiers. Many
American soldiers embraced the more limited interpretation of their charge and resented
the British decision to create a so-called defensive front that extended over 300 miles. The
British claimed that broader perimeter fighting was necessary to support Russian fighters
in the field, but Wilson eventually accused the British of using this rationale as a pretext
for trying to open up a new eastern front against Germany.

The president quickly lost faith in the North Russian expedition, especially when it became clear that, as he feared, foreign support of the counter-revolutionary movement unintentionally benefited the Bolshevik cause. Too small to convince fearful or indifferent Russian peasants to take up arms against a larger and more persistent Bolshevik force, the presence of Allied forces on Russian soil instead generated fears that the West wanted to conquer Russia. The Bolsheviks easily rallied peasants to their ranks around the cry of purging all foreign forces from Russia and castigated anyone who cooperated with the Allies as collaborators in a western colonization scheme. Some easy victories by Bolshevik forces against the under-manned Allies made the Bolsheviks appear stronger militarily than they really were, further discouraging disaffected Russians from joining a counter-revolutionary group. In the end, the Allies only succeeded in arousing nationalistic rather than democratic sentiment among the local population, a development that quickly doomed Wilson's desire to plant the seeds of democracy in Russia.

With his hopes dashed in North Russia, Wilson refused requests for additional deployments. Yet Wilson's lost interest in the mission did not change the reality for troops on the ground, especially when ice blocked the port in November and trapped American soldiers in North Russia until the spring thaw. Morale plummeted as winter snows and frigid temperatures enveloped the region and overland supply lines broke down. Wearing sheets of white camouflage over their thick winter coats and boots so they would blend with the snow, American soldiers trudged miles through frozen terrain to fight against a constantly growing Bolshevik force. Aware that the war had ended in France, these troops expressed mounting anger over their prolonged deployment on a mission with questionable aims. While some American soldiers secretly mused in their diaries about arranging informal truces with the Bolsheviks to let them live through the winter until they could be withdrawn in the spring, others mimicked the savagery of their opponents by killing prisoners. In mid-January, the Americans suffered a rout at Shenkursk where the Sixth Soviet Army pushed the Americans back fifty miles before they could stabilize the front. This defeat had a devastating effect on troop morale, and grumblings that had previously been made privately now spilled out into the open. Direct challenges to orders, attempts to secret out uncensored letters home, self-inflicted wounds, and fraternization with enemy Bolshevik forces all revealed the extent of troop discontent. Troops circulated clandestine petitions to demand their recall and challenged the government to explain the purpose of their mission. "We have earnestly endeavored to find some justification for our being here," First Lieutenant Carl H. Christine declared in one petition, "but we have been unable to reconcile this expedition with American ideals and principles instilled within us."[54] Another petition noted that "the interest and honor of the USA are not at stake [because] we have accomplished the defeat of the German's whitch [sic] was our mission."[55]

At times, disgruntlement bordered on mutiny. In March 1919, a company of men refused to load their sleds and return to the front. The army vigorously denied that a mutiny had occurred, claiming that the men had willingly returned to the front after their commanding officer agreed to listen to their questions. When word of the confrontation reached the United States, the public clearly sympathized with the soldiers and denunciations of the American presence in Russia increased in the press and in Congress. Seven months after the armistice, American forces left North Russia. When they stopped in France on their way home, several soldiers walking down the gangplank sarcastically asked if the war was over.

In 1920, the Secretary of War reported that 353 American soldiers had died in Siberia and North Russia. American officials listed all men missing in action as dead, despite confirmed reports that the Soviet Union was holding Americans as prisoners-of-war to use as bargaining chips in negotiations with the United States. The United States refused to grant the Soviet Union diplomatic recognition or resume trade relations even though the Soviets threatened to execute these prisoners. In 1921, as part of the Riga Agreement that sent humanitarian aid to starving Russian children, the Soviet Union released more than a hundred American prisoners of war to a surprised American delegation that was expecting around twenty men. The Soviets, however, held onto a few Americans prisoners to use in future negotiations with the United States. Classified reports of Americans languishing in Russian prisons continued to surface well into the 1930s even after the United States formally recognized the Soviet Union but no more were ever released. Concern about the uncertain fate of the missing led to two missions by the U.S. Graves Registration Service in 1929 and 1934 to identify the remains of American servicemen killed in Archangel. Of the 146 men killed there, these missions claimed to have identified all but forty-one.

CONCLUSION

The experience overseas encompassed a wide variety of combat experiences on sea, land, and in the air. Soldiers both fought in the trenches and worked behind the lines to create the enormous infrastructure needed to send messages, men, and material throughout France. A few thousand men spent the war shivering in North Russia and Siberia, and the questionable nature of their mission made these the only troops of the war who came close to staging a mutiny. Although the trenches certainly created miserable living conditions, most American soldiers remained dedicated to fighting and winning the war.

NOTES

1. Mark Meigs, *Optimism at Armageddon: Voices of American Participants in the First World War* (New York: New York University Press, 1997), 49.

2. Meirion and Susie Harries, *The Last Days of Innocence: America at War, 1917–1918* (New York: Vintage Books, 1997), 382.

3. John T. Winterich, (ed.), *Squads Write! A Selection of the Best Things in Prose, Verse & Cartoon from The Stars and Stripes* (New York: Harper & Brothers, 1931), 112.

4. Edward Coffman, *The War to End All Wars: The American Military Experience in World War I* (New York: Oxford University Press, 1968), 110.

5. Robert H. Zieger, *America's Great War: World War I and the American Experience.* (Lanham, Md.: Rowman & Littlefield, 2000), 113.

6. Coffman, *The War to End All Wars*, 107.

7. Coffman, *The War to End All Wars*, 109.

8. Coffman, *The War to End All Wars*, 110.

9. Coffman, *The War to End All Wars*, 118.

10. Stephen Harris, *Harlem's Hell Fighters: The African American 369th Infantry in World War I* (Washington, D.C.: Brassey's, 2003), 145.

11. Harris, *Harlem's Hell Fighters*, 147.

12. Harris, *Harlem's Hell Fighters*, 149–50.

13. Harris, *Harlem's Hell Fighters*, 149.

14. Harris, *Harlem's Hell Fighters*, 152.

15. Carol R. Byerly, *Fever of War: The Influenza Epidemic in the U.S. Army during World War I* (New York: New York University Press, 2005), 103.

16. Christopher M. Sterba, *Good Americans: Italian and Jewish Immigrants during the First World War* (New York: Oxford University Press, 2003), 184.

17. Alfred E. Cornebise, *The Stars and Stripes: Doughboy Journalism in World War I.* (Westport, Conn.: Greenwood Press, 1984), 70.

18. Col. Robert Wyllie, "The Romance of Military Insignia," *The National Geographic Magazine*, Vol. XXXVI, no. 6 (December 1919).

19. Richard Schweitzer, *The Cross and the Trenches: Religious Faith and Doubt Among British and American Great War Soldiers* (Westport, Conn.: Praeger, 2003), 220.

20. Sterba, *Good Americans*, 96.

21. Cornebise, *The Stars and Stripes*, 106–7.

22. Sterba, *Good Americans*, 185.

23. Jennifer D. Keene, "Protest and Disability: A New Look at African American Soldiers During the First World War," in *Warfare and Belligerence: Perspectives in First World War Studies*, ed. Pierre Purseigle (Boston: Brill, 2005), 233.

24. Arthur W. Little, *From Harlem to the Rhine: The Story of New York's Colored Volunteers* (New York: Covici, Friede, 1936), 195.

25. Little, *From Harlem to the Rhine*, 196.

26. Ronald Schaffer, *America in the Great War: The Rise of the War Welfare State* (New York: Oxford University Press, 1991), 158.

27. Coffman, *The War to End All Wars*, 289.

28. Jennifer D. Keene, *Doughboys, the Great War and the Remaking of America* (Baltimore, Md.: Johns Hopkins University Press), 46.

29. Sterba, *Good Americans*, 183.

30. Keene, *Doughboys, the Great War and the Remaking of America*, 46.

31. Sterba, *Good Americans*, 183.

32. Keene, *Doughboys, the Great War and the Remaking of America*, 49.

33. Sterba, *Good Americans*, 183.

34. Harry Haywood, *Black Bolshevik: Autobiography of an Afro-American Communist* (Chicago: Liberator Press, 1978), 58.

35. Noble Sissle, "Memoirs of Lieutenant Jim Europe," (1942), p. 168, box J-56, National Association for the Advancement of Colored People Papers, Part II, Library of Congress, Washington, D.C.

36. Robert B. Bruce, *A Fraternity of Arms: America and France in the Great War* (Lawrence, Ks.: University Press of Kansas, 2003), 10.

37. Jamie Cockfield, "Eugene Bullard, America's First Black Military Aviator, Flew for France During World War I," *Military History* (February 1996): 74.

38. Harries, *The Last Days of Innocence*, 201.

39. Coffman, *The War to End All Wars*, 199.

40. Coffman, *The War to End All Wars*, 200.

41. Schaffer, *America in the Great War*, 193.

42. Coffman, *The War to End All Wars*, 202.

43. Harries, *The Last Days of Innocence*, 47. Thomas C. Leonard, *Above the Battle: War-Making in America From Appomattox to Versaille*s (New York: Oxford University Press, 1978), 141.

44. Harries, *The Last Days of Innocence*, 369.

45. Coffman, *The War to End All Wars*, 210.

46. Frank Freidel, *Over There: The Story of America's First Great Overseas Crusade* (Boston: Little, Brown, 1964), 102.

47. Sterba, *Good Americans*, 184.

48. Chief Surgeon, First Army Corps, to Chief Surgeon, S.O.S, October 21, 1918, reprinted on Doughboy Center website, www.worldwar1.com/dbc/burial.htm.

49. Freidel, *Over There*, 98.

50. Susan Zeiger, *In Uncle Sam's Service: Women Workers with the American Expeditionary Force, 1917-1919* (Philadelphia: University of Pennsylvania Press, 2004), 84.

51. Freidel, *Over There*, 98.

52. William S. Graves, *America's Siberian Adventure, 1918–1920* (New York: Peter Smith, 1931), 4.

53. George F. Kennan, *Soviet-American Relations, 1917–1920*, vol. 1 (Princeton, New Jersey: Princeton University Press, 1956), 56.

54. Jennifer D. Keene, *The United States and the First World War* (New York: Longman, 2000), 68.

55. Keene, *Doughboys, the Great War and the Remaking of America*, 147.

6   THE WOUNDS OF WAR

Death, wounds, and disease were all serious risks for the soldier at war. The First World War ushered in a new term, *shellshock,* to describe the mental breakdown some soldiers suffered after prolonged exposure to artillery shelling and the horrors of combat. The American Army suffered 53,402 battlefield deaths during the war with another 204,002 men physically wounded in combat. The outbreak of the deadly Spanish Influenza epidemic pushed the numbers of wartime deaths even higher. Over 63,000 men died of illness, including many who succumbed to influenza-induced pneumonia. Soldiers both at the front and behind the lines, therefore, had constant interaction with the sick, wounded, and dead even if they personally managed to stay healthy for the duration of the war.

DISEASE

In this era before the advent of antibiotics, disease could quickly lead to disaster. Traditionally, disease killed as many soldiers as enemy bullets in time of war. Initially, medical officers had reason to hope that the First World War would break this pattern. At the conclusion of the Spanish-American War, an epidemic of yellow fever and malaria swept the ranks of men stationed in Cuba, dampening public euphoria over the nation's quick victory against Spain. William C. Gorgas emerged as a national hero for discovering that mosquitoes carried the deadly yellow fever virus. Gorgas led two well-publicized mosquito eradication campaigns in Cuba and the Panama Canal that virtually eliminated yellow fever, dramatically reducing the human cost of occupying these areas. Building on these experiences, medical officials throughout the war rigorously policed training camps to eliminate stagnant pools of water and put screens in barrack windows to reduce the risk of mosquito-born illnesses.

Other medical breakthroughs in the prewar era gave medical officers further hope that epidemic diseases within the wartime army might become a relic of the past. Across America, urban reformers had successfully demonstrated that municipal sewer systems and sand filtration of water practically eliminated the threat of cholera, dysentery, and typhoid. Consequently, soldiers entered camps where water purification and efficient waste disposal systems reduced their chances of contracting diseases that had ravaged soldier populations in the past. Owing to scientists' newfound ability to identify types of bacteria, medical officers could determine if typhoid germs had infected a training camps' water supply before the disease killed any soldiers. In the prewar era, scientists also discovered that body lice transmitted typhus. It was now possible to control typhus within military camps and overseas by mandating regular antilousing treatments that included sterilizing soldiers' clothing and bathing in a solution to kill the vermin on their bodies. Vaccinations became a routine part of the soldier's entry into the military as well, with troops receiving vaccines for tetanus, typhoid, and smallpox. Men also underwent regular medical examinations to detect venereal disease and had access to a chemical prophylaxis treatment that dramatically reduced the chances of contracting a sexually transmitted disease if the serum was injected into the penis within 3 hours of intercourse.

Medical officers, therefore, had sound reasons for expecting to open a new chapter in military medical history by keeping illness and disease to a minimum in the wartime army. Even before the outbreak of the influenza epidemic, however, these rosy predictions proved too optimistic. Overcrowding, poor personal hygienic habits, and the constant shuffling of the soldier population all created the perfect conditions for infectious diseases to flourish. Recruits, complained one medical officer, "were shifted from camp to camp by the thousands, taking with them such diseases as they were incubating, thus infecting all camps."[1] Whipping an army into shape quickly meant long days of training and marching in all kinds of inclement weather. Exposed to the elements day after day, exhausted soldiers slept fitfully in poorly ventilated and overcrowded barracks. These men were "easier victims for infections, and the infections came," noted this same doctor.

Controlling outbreaks of airborne diseases such as measles, influenza and pneumonia proved the biggest challenge for the Army Medical Corps. As one medical officer aptly predicted, "respiratory, not intestinal, disease will be the scandal of the World War."[2] These concerns prompted medical officials to propose some changes in the training regime and living environment. Gorgas, now the Surgeon General of the Army, recommended building more barracks to reduce overcrowding and creating detention camps to quarantine men exposed to infectious diseases. He also urged the army to modify the training schedule to reduce exhaustion among newly inducted troops. Building up their physical stamina, he reasoned, would make them less susceptible to infectious diseases. These recommendations received scant consideration in a War Department determined to send large numbers of trained troops overseas as quickly as possible. Lengthening the training regime threatened to delay the stream of American troops headed for France, an unacceptable military and political alternative in 1917. Barrack construction lagged throughout the war as the military, in competition with civilian businesses for scarce resources, faced problems securing the materials and labor needed to build an adequate number of structures. Large numbers of troops training in southern training camps never set foot in a barracks stateside, living instead in tent cities meant to serve as temporary quarters while barracks were being built.

The cost of ignoring this medical advice became immediately apparent in 1917 when epidemics of measles, mumps, scarlet fever, meningitis, and pneumonia swept the training camps. Measles exacted the worst toll on the growing army, requiring over 48,000 hospital admissions and accounting for 30 percent of the deaths in the army that year. The isolated and insular lives of many rural recruits before the war dramatically increased their risk to infection. Coming from thinly settled southern, rural areas, a good proportion of troops were exposed to measles for the first time when they entered the army. Measles alone was not deadly, unless complications of pneumonia set in during the normal 14-day course of the illness. Medical workers did their best to prevent the spread of the disease by placing patients behind screens in hospitals, rigorously disinfecting their bedding and clothes on a regular basis. Only medical workers who had acquired immunity through a previous bout with the measles cared for stricken soldiers. Doctors also tried to make patients as comfortable as possible while their bodies fought the infection by keeping them on a liquid diet and protecting their eyes from direct light. To guard against pneumonia, patients remained in the hospital for 10 days after their fevers broke to ensure a complete recovery.

Stateside epidemics often played havoc with the military's proposed training regime, calling into question how much time the army actually gained by refusing to reduce the daily workload placed on soldiers. In camps struck by an epidemic, training and transport schedules became meaningless once large numbers of troops were placed either in the hospital or under quarantines. Troops whose training was compromised occasionally had time to make up these deficiencies before heading off to France, but not always. In the fall of 1918, the American army launched its major offensive along the Western Front with many undertrained men. The ever-present problem of epidemics in the training camps helped create this backlog of men with insufficient training.

With the war effort barely underway, families of ill men became increasingly alarmed over the prevalence of sickness in the nation's training camps. Pressing for better medical care, these families' concerns received a sympathetic airing in Congress. In December 1917, Congress began a broad inquiry into the War Department's bungling and ineptness. Initially focused on remedying supply shortages in the camps, the investigating committee broadened its mandate to consider health issues after Representative Augustus Gardner of Massachusetts, who had left Congress to join the army, died from pneumonia in Camp Wheeler, Georgia on 14 January 1918. Under scrutiny, camp commanders assured Congress that they would work harder to reduce overcrowding and fatigue and increase the numbers of medical personnel caring for ill troops.

The Influenza Pandemic of 1918–1919

Unfortunately, building more barracks and recruiting more doctors did little to halt the progress of the worldwide influenza pandemic that traversed the globe in 1918–1919. The most costly and deadly disease of the war, influenza sickened at least one quarter of the world's population including 25 million people in the United States. Even President Woodrow Wilson became ill with the flu while attending the Paris Peace Conference in 1919. Approximately 3 percent of flu victims perished, taking the lives of 675,000 Americans. Nearly 26 percent of the American army, or roughly 1 million men, became ill with influenza. Most recovered, but one-quarter developed secondary complications such as pneumonia. Once an ill soldier contracted flu-related pneumonia, he had only a 50 percent chance of recovering.

The speed and intensity of the epidemic shocked medical officers, who watched helplessly as the disease felled otherwise healthy and hardy young men within a matter of days. The virus struck without warning. Within hours, fevers shot up to 106 degrees and made victims delirious. If pneumonia developed, patients literally suffocated as liquid filled their lungs and turned healthy pink tissue into blue sodden masses almost

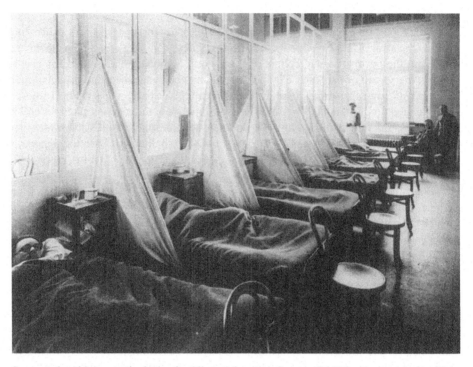

Screens placed between the beds of soldiers sick with influenza did little to stop the virus from spreading. (*Courtesy of the National Museum of Health and Medicine, Armed Forces Institute of Pathology, Washington, D.C.*)

overnight. As they struggled for air, influenza patients often developed a bluish tinge to their skin and began coughing blood. By the time ill men arrived at the hospital, one army physician noted, "it is only a matter of a few hours until death comes, and it is simply a struggle for air until they suffocate."[3] Without access to antibiotics, there was little doctors could do. Instead, a patient's best hope for recovery lay with good nursing. The epidemic gave female nurses a chance to demonstrate that their care made a real difference, fortifying their claim for greater professional responsibility and authority within army hospitals. Seeing patients recover under their care also gave these nurses enormous professional satisfaction.

The intensity with which influenza struck young adults surprised medical professionals because influenza usually killed the very young or very old. Besides attacking these traditionally vulnerable populations, this strain of influenza ravaged what was normally the healthiest and most resilient segment of the population. The ghoulish scenes in many training camp hospitals resembled situations more normally associated with the aftermath of combat. "One can stand to see one, two or twenty men die, but to see these poor devils dropping like flies sort of gets on your nerves," wrote one physician in a letter to a colleague.[4]

Nearby relatives usually had time to travel to the bedsides of stricken soldiers to see them one last time before they died. Some families arrived at the camp after receiving word that their loved one was ill, only to learn that the soldier had already died. Others, one Red Cross volunteer recalled, crowded "beside the cot of a dead or dying boy, still and stunned by the suddenness of it, or grief stricken and inconsolable."[5] One mother, he recalled, held the hand of her son while he died. Another father arrived at a training camp to claim his son's body only to discover that he was still alive, lying among a row of corpses placed on a screened porch.

The influenza epidemic reached its peak in stateside training camps during the week of 4 October 1918, with 6,160 recorded deaths and a week later spiked in the AEF with 1,451 reported fatalities. Within the AEF, a total of 340,000 soldiers were hospitalized with influenza. Overseas, the height of the influenza epidemic coincided with the Meuse-Argonne campaign. At the very moment that American soldiers undertook their most sustained and heaviest fighting of the war, thousands lay in base hospitals too ill to fight. Between 1 September 1918 and 11 November 1918, approximately 9,000 soldiers in the AEF and 23,000 soldiers stateside died of the flu. During this same period, approximately 35,000 soldiers died of combat wounds. In the fall of 1918, encountering death became a daily experience for troops whether at home or overseas, at the front or behind the lines.

Not all ill soldiers made their way to hospitals for treatment, suggesting that the rate of infection in the army was even higher. Soldiers had reason to avoid army hospitals if they had the flu. In September 1918, the army only had enough beds for 11 percent of AEF troops, leading to severe overcrowding as the flood of battle casualties and flu victims arrived. "Everything is overflowing with patients," noted one surgeon in his diary. "Our Divisions are being shot up; the wards are full of machine gun wounds. There is rain, mud, 'flu' and pneumonia."[6] It took a few weeks for medical personnel to realize that severely ill flu victims could not withstand the exhausting and uncomfortable trip to the rear. Finally, the AEF chief surgeon told the medical staff that "moving a case of pneumonia to make room for a battle casualty may kill the pneumonia patient and not aid the wounded, and the practice should not be tolerated."[7]

The appearance of a devastating influenza epidemic during the most deadly war to date was not coincidence. The wartime transport of troops and goods, along with the horrendous living conditions in the front lines created circumstances perfect for the transmission and incubation of the deadly virus. A strain of avian flu virus that mutated to attack human beings first appeared in Kansas and Georgia in March 1918, striking civilian students and soldiers in area training camps. American troops then carried influenza germs on troop ships to Europe where they thrived in the wretched conditions of the trenches before the virus seemingly disappeared over the summer. When the flu reappeared in the fall, the virus had become much more virulent and aggressive. Circumventing the world, including every region of the United States, the flu finally burned itself out by mid-1919, having infected all susceptible human beings.

Medical officers struggled to explain the epidemic during a time when the existence of viruses was unknown (scientists did not identify disease-causing viruses until the 1940s), theorizing that bacteria or an unseen organism caused influenza. Doctors developed a droplet theory to explain how the disease spread, reasoning that sneezes, coughs, spitting, or direct contact with the germ through handshakes or touching contaminated objects passed the flu from person to person. Physicians consequently devised some useless precautionary measures to prevent transmission of the airborne virus such as wearing masks, placing screens between patients, and boiling their dishes and utensils. Thousands of soldiers also received experimental and apparently ineffectual flu vaccines. Medical officers instructed troops to cover their mouths when sneezing or coughing and to breathe through their mouths to prevent droplets from contaminating the surrounding environment.

In an ironic twist, the exclusion of black troops from some indoor recreational events may have actually protected them from contracting the air-borne virus. Medical officers at one overseas camp noted that black soldiers who watched a YMCA performance from outside a tent while their white comrades crowded together inside stayed healthy when influenza swept through the camp in the next few days. In this case, their enforced segregation from ill white troops in their recreational, working, and living environments served as a de-facto quarantine that had at least one unintended benefit for these troops. Medical investigators never formally studied the correlation between segregation and flu transmission suggested by such anecdotes. Any indirect health benefits bestowed by racist army policies ended the moment a black soldier fell ill and went to an army hospital. At the height of the epidemic in October 1918, 11.1 percent of black patients died, as compared to 9.5 of white patients. Medical officers claimed that as a weaker race, blacks were more susceptible to pneumonia. In reality, reluctant to seek care from unsympathetic white doctors or sent back to their units by medical officers who dismissed their complaints as insignificant, many black soldiers entered the hospital sicker than white soldiers. Living in tents instead of barracks, insufficient clothing and food, and hard outdoor manual labor in inclement weather, were all conditions that also served to intensify the course of the disease for black troops.

The third wave of influenza hit the debarkation camps in France hard during the demobilization period. This final gasp of the epidemic created much bitterness among troops who watched their comrades fall ill and die while awaiting transport home. "Perhaps nothing touched the hearts of the American people more than did the deaths of those who had survived strenuous training, an ocean voyage fraught with peril, enemy shells, and disease, only to succumb to illness after all warfare was over," noted one officer.[8]

THE WOUNDED

When it came to treating the wounded, individual soldiers and AEF commanders approached the issue from dramatically different perspectives. From the standpoint of the wounded man, immediate evacuation and care were essential to head off a possible death from shock, blood loss, or infection. Army commanders, eager to maximize the number of troops in the field, understood that four healthy and able-bodied soldiers carried every wounded man off the field. One wound, therefore, reduced a unit's effective strength by five men.

Every soldier carried a first aid pack to dress his own wounds or those of comrades, and medics also followed units into battle. Most commonly, soldiers had to wait several hours and sometimes as long as a day before undertaking the painful and taxing stretcher journey to a rear area dressing station before traveling in an ambulance over rutted roads to the evacuation hospital. Once they arrived at this "chamber of horrors" as one sergeant called it, patients witnessed "the constant flow in and out of the operating room of desperately wounded men, the screaming when dressings were changed on the stump of an arm or leg recently amputated, a head gashed up, part of a face blown away, or a stomach punctured by a dozen pieces of shrapnel; the insane gibbering, mouthing, and scorching profanity of men partially under ether."[9] Ideally, the field hospital was close to a rail line, allowing for a more comfortable ride to the base hospital further in the rear.

Some important medical developments improved the treatment of combat wounds. X-ray technology helped surgeons locate and extract bullets and shrapnel. The ability to give patients blood transfusions and administer tetanus antitoxins greatly increased a soldier's chances of surviving an operation. Similarly, doctors employed the

Every seriously wounded man required four able-bodied men to carry him to the rear. Army commanders worried that this mode of transport depleted their ranks at the front, while wounded men focused on the painful agony of a jostled journey. (*Courtesy of the National Archives*)

Carrel–Dakin treatment to cleanse wounds that involved cutting away dead tissue, irrigating wounds, and testing the tissue daily for bacteria before finally closing the wound. This type of wound care dramatically reduced the incidence of gas gangrene, an infection caused by bits of shrapnel carrying dirt or cloth into the flesh that led to amputations of infected limbs. Even with these advancements, however, nearly 1,700 men lost arms, legs, or hands to amputation. Soldiers circulated the lurid tale of a "basket case," a man who had lost both arms and legs, and this legend became the basis for the central character in a postwar antiwar novel, *Johnny Got His Gun*. The Surgeon General disputed the factual basis for this story, proclaiming that "I have personally examined the records and am able to say there is not a single 'basket case' either in the army at home or the AEF."[10]

Losing just one limb was traumatic enough. When word came that Private Joseph Maleski's unit would soon enter the line, he was excited. "I knew I felt good. This is what I had enlisted for. This is what I came for. I was going to get a crack at the Germans," he recalled. As his unit charged successfully across an open field and into the woods around Chateau-Thierry, he and his comrades began laughing about their good fortune. "One would say 'That fellow can't spell our names' and another would answer 'Yes, his shells can't hit us unless they have our names on the cover.'" This banter reflected the common soldier superstition that dying or surviving had more to do with fate than luck. Unfortunately, the shell with Maleski's name on it soon found him and shattered his leg. Are you in much pain, asked a surgeon at the field hospital. No, Maleski replied, but then admitted that he couldn't feel his toes. "When I woke up the surgeon asked me how I felt. 'All right.' 'Any pain?' 'No sir.' 'Can you feel your toes now?' 'Yes sir.' He laughed and went on to the other men. The third day I was there he asked the same questions and I gave the same answers. Then he didn't laugh any more. His face became very serious and he said: 'I guess my boy I'll have to tell you now. You haven't got any toes. We had to cut your leg off about the knee to save your life."[11]

Medics could do less for soldiers suffering from gas exposure. Men who arrived in the hospital with blistered bodies from mustard gas were stripped and quickly washed. After victims left the showers, medics sprayed their eyes, nose and throat with bicarbonate of soda. If the soldier had ingested contaminated food or water, then olive or castor oil was given to coat the stomach. To counter the effects of inhaled gas, soldiers were treated with alkaline, oxygen, or bled. Lightly afflicted gas casualties responded well to these treatments, but for men suffering from prolonged or intense contact with gas, modern medicine had few answers.

Shellshock

By the time the United States entered the conflict, the appearance of a new battlefield psychosis was a well-established fact. Afflicted soldiers stumbled out of battle with glazed eyes that conveyed their terror and anguish, some twitching uncontrollably. A few men went temporarily blind, and others could not speak. Soldiers called this mental collapse "shellshock," reflecting the initial belief that sound waves or outright wounding by artillery caused the onset of these neurological problems. By 1917, military psychiatrists had discarded an actual physiological explanation for shellshock, viewing it mostly as a psychological reaction to the horrors of war. The term shellshock stuck, however, and soldiers used it to succinctly describe a host of symptoms associated with combat-related mental breakdowns. Today, the term posttraumatic stress disorder (PTSD) is used to describe similar problems for soldiers.

Throughout the war, army psychiatrists debated whether the wartime environment or a soldier's predisposition to mental illness caused shellshock. Many American army psychiatrists were specialists in abnormal psychology, and therefore predisposed to believe that mental collapse revealed innate flaws in the emotional fiber of individual soldiers. These psychiatrists believed that weeding out men with weak psychological profiles, including a family history of mental illness, would effectively reduce the incidence of mental breakdowns on the battlefield. Many military psychiatrists consequently spent the war screening recruits for mental defects, tolling in training camps rather than at the front. The army did release 11,000 men from the training camps as mentally unfit to serve, which may or may not have reduced the number of psychiatric casualties at the front.

There was some evidence that the stress of war caused the return of a previous mental aliment in a grotesquely exaggerated way. Afflicted men who had stammered as children found themselves rendered mute or burdened with uncontrollable tics. Men with any type of phobia experienced heightened fears once exposed to the trauma of combat. Psychiatrists paid particular attention to men who reported suffering from an obsessive fear of the dark as children. Once shellshocked, these men not only refused to venture out at nightfall but also became afraid to leave their wards alone.

In compiling these anecdotal case studies, psychiatrists made no effort to locate men who, although afraid of the dark as children, never experienced a mental collapse at the front. Even assuming that this past history put soldiers at greater risk for mental collapse, the army could hardly afford to discharge all men who had been afraid of the dark as children. An exhaustive stateside study of one regiment, for example, revealed some degree of mental instability in the family histories of nearly 50 percent of the men. Discharging over half of the men inducted into service would bring the war effort to a halt.

Subsequent studies of men who actually suffered from shellshock suggested that screening out men with a family history of mental disease might reduce, but not eliminate, the problem of mental collapse at the front. When psychiatrists in Base Hospital 117 investigated their patients' backgrounds, they discovered that one third had no evidence of mental instability in either their personal or family histories. Determining how a man would react to prolonged service at the front proved difficult to predict. "I have seen some men who are recommended for the Croix de Guerre on other fronts go to pieces later and be sent to the rear," noted one sergeant in the 42nd Division.[12] The stress of having to appear brave and resolute when all one really wanted to do was run and hide eventually took its toll on these soldiers, perhaps explaining why men could perform well during one mission only to crack on the next. Some men who succumbed to shellshock in the summer and fall later recalled that they felt themselves "slipping" much earlier as exhaustion and depression set in. Often it took just one traumatic event to finally bring these tensions to the surface and cause a breakdown. One Marine Corps private fought well under shellfire and witnessed the wounding and killing of comrades for several months without any noticeable change in his battlefield demeanor. Then, over the course of a few days, he had a few encounters that brought home the reality of death and dying at the front. Advancing over several miles to relieve a French unit, he saw the decapitated bodies of dead Frenchmen whose headless bodies and open eyes began to haunt him. The breaking point came when his commanding officer sent him on a burial detail despite his extreme aversion to handling corpses. The marine became preoccupied with death, tormented by nightmares that featured images of the dead Frenchmen. Under shelling, he subsequently lost his composure and his violent shaking left him too weak to stay with his unit. Evacuated to a rear area hospital, the nightmares continued and each time some one dropped a spoon or slammed a door the man sought refuge under a chair or bed.[13]

Troops overwhelmingly viewed shellshock as legitimate war injury. Because shellshock could seemingly strike anyone, soldiers tended to view its victims sympathetically. Rather than dismissing shellshocked men as cowards intent on deserting their comrades in the heat of battle, soldiers appreciated that every man had his breaking point. Indeed, men afflicted with shellshock did not always head to the rear. Supreme indifference to dying was one clear sign that a man was headed for a breakdown, and this fatalism or depression induced irrational behavior such as running around like a crazed lunatic during shelling or uncontrolled cursing, crying, or screaming. In the throes of a mental collapse, shellshocked soldiers lost the self-discipline required to maintain one's composure while under fire. Shaking uncontrollably, experiencing convulsions, frothing at the mouth, these men were quickly removed from the front lines lest they spread fear and panic among the troops.

Some men initially diagnosed as shellshocked simply needed bed rest and hearty meals to recover, while others required long-term care in army hospitals. Before September 1918, the army offered no systematic care for soldiers suffering mental collapse. Shellshock accounted for nearly 20 percent of the hospital admissions during the fighting at Chateau-Thierry in June 1918. Medics sent afflicted troops to general hospitals where doctors quickly pushed aside psychiatric cases to deal with visibly wounded men. Unsurprisingly, this indifferent treatment resulted in few of these soldiers ever returning to duty.

Treatment for shellshock improved dramatically when the Americans took over their own sector of the front. As the AEF headed into battle in the fall of 1918, the medical corps dispersed its 263 military psychiatrists among field and neurological hospitals near combat zones and base hospitals in the rear, including one special thousand-bed base hospital for men suffering from war neurosis. After the war, army psychiatrists claimed that this triage approach provided satisfactory care for nearly 65 percent of shellshock men who received treatment in field hospitals about a mile or two behind the front and sometimes returned to their units in a matter of hours. More serious cases traveled to the neurological hospitals located 10 miles in the rear, where 59 percent of shellshock cases required only a week or two of treatment. Front-line triage successfully prevented shellshock from draining the front lines of men during the last few months of the war.

A variety of psychological conditions fit under the umbrella term of shellshock, a term that army officials tried to purge from the official vocabulary. Because soldiers saw shellshock as a legitimate war injury, medical personnel never used the term out of fear, that once diagnosed with shellshock, ill soldiers would embrace their condition as a morally acceptable way to leave the fighting and resist treatment. Medical corpsmen routinely pinned or hung a medical tag on each injured man that described his ailment and authorized his removal to a rear area medical facility. Medics never labeled a man a shellshocked, but instead used the acronym "N.Y.D. (Nervous)." Behind the lines, psychiatrists continued to substitute other terms for shellshock, embracing more specific diagnoses that offered a possible way to treat the patient. They described patients as suffering from intense fatigue when soldiers lost their ability to think clearly or experienced intense and blinding headaches. Psychiatrists considered soldiers psychathenic if they felt paralyzed by fear, certain that any action would bring about an undesirable result. Some men suffered from hysteria, shaking and sweating profusely at the slightest loud noise. Still others developed anxiety neurosis when they could no longer reconcile their desire to live with their duty to expose themselves to constant danger in combat.

Behind the lines, doctors strove to give victims the rest and comfort they needed to recover without coddling men to the point that they lost all incentive to rejoin their units at the front. Psychiatrists first provided each soldier with a bath, ample food, and 24 to 48 hours of uninterrupted sleep, then began urging soldiers to talk about their fears and anxieties. Once patients had regained their strength, they began a daily routine of exercise and recreation while psychiatrists offered rationale, scientific explanations for their distress. Psychiatrists and orderlies steadily reminded men of their responsibilities to the cause, the nation, and their comrades left behind to continue the fight. Medical personnel rehashed the glory of individual regiments, propaganda posters decorated the walls of recreation rooms, and chaplains emphasized the importance of courage and patriotism in their sermons to shellshocked patients. When columns of enemy prisoners marched by one hospital during the Meuse-Argonne campaign, doctors brought shellshocked patients outside to watch the procession, hoping to reignite their interest in joining the victorious crusade.

Base Hospital 117, the specially designated hospital for prolonged psychiatric cases, was located in the village of La Fauche by the foothills of the Vosges Mountains. Easily accessible by rail and roads to the American sector of the Western Front, the village was also far enough from the front lines to provide the isolation and serenity needed for treatment. The men admitted to Base Hospital 117 had spent an average of 57 days at the front, although 7.59 percent suffered their mental breakdowns behind the lines before they ever engaged in combat. The daily regime prescribed for patients reflected the dictum "healthy bodies, healthy minds." The treatment program included "the therapeutic application of work," which kept the men engaged in manual labor and arts and crafts projects to keep their minds busy and hands occupied. Shellshocked soldiers learned to weave, built roads, and worked on the hospital farm. Dr. Thomas W. Salmon, who sketched out this treatment plan, believed that "continual 'resting,' long periods spent alone, general softening of the environment, and occupations undertaken simply because the mood of the patient suggests them, are positively harmful."[14]

This regime of counseling, rest, good food, and exercise close to the front proved quite effective. Typically, patients with mental delusions brought upon by a head wound or concussion recovered the fastest, while those suffering solely from anxiety healed more slowly. The military decided against court-martialing men who resisted returning to their units. Instead, doctors denied these patients privileges and gave them unpleasant tasks in the hospital like digging latrines. Doctors and staff became more distant and unfriendly as well. By making the hospital environment less hospitable, doctors succeeded in convincing many to return to the front. The army reassigned those who refused to return to the front to noncombatant duty in the Services of Supply.

Despite the generally effective treatment regime that military psychiatrists devised to rehabilitate shellshock victims, battlefield conditions in the fall of 1918 often prevented medics from putting them into practice. The steady advances of American forces made it difficult to maintain adequate advance psychiatric treatment facilities. Often, doctors were forced to send shellshock victims far to the rear. As predicted, these men rarely rejoined their units at the front. Overall, the army evacuated 106,000 psychiatric casualties from the front, returning 36,606 to the frontlines. This experience convinced army psychiatrists that conditions on the battlefield often precluded effectively treating shellshock. They remained convinced, therefore, that devising more effective screening methods to weed out mentally unbalanced soldiers offered the best way to reduce shellshock in future combat forces.

DISABLED VETERANS

In a letter home in the fall of 1918 to his local newspaper, Sergeant Judson Hanna tried to prepare his Pennsylvanian community for the changes that they would certainly notice in those who had fought on the Western Front. "Some men who went though the big barrage still show the effects of it. Let a door slam, and a big healthy man will jump as if stung," he wrote. But general nervousness was the least of the combat veteran's problems, this soldier wrote. Often their experiences under fire had reshaped their entire personalities. To support this contention, Hanna described the changes he noted in a friend after he was covered with dirt from exploding bombs during an artillery barrage. As he hugged the ground, this friend felt a shell fall right beside him. "The soldier waited in this makeshift grave for the bomb to explode, knowing the uselessness of trying to escape, and trying to prepare his mind for the bumping off of his body. Those seconds of agonized waiting for an expected tragedy may change a whole man's character. This bomb was also a dud, but the man today goes around with a strained face and seems always listening for something," Hanna observed.[15]

A shattered church behind the lines served as a temporary hospital for troops wounded near Neuvilly, France. (*Courtesy of the National Archives*)

Veterans Disabled by Shellshock

Military psychiatrists defined their mission as restoring men to duty. How effectively these doctors cured their patients was another matter. Several studies in the 1920s suggested that shellshocked soldiers continued to experience mental health problems long after they left the service. Psychiatrists readily admitted that elements in the civilian environment could easily trigger the reemergence of symptoms in a shell-shocked veteran. Fourth of July fireworks terrified many shellshock victims, while others found it difficult to even endure thunderstorms. "I used to work a pneumatic drill, but I cannot any longer; the constant action is so much like a machine gun," noted one veteran in a postwar interview.[16] For the next 20 years, veterans' hospitals annually treated between 8,000–10,000 patients suffering from neuropsychiatric disease. Countless other distressed veterans either suffered in private or sought care from their own physicians. For years, men who appeared normal to the casual observer continued to suffer from nightmares, an inability to concentrate, and a heart-stopping moment of terror when surprised by a train whistle. Workplace accidents plagued many shell-shocked veterans who worked full- or part-time. "I make mistakes I ordinarily would not make," noted one veteran, unable to steady his mind for long periods.[17] The strains of supporting a family in the immediate postwar recession and during the Great

Depression could also trigger a relapse. Dr. Norman Fenton, a psychiatrist who treated soldiers in France noted that:

> After the war many men went back to, or met anew, conditions of living much harder than those in the army. . . . They returned and went to work at something often more exacting than the army, say in a mine or a machine shop. They worked long hours, were fagged, and unhappy at the end of the day. They had little time for recreation, no Y.M.C.A. or Red Cross with free movies or other entertainment—just the hard struggle of modern industrial life to which they were no longer adjusted, and to which a period as war neurotics had seriously lessened their chances of readaptation. The raw materials for the recall of their neuroses were at hand.[18]

When considering shellshocked soldiers as a group, the general public viewed them sympathetically, convinced, as one wartime psychiatrist noted, "that exploding shells and the horror of battle were capable of causing insanity and might often lead to nervousness, weakness, and eccentricity."[19] At the same time, however, each individual veteran could recall an encounter with a fellow citizen who regarded the injured man with a degree of suspicion, never exactly sure when he might explode. Indeed, the association of shellshock with insanity caused great difficulties for men seeking employment with honorable discharge papers that specifically noted their wartime affliction. "One employer upon seeing the magic words said, 'I'd like to reemploy you, but I'm afraid you'd get to breaking things and hugging the girls, etc.'," recounted one veteran.[20]

Their diagnosis of shellshock offered these men a reasonable explanation for why they encountered so many difficulties in resuming normal postwar lives. Rather than blaming their mental breakdowns on cowardice or a fragile psychological make-up, afflicted veterans faulted military leaders for their bad judgment in subjecting troops to days upon days of incessant artillery shelling. In the postwar era, pacifist and isolationist groups used the image of the shellshocked soldier to indict military and political leaders for their wartime missteps. In reexamining the reasons for going to war and the methods employed along the Western Front, pushing otherwise brave and capable men beyond the limits of human endurance became the symbol of all that had gone wrong during the war.

Veterans' Difficulties

Reflecting the intensity of their battlefield experience, over 300,000 soldiers returned home with debilitating physical and mental disorders. The physically disabled faced severe challenges living with their combat-inflicted handicaps. Advances in front-line medical treatment meant that many men with disfiguring or painful wounds survived the war, when in previous conflicts they had perished. Having put the overwhelming majority of its resources into mobilizing the army, the government gave scant attention to the problems of rehabilitation or long-term medical care for wounded veterans. The number of injured men returning home was twice the size of the regular army, and government officials scrambled to provide enough hospital beds and retraining programs for them. With no one agency in charge of handling disabled veterans' claims, these men, many of them poorly educated, encountered a bureaucratic labyrinth that created further confusion and delay in receiving appropriate care. Many only tried once to apply for government benefits, and, if refused, as many were, they never applied again.

Several social welfare organizations provided assistance to disabled veterans trying to negotiate their way through the tangle of government bureaucracy, including the American Red Cross, the American Legion, the YMCA, and Knights of Columbus. A wounded veteran first applied to the War Risk Insurance Bureau for disability compensation. The Bureau then sent the ex-serviceman to a physician who established the extent of his disability and decided whether further hospitalization might render him one-hundred percent fit for work. After a series of additional examinations by specialists, the disabled man received a disability rating that determined the monthly subsidy he received to compensate for his decreased earning capacity. A veteran with 100 percent disability rating, for instance, received a larger monthly stipend than one rated 50 percent disabled.

The claims process privileged men with physical wounds over those suffering from shellshock. Without visible evidence of their affliction, medical examiners often viewed these men as malingers simply trying to avoid work for the rest of their lives. Shellshocked men also experienced trouble obtaining a disability rating if they had left the army before completing the prescribed year of treatment. Anxious to return to civilian life, some men voluntarily waived all claims to a disability rating so they could obtain an honorable discharge as soon as possible. When these veterans subsequently relapsed, the government disavowed any further responsibility for their mental health problems.

Some disabled veterans devoted precious hours to challenging these ratings. Both white and black disabled veterans often felt that government officials failed to appreciate the true extent of their war-related injuries. African American veterans faced an additional obstacle, however, because in the decentralized federal system unsympathetic southern bureaucrats and doctors determined the amount of monthly disability allowances and if a veteran was eligible to receive care in a veterans' hospital. "Since the war, some of the Southern crackers are using different means to keep we colored soldiers out of the hospitals and from getting vocational training. Their reason for keeping us out of training is to rate us in compensation as low as possible," Joel Moore charged in a letter to the National Association for the Advancement of Colored People (NAACP) in 1924.[21] When the NAACP complained to governmental authorities, officials countered that many black veterans received timely and beneficial treatment in government hospitals. Yet, even if a veteran obtained appropriate care, he usually received it in a segregated ward that he often reached by traveling in a Jim Crow train car.

Rehabilitation Programs

In theory, the government offered disabled veterans the chance to learn a new skill or trade better suited to their new physical or mental condition. Throughout 1919 and 1920, men ready to begin their rehabilitation programs languished on meager disability allowances as corruption and mismanagement plagued the Federal Bureau of Vocational Education. Although the Bureau hired at a tremendous rate, with one clerk for every ten disabled veterans, only 217 men completed retraining programs in 1919. In response, the Disabled American Veterans of the World War (DAVWW) formed to help increasingly frustrated white and black veterans gain the care they needed and deserved. The DAVWW emerged from the efforts of local disabled veterans groups in Ohio to help returned servicemen negotiate the labyrinth of federal bureaucracy. Taking the lead to form a national organization, these groups held a national caucus that formed the DAVWW. In an early success, the DAVWW convinced Congress to consolidate the Federal Board of Vocational Training, the Public Health Service, and the War Risk Insurance agencies into the Veterans Bureau in 1921. Throughout the 1920s, the DAVWW worked with the Veterans Bureau to streamline the claims process and lobbied effectively for more generous rehabilitation programs and disability ratings. As a reflection of their effectiveness, a host of programs for disabled soldiers at colleges, trade schools, and business schools, and special veterans' vocational schools finally became available in the mid-1920s and by the early 1930s the government devoted one-quarter of the federal budget to veterans' services.

Officials running rehabilitation programs advised men against setting their sights too high. After consultation with a physician and vocational advisor, for example, a former machinist who wanted to learn to play the piano was directed into a piano-tuner's course instead. Corruption continued to reduce the resources available for veteran rehabilitation, with nearly 2 million dollars disappearing from the Veterans Bureau budget between 1921 and 1923.

Rehabilitation offered disabled men the promise of living an independent life as a contributing member of society. In published testimonials, doughboys provided sooth-ing assurances that their lives could indeed proceed normally after the war. "I will never become a charge upon public society," declared Private Ray Wunderlich, a machinist in civilian life who lost a leg at Belleau Wood. "When the government fits me with a new limb I'll be as good as new all over, and as soon as I can learn to use it handily, I'll go back to the machine shop once more."[22] An army propaganda film even showed a group of amputees playing baseball. One-legged soldiers hopped around the bases while their wheelchair-bound comrades cheered them on.

In veterans' hospitals, men learned to use prosthetic limbs, underwent reconstruc-tive surgery, and received care for reoccurring respiratory ailments. The five hundred men blinded and three hundred partly blinded underwent training in completing daily tasks at the Red Cross Institute for the Blind near Baltimore. During their hospital stint, the men learned to accept the well-intentioned, but sometimes grating, charity of Baltimoreans who visited once a week bearing gifts of cigarettes and candy and invita-tions for outings. As one man wrote with a trace of bitterness, "today is Sunday and this is the day the people come out and feed the blind apes peanuts."[23]

Most blinded men reentered civilian life successfully. Attempting retraining for a new trade or profession often proved more difficult for veterans suffering from shellshock. As one man explained, "it's no use. I can't study–there are always planes flying in my head."[24] After the war, Dr. Norman Fenton traced the subsequent lives of shellshocked veterans who had been treated in Base Hospital 117, the designated treatment facility for wartime neuroses. When Dr. Fenton contacted these men in 1919, only 60.9 percent of them thought they were living normal lives, by 1924–1925 over 80 percent felt they were func-tioning well in civilian life even if all or some symptoms and nervous habits lingered. Of the 830 men who responded to Fenton's questionnaire in 1924–1925, 19.5 percent had learned a new trade through a government rehabilitation program, 32 percent had spent time in a government hospital (some more than once), while 37.3 percent reported receiv-ing disability compensation from the government.[25] A tranquil, rural setting seemed to offer the best opportunity for men suffering from mild, but annoying, symptoms to lead relatively normal postwar lives. Fenton speculated that improved social services for dis-abled veterans, a more prosperous economic climate, and the simple passage of time had combined to improve daily life for these veterans.[26]

Nearly 128,000 disabled veterans completed government rehabilitation programs from 1919–1928, meaning that over one half of the wounded returned home without receiving any further assistance in resuming civilian lives. The welcome home was not always cordial. Many Americans wanted to put the war behind them as quickly as possible. Rather than fully confronting the emotional and financial cost of war, some towns elected to keep the wounded out of sight. In the immediate postwar years, for example, some cities passed ordinances that required veterans with severe facial wounds to wear masks or hoods in public so their disfigured faces would not scare women or children. In Chicago, the "Being Ugly on the Public Way" law threatened veterans with criminal prosecution if they failed to comply.[27] Surgeons and craftsmen created specially designed masks that hooked around a patient's ear to add an anatomically correct chin, nose, or cheek to a face destroyed by gas or shrapnel. Avoiding stares in public certainly helped disfigured veterans reenter civilian life, who nonetheless felt humiliated by city ordinances mostly intended to protect the feelings of civilians who had stayed at home during the war.

In another act of callousness, some Americans began questioning the moral fiber of disabled veterans who received government pensions. The sympathetic view of disabled veterans as wounded warriors gradually diminished. In a sign of how time had eroded wartime memories, one advocate for the disabled wrote to Congresswoman Virginia Jenckes (D-Ind.) to relate the following story in 1931:

> I passed several small boys playing along the street, one of these small lads had on (probably his dad's) an overseas hat, a lad a little larger than the one wearing the hat made a remark about the hat, where-upon the little fellow wearing the hat was to heard to remark, my dad was a soldier he was over fighting the [G]ermans, and he has bullet wounds to prove it, the larger lad says that is nothing, he is a big bum anyway, the little fellow wants to know why his dad is a bum, and the larger lad repl[ies], why my father says he is, because he lays around and want[s] work.[28]

CONCLUSION

Medical advances before and during the First World War ensured the survival of many wounded and ill soldiers, who returned home bearing the scars of their war-related injuries. Throughout the war, doctors struggled to contain epidemics caused by overcrowding, poor ventilation, and the unprecedented tenacity of an influenza virus that encapsulated the globe in 1918–1919. On the battlefield, doctors had better success in saving the lives of men wounded in combat owing to technological advances in X rays, blood transfusions, and wound-cleansing treatments. Shellshocked soldiers also responded well to a regime that kept them near the front and restored their physical health before tackling their psychological fears and phobias. Although many shellshocked soldiers returned to their units, thousands returned home too fragile to withstand the strains and stresses of daily civilian life. The government promised an impressive array of programs intended to rehabilitate and financially support disabled veterans, but it took extensive lobbying by veterans' groups for the government to finally begin fulfilling these pledges. For the disabled veterans, government bureaucracy and diminishing public sympathy helped define their postwar lives.

NOTES

1. Carol R. Byerly, *Fever of War: The Influenza Epidemic in the U.S. Army during World War I* (New York: New York University Press, 2005), 53.
2. Byerly, *Fever of War*, 53.
3. Byerly, *Fever of War*, 78.
4. Byerly, *Fever of War*, 78.
5. Byerly, *Fever of War*, 136.
6. Byerly, *Fever of War*, 115.

7. Byerly, *Fever of War*, 115.

8. Byerly, *Fever of War*, 147.

9. Ronald Schaffer, *America in the Great War: The Rise of the War Welfare State* (New York: Oxford University Press, 1991), 171.

10. Dixon Wecter, *When Johnny Comes Marching Home* (Cambridge, Mass.: Houghton Mifflin, 1944), 385.

11. *Pennsylvanian Voices of the Great War: Letters, Stories, and Oral Histories of World War I*, ed. J. Stuart Richards (Jefferson, North Carolina: McFarland & Co., 2002), 108.

12. Schaffer, *America in the Great War*, 200.

13. Schaffer, *America in the Great War*, 204.

14. Norman Fenton, *Shellshock and Its Aftermath* (St. Louis, MO.: C.V. Mosby Co., 1926), 33.

15. *Pennsylvanian Voices of the Great War*, 164.

16. Fenton, *Shellshock and Its Aftermath*, 92.

17. Fenton, *Shellshock and Its Aftermath*, 91.

18. Fenton, *Shellshock and Its Aftermath*, 165.

19. Fenton, *Shellshock and Its Aftermath*, 86.

20. Fenton, *Shellshock and Its Aftermath*, 87.

21. Jennifer D. Keene, "Protest and Disability: A New Look at African American Soldiers During the First World War," in *Warfare and Belligerence: Perspectives in First World War Studies*, ed. Pierre Purseigle (Boston: Brill, 2005), 235–6.

22. Wecter, *When Johnny Comes Marching Home*, 388.

23. Wecter, *When Johnny Comes Marching Home*, 390.

24. Wecter, *When Johnny Comes Marching Home*, 392.

25. Fenton, *Shellshock and Its Aftermath*, 127–8.

26. Fenton, *Shellshock and Its Aftermath*, 145–7.

27. Thomas A. Hoff, *U.S. Doughboy, 1916–1919* (Oxford: Osprey Publishing, 2005), 41.

28. Jennifer D. Keene, *Doughboys, the Great War and the Remaking of America* (Baltimore, MD.: Johns Hopkins University Press, 2001), 183.

7   COMING HOME

Fighting along the Western Front ended on 11 November 1918. As diplomats from the Allied nations negotiated the terms of the peace treaty in the palace of Versailles, American troops joined French and British troops in undertaking a limited occupation of the German Rhineland. Anxious to return home, soldiers balked at the continuation of a heavy training regime designed to keep them fit to fight in case Germany refused to sign the peace treaty and the war resumed. With the German army melting away and friction between the American troops and the French civilians on the rise, army officials devised a comprehensive program of sightseeing and continuing education to give troops a positive view of French culture and to ease the transition to civilian life. As men began to leave the army, they faced the challenges of reconnecting with their families, finding a job, and putting the war behind them. The American Legion formed to help men with some of these endeavors, and also took the lead in urging local and federal governments to properly commemorate those who had fallen in defense of their country. The creation of overseas American military cemeteries, the erection of doughboy statues that listed the dead, and interring the body of an unidentified soldier in Arlington National Cemetery were all ways in which the nation remembered those troops who died during the war.

THE ARMISTICE

The Armistice brought an end to the fighting in France on 11 November 1918. At 11 A.M., the guns fell silent along the Western Front. Men climbed out of their trenches to shake hands with enemy soldiers. Only a few hours earlier, shells had rained along the Western Front. Ordered to shell and attack the German line in the morning, "to prevent," one officer surmised, "the Hun from pulling over any tricks at the last minute," some American men died on the final day of the war.[1] Intoxicated with victory, French troops shouted "Vive la France et les Etats-Unis" as they embraced American soldiers and thanked them for their help in the war. German soldiers expressed surprisingly little bitterness over their nation's loss, eager instead to denounce the Kaiser before asking American soldiers for tobacco and cigarettes. Eager for souvenirs, American troops began a frantic exchange with German men for helmets, belt buckles, and rifles. That evening both sides shot colored signal flares into the sky to create a vivid fireworks display that celebrated their survival in the bloodiest war to date. Fires burned well into the night while men sang songs and played music, no longer concerned that lights or noise might reveal their position. Unperturbed by shells, gas, or bullets "the relaxation from the terrible nervous strain seems to effect [*sic*] everybody the same for we are now all full of smiles," one medical officer wrote to his family.[2]

Demobilizing the Military

The sudden end of the war took American military officials by surprise. Expecting the fighting to continue into 1919, the War Department focused its efforts throughout the fall of 1918 on building-up and training American forces. Army officials gave very little thought to the difficulties of demobilizing a mass army in an efficient and equitable manner. Once the fighting ceased, however, both men in uniform and their families at home began to clamor for an immediate release from service. Discharging the 1.5 million men still in the training camps was a relatively easy proposition, and most headed home by February 1919. After that, men returned from overseas in the following order: casuals, surplus and special service troops (including Divisions that had been broken up to send replacement troops to front-line units), troops in England, U.S. Air Service personnel, troops in Italy, combat Divisions, and, lastly, Service of Supply troops.

The delay in returning men from overseas gave the military time to build the large debarkation centers near French ports it needed to process troops before they returned home. Besides these logistical concerns, the government also had some strategic and economic reasons for postponing the trip home for American troops. Staggering the reentry of returning soldiers into the job market eased the economic strain of finding immediate employment for 4 million men in a postwar economy hit by recession when many lucrative war industry jobs evaporated. It was also important to keep a combat-ready force in Europe to occupy the Rhineland alongside French and British troops and potentially resume the fighting if Germany rejected the eventual peace settlement.

Training after the End of the War

Army officials initially saw the armistice as an opportunity to improve the fighting prowess of their army and mandated a steady daily diet of drills, target practice, and tactical exercises. This continued training was justified, GHQ contended, in case peace negotiations broke down and the army was forced to fight again. When the melting away of the German army made such a scenario unlikely, army officials privately acknowledged that they expected ongoing training to enhance the future security of the nation by creating a professionally trained corps of reserves the government could call back into service if needed. Soldiers tended to see ongoing training as meaningless busywork. Raymond B. Fosdick, chairman of the Commission on Training Camp Activities, agreed. "To see a battery that has fired 70,000 rounds in the Argonne fight going listlessly through the movements of ramming an empty shell into a gun for hours at a stretch, or training the sights on an enemy that does not exist, is depressing enough to watch, and its effect on the spirits of the men is apparent," he observed.[3] By February, soldier discontent over continued training reached near-crisis proportions and Pershing turned to Lieutenant Colonel Theodore Roosevelt, Jr., the son of the former president, for advice on how to handle the precipitant drop in morale within his victorious army. In response, Roosevelt, Jr. conferred with his fellow National Guard officers before suggesting that Pershing reduce training time, offer more recreational activities, award more men medals, and publish the order in which units would head home. This same group also used the meeting to lay the groundwork for establishing an organization for World War I veterans named the American Legion.

Before releasing soldiers from service, army doctors examined troops and ideally noted clearly on each man's service record what illnesses or wounds he had sustained while in the service. Complete and accurate medical paperwork would, the government believed, reduce the number of fraudulent claims made in the postwar period for disability allowances or service-related health problems. Unfortunately, many soldiers still returned home with inaccurate discharge papers that hampered their efforts to receive the help they deserved for health problems connected to their wartime service.

Army officials quickly learned that releasing men involved more than processing paperwork. In the first round of discharges directly from the training camps, army officials discovered that instead of heading straight home many ex-servicemen took a short detour to nearby cities intent on enjoying themselves with their final army pay. In an effort to hasten their trip back home, the army began selling discounted train tickets to troops that they had to use within a few days. "How ya gonna keep 'em away from Broadway/Jazzin around and paintin' the town," the lyrics of a popular wartime song "How ya gonna keep 'em down on the farm (After they've seen Paree)" aptly summed up the dilemma facing the government and the nation.

Postwar Soldier Attitudes toward the Germans and French

In the winter of 1918, two hundred thousand American troops headed to the Rhineland to guard a bridgehead around Coblenz. They were there to prevent the German army from crossing the Rhine if peace talks broke down. Many American soldiers who spent time in the occupying army quickly discarded feelings of hate or animosity towards the German people. Instead, occupying troops embraced the Germans as an industrious and friendly people eager to develop democracy. In sharp contrast to this new-found enthusiasm for German society, American soldiers still in France voiced increasing complaints and dissatisfaction with French civilians. The quick reconciliation between American troops and their German foes worried American military officials almost as much as the virulent anti-French feeling that emerged within the ranks. Incensed that the French civilians barely acknowledged their role in winning the war, gossip in the ranks swirled with rumors of the French government charging the Americans rent for their section of the trenches and plotting to keep American soldiers permanently in France.

The reasons that soldiers gave for preferring the Germans to the French in the postwar period were based almost entirely on their daily encounters with each respective population. The feeling that French shopkeepers and peasants took advantage of American troops by charging high prices for their wares particularly incensed many men. American soldiers arrived flush with money in 1918, and French merchants were quick to realize that, if they charged more, American soldiers had the means to pay. By contrast, military regulations in the occupation zone prevented merchants from gouging soldiers. In addition, the stark contrast offered between the rural, and in American eyes, backward regions of France and pristine German towns gave American troops the impression of entering a society that more closely resembled their own when they took up residence there. As Alexander Woollcott explained, "the American soldier is at ease in Germany because it is a country contemporary with his own, that is, a country which by expanding during the same half century that saw America's expansion, is similarly adorned and equipped." The Americans might be "kin in thought" with the French because of their shared commitment to democracy, Woollcott concluded, but they were "kin in custom" with the Germans when it came to material comforts and cultural habits.[4]

When soldiers began commenting in letters home that, "we fought the war on the wrong side," American and French officials knew that it was time to act.[5] Both pro-German and anti-French feeling, officials feared, would have negative repercussions on the peace process. Overt fraternization might reduce American soldiers' willingness to pick up arms once again in the unlikely event that the German government refused to sign the Versailles Peace Treaty and hostilities resumed. Likewise, if servicemen returned home with strong anti-French feeling, they might perhaps prejudice the American people against ratifying the punitive peace treaty or undermine postwar relations between the United States and France.

Both American and French officials took this situation seriously enough to initiate a series of programs intended to improve troops' relations with French civilians. French officials organized multiple ceremonies to bestow French military honors on American units and honor the achievements of American soldiers on the battlefield. At the same time, strict orders prohibited fraternization between American soldiers and German civilians. These orders by no means succeeded in eliminating all contact, but at least signaled to troops that overly friendly relations were ill advised. To improve soldiers' views of the French, American officials sent groups of troops on sightseeing trips around the country in the hopes that, by getting them away from the devastated regions of France and the hardened peasants that inhabited these areas, American soldiers would learn to see France in a new light. *The Stars and Stripes* also advised soldiers to remember the war a bit more. Consider why French villages were so dirty and broken when compared to the neat and tidy German towns along the Rhineland, the editors wrote:

> When Bismarck enunciated the principle that the best place to have a war was in somebody else's territory he said a sage and far-sighted mouthful . . . The Chemin des Dames is gutted and black with the ugly aftermath of war; the Rheinstrasse is as neat as ever. In Coblenz you will walk along a clean street (that was never splattered by a Bertha's iron scales [a reference to the shelling of Paris in 1918]) into a neat café (that never shook from a Gotha's bomb) and drink a tall one from a brewery which has been assaulted by nothing worse than a wax tax. It is good. It is comfortable. It is clean. With its roofs and walls intact, why shouldn't it be?[6]

The army sent soldiers to officially run recreational areas in picturesque regions such as Brittany and the Pyrenees. The Riviera emerged as one of the most popular destinations for these soldier tourists, which they reached by taking a special leave train from Paris. Army officers also made passes readily available for soldiers who wanted to visit Paris. "Soldiers 'on three days' leave' wanted to see luxurious Versailles whatever else was omitted . . . ," one soldier noted. "All wanted to go to the tombs of Lafayette and Napoleon. One would find the Chapel of the Invalides (where Napoleon was buried) crowded with soldiers looking down upon the great sarcophagus, while a Y man related the history."[7]

Waiting to Go Home

Dissatisfaction in the armistice period also found American targets. Overcrowding and inclement winter weather created unhealthy conditions in the debarkation camps around Brest that soon bred disease and misery within many units. Officials had hoped to create a model of efficiency in these camps, but the combination of cold, rain, and influenza turned the journey home into a nightmare for many troops. Men exploded in fury when comrades survived combat at the front only to succumb to complications from the flu while waiting to return home. The combination of poor camp conditions, deaths from flu, and general uncertainty about when they were scheduled to sail home created a furor in the camps overseas and at home. An official War Department investigation into debarkation camp conditions came too late to bring much relief for most American troops. Instead, Congress became a forum where the complaints of troops and their families received a daily airing.

Throughout the spring, Army officials used entertainment and education to ease troops' discontent as they awaited orders to return home. Soldier troupes gave nightly comedic and dramatic performances dubbed "Olive Drab" shows. No professional actor could "hand an outfit as many laughs as its own privates in petticoats, [or] its own sergeants in skirts," one official commented.[8] Some soldier productions were quite elaborate. The U.S. Army Ambulance Service put on a show entitled *Let's Go* that featured performers wearing donated theatrical costumes worth nearly 30,000 francs when they sang a song called "Bring Me a Blonde."

The AEF also instituted a variety of educational programs to occupy soldiers' time. Non-English speaking soldiers and illiterate troops were required to attend classes at newly created post schools. Many other soldiers decided that taking a course in U.S. history or French was preferable to spending time on the drilling field. The AEF offered correspondence courses for soldiers stationed on bases too small to support a school, and even secured a limited number of spots for officers to attend the Sorbonne, Oxford, and Cambridge, as well as other British and French universities. Almost 2,000 soldiers attended lectures at the Sorbonne, living in the Latin quarter in Paris and perfecting their French at the Alliance Français. How seriously soldiers took these educational opportunities is another matter. One veteran who attended a French university in Toulouse later recalled, "We had only one thing on our minds and that was to get home. . . . We enjoyed a good time, but most of us studied but little. It was a good place to swap stories."[9]

The army's most ambitious scheme involved the creation of the AEF University at Beaune, a French town near Dijon. There, the AEF took over an abandoned hospital complex and made plans to construct the largest university in the world by enrolling 15,000 students in 14 separate colleges staffed by nearly 500 professors. The university venture was short-lived, but still successfully offered a range of courses in business, engineering, agriculture, and the liberal arts to nearly 10,000 men. By the spring, the educational offerings also included some vocational training in agriculture, metal trades, auto repair, and blacksmithing.

The ever-shrinking army made these educational ventures hard to maintain past the summer of 1919. The vast majority of soldiers were on their way home before the peace treaty was even signed. By the end of June 1919 nearly 2.7 million troops had received their discharge papers, a clean uniform, shoes, their final army pay and a $60 bonus to ease their journey home. Discharging men from the military was just one part of the demobilization process. Helping them readjust to civilian life was another. The YMCA stepped in with lectures intended to help men resume their good manners and modes of speech. "When you get back . . . " one Y secretary lectured a group of soldiers, "You'll sit down at the family breakfast table. . . . Your mother will want to be filling up your coffee cup again, and your little brother will be crowding up against one side of you and

A group of soldiers enthusiastically bid military life good-bye. (*Courtesy of the National Archives*)

your kid sister against the other, and you'll look across the table and say, 'Goddammit, Ma, where in the hell's the butter.'"[10] Soldiers also understood that the return home would require some mental readjustment on their part. "Before I reached home," one soldier recalled in his memoir, "I decided that I must clear my mind of all the terrible experiences of the past two years, as much as possible." It would be unjust, this soldier felt, "to make my family and friends sad and uncomfortable by inflicting upon them the horrors in which they had no part."[11]

Besides encouraging soldiers to resume their former habits of dress and speech, officials also wanted veterans to return to their previous jobs and homes. Many veterans had other ideas, hoping to use military service as a stepping stone into a new occupation or residence. To dissuade thousands of discharged servicemen from descending on cities already reeling from postwar layoffs and strikes, officials tried to steer soldiers back to their former lives as quickly as possible. The War Department's Employment Service publicly promised to match every veteran with a job, but privately grumbled that much unemployment among veterans stemmed from the inflated ideas they had of their abilities. Soldiers received a pamphlet upon leaving the service entitled, "Soldiers! Your Job and How to Get It," which acknowledged that "you have probably been broadened by your Army experience" before advising troops that "this does not mean that you will better yourself by taking up a new kind of work . . . advancement will come more rapidly if you go back to the job where you are known."[12] Colonel Arthur Woods, director of the War Department's Employment Service, sent agents from the Agriculture Department to encourage former farmers to return home to rural communities and established employment boards in major cities. The Employment Service took credit for placing nearly 70 percent of the 1.3 million ex-servicemen who sought work through the agency in jobs throughout the United States. Using the slogan, "Local Jobs for Local Men," the Employment Service encouraged businesses to rehire returning veterans and urged towns and cities to give veterans preference for employment on public works projects.

In 1919, several hundred soldiers submitted essays in a writing contest entitled "Home—Then What?" Editors from the Paris bureaus of *The New York Herald*, *The Chicago Tribune*, and *The London Daily Mail* judged Private Marcelle H. Wallenstein from Atchison, Kansas the winner for his conclusion that "the more we see of the world the better we love America."[13] The second prize winner, Joshua B. Lee from Norman, Oklahoma, seconded these patriotic sentiments and further underscored the benefits that individual soldiers and the nation drew from military service. "We are heavier, we are taller, we are stronger, and returning, we will infuse the iron of our blood into the nation and give her vigor," Lee promised.[14] Despite such lofty pronouncements, it was hard for veterans to retain a completely positive memory of their time in the army when they faced the realities of beginning their civilian lives anew in a society that seemed anxious to forget the war as quickly as possible.

VETERANS OF WORLD WAR ONE

The American Legion

Some veterans kept the camaraderie of their wartime years alive by joining the American Legion. Founded by a group of National Guard officers in Paris in 1919, the American Legion was devoted to preserving comradeship among ex-servicemen, law and order, and democracy. In the postwar period, the Legion devised both a broad-based political agenda and lobbied to secure veterans' benefits. In the immediate postwar period, a host of smaller veterans' groups competed for members and power. By the early twenties, however, more politically connected and financially secure American Legion emerged as the principal spokesman for World War I veterans. Throughout the twenties and thirties, the Legion conferred directly with the White House and Congress on a range of social and political issues relating to veterans.

Adopting the motto "For God and Country," the Legion advocated 100 percent Americanism, a political stance that urged the complete assimilation of immigrants and unwavering loyalty to the United States. Many individual posts took an active role in combating radicalism during the first Red Scare in 1919–1920 by attacking suspected Bolsheviks and breaking strikes. The Legion maintained strong ties with law enforcement agencies throughout the interwar period, and, in 1940, the Federal Bureau of Investigation recruited 33,000 legionnaires as official informants. Between 1920 and 1941, the Legion also consistently championed a strong defense budget and immigration restrictions.

Charters for individual posts came from each state's Legion headquarters, a policy that allowed Southern states to reject applications from black posts. In 1925, the Legion recognized 100 black posts, with an overall membership of 1,862 out of 380,000 potential members. Race was not the only one issue that divided Legion posts. The Legion's 11,000 posts ranged from conservative posts that readily cooperated with the Ku Klux Klan to urban chapters linked to unions. In the postwar world, veterans allied themselves with a diversity of political causes, only finding true unity around issues related to veterans' benefits and commemoration of the war.

Despite the Legion's official emphasis on law and order, most annual conventions gained national renown for the drunken parties that authorities tactfully ignored during this period of national prohibition. Many veterans viewed prohibition as an illegal measure enacted while they were out of the country fighting the war. Although dry Legion posts existed, most functioned as de facto bars where veterans could drink freely with their friends without worrying about interference from the police. In 1931, the Legion formally denounced prohibition, at long last bringing its official policy in line with the private practice of its members.

The Legion never formally endorsed candidates running for office and prohibited public officials from holding official positions within the organization. Many prominent politicians who had served during the war, however, exerted considerable influence behind the scenes in the Legion. Legion posts often provided a launching pad for veterans interested in a career in local politics. Legion posts also emerged as important civic boosters within their communities. They sponsored boy scout troops, built parks and playgrounds, organized baseball leagues, held patriotic ceremonies, promoted proper flag etiquette, ran child-welfare programs, and offered disaster-relief.

The Legion devoted enormous energy to securing aid for disabled veterans, hospital care for needy veterans, and bonus service pay for all World War I veterans. The postwar campaign for adjusted compensation (sometimes called a "bonus") originated as a grassroots demand from within the Legion. Initially, the Legion's leaders proclaimed that veterans were satisfied with the $60 mustering-out pay and help finding jobs provided by the government. Soon, however, veterans began grumbling about the high wages and large profits that civilians at home had accumulated during the war. Their increased difficulties in finding steady employment as the economy slid into a recession prompted many veterans to call for an adjusted compensation payment from the government. In their view, the government had paid soldiers too little during the war and now needed to retroactively increase their soldier pay. By the early 1920s, the Legion firmly supported paying veterans adjusted compensation. The Legion argued that the government should retroactively adjust soldiers' wartime wages to equalize the financial burden borne by soldiers and civilians during the conflict. In making this claim, the Legion leadership echoed the demands of its members. "As I recollect" one legionnaire declared, men "were yanked out of their ordinary walks of life, deprived of their earning capacity and in many tens of thousands of cases were obliged to leave dependents with no adequate means of support" while people at home enjoyed record wages.[15]

The Bonus March

In 1924, veterans finally received adjusted compensation in the form of a bond that matured in 1945. The accepted compromise that delayed payment for 20 years eventually fell apart during the Great Depression. In 1932, approximately 30,000 "Bonus Marchers" descended on Washington, D.C., to demand immediate payment of their adjusted compensation certificates. Discrimination within the Legion tended to marginalize black legionnaires, but they did find common cause with white veterans over the issue of adjusted compensation, and many black veterans actively participated in the so-called Bonus March. The Bonus March came to a bloody end when the army forcibly evicted the protesting veterans from the city. In 1936, in the wake of large-scale deficit spending for New Deal programs, Congress finally agreed to pay veterans the full value of their adjusted compensation certificates. "The bonus, when it came, was too little and too late," concluded one veteran. "Too little for justice, too late to be of any help in readjustment."[16]

The GI Bill

The majority of veterans never joined the Legion or other veterans' organization such as the Veterans of Foreign Wars (VFW). Out of 4 million potential members, Legion rolls ranged from 843,000 in 1920 to 609,000 in 1925, to an interwar high of 1 million in 1931. The Legion's opposition to immediate payment of the bonus resulted in a severe dip to 770,000 in 1933, the exact moment that the rolls of the VFW soared because of its support for immediate payment.[17]

Through the Legion, World War I veterans made their greatest postwar contribution to American society by authoring and lobbying for the Servicemen's Readjustment Act in 1944, also known as the GI Bill. This legislation helped the country avoid the mistakes made after World War I when veterans faced a difficult readjustment. The GI Bill gave World War II veterans access to unemployment compensation, low-interest housing and small business loans, college tuition, and health care. By World War II, offering recompense to make up for missed financial and educational opportunities became a broadly accepted justification for subsidizing this extensive and expensive system of veterans' benefits. "The fact that selective service has become the basis for recruiting our armed forces—that a man's losses in time, opportunity, or health while in the service are no longer voluntary but risks exacted by the State—has fostered a greater sense of Federal responsibility in his retraining and reemployment," historian Dixon Wecter noted in 1944.[18]

African American Veterans

Military service gave large numbers of black soldiers their first experiences out of the South when they trained in northern training camps or served overseas in France. Both experiences let African American troops live in societies, which, if not completely free of racial prejudices, were at least devoid of legalized segregation and disenfranchisement. These experiences made the prospect of returning to the Jim Crow south unappealing to many black veterans. "We offered our lives to save this country and we are willing to give our lives for our rights," one African American soldier proclaimed.[19]

Many civil rights leaders initially hoped that a grateful nation would reward African Americans for their wartime loyalty by recognizing their civil rights. Limited opportunities to fight, however, meant few chances for African Americans to demonstrate their bravery to white America. Instead of receiving acclaim, the achievements and contributions of black soldiers went unappreciated by mainstream society. To bolster their postwar campaign to end discrimination and segregation, civil rights groups actively recruited black veterans into their organizations. Imbued with the democratic rhetoric to "make the world safe for democracy" and memories of positive social mingling between the races overseas, many black veterans enthusiastically joined the civil rights movement and infused it with a new sense of urgency and militant spirit.

On 17 February 1919, New York City welcomed home the men of the 369th Infantry Regiment (the former New York 15th Infantry Regiment) with a 7-mile ticker tape parade down Fifth Avenue. Even white New Yorkers turned out in droves to cheer their native sons' homecoming. A shockingly different reception awaited black veterans headed home to the South. Army officials advised the returning black servicemen not to wear their uniforms home, lest they antagonize white southerners determined to remind these black soldiers of their proper place at the bottom of the social ladder. Southerners did more than threaten violence. Of the seventy-seven black civilians killed by mobs in 1919, ten were former soldiers. Little wonder that many black veterans resolved to seek their fortunes in the North. Most veterans, however, returned to the South where 80 percent of the nation's black population still lived.

Whether they settled in the North or South, black ex-servicemen helped introduce an ethos of fighting back into an awakened and often militant postwar civil rights movement. These men arrived home determined to improve life for themselves and their families. Black veterans participated actively in postwar racial rioting, ensuring that white attacks met with resistance. In Chicago, Washington, D.C., Birmingham, Alabama, Philips County, Arkansas, and Tulsa, Oklahoma, black veterans demonstrated their resolve to defend themselves with force against white mobs. Their actions revealed the truth of W.E.B. Du Bois's famous postwar declaration, "We return, We return from fighting, We return fighting." [20]

Staying true to their democratic principles, asserting their rights, and standing up like men were all ways that their wartime experiences informed the postwar political activities of black veterans. Regimental associations also constructed memorials to fallen comrades on battlefields in France, held reunions to bring together former comrades, and raised funds for disabled soldiers and war widows. In these activities, black veterans shared the same desire as their white counterparts to find a place for war remembrance in postwar American culture.

REMEMBERING THE WAR

Throughout the interwar years, veterans took an active interest in keeping the memory of the war alive. The Legion built monuments and memorial buildings to commemorate the war and successfully pushed for Armistice Day to become a national holiday in 1938. Throughout the nation, statues of doughboys went up in town squares, adorned with plaques that bore the names of the local boys who had lost their lives in the war. E.M. Viquesney's *Spirit of the American Doughboy* emerged as a popular choice for many towns. Viquesney's bronzed doughboy strides into battles with a grenade in his upwardly extended right hand and a bayonet attached to a 1903 Springfield rifle in his left. Ready for combat, the soldier is adorned with a steel helmet and wears wrapped leggings above his boots, a haversack on his back, and a gas mask pouch on his chest. A canteen, mess kit, and first aid kit hang from his body. The soldier strides among the barbed wire and charred stumps of No Man's Land, and he gazes purposefully into the distance, ready to engage the enemy. The hollow statue weighed only 200 pounds, and reputedly accounted for 10 percent of the monuments erected to the honor the memory of First World War soldiers. Miniature replicas of the statue advertised in the *American Legion Monthly Magazine* also found ready customers throughout the United States, as did memorial plaques, lamps, and candlesticks fashioned from the *Spirit of the American Doughboy* design. Viquesney created

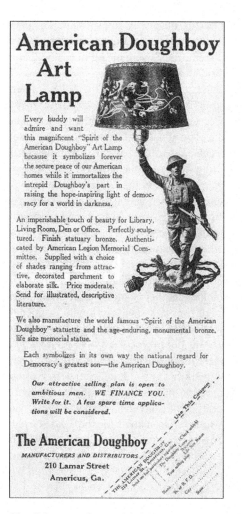

"The Spirit of the Doughboy" became the model for numerous monuments erected in town squares throughout the United States. It was also marketed in miniature form as a desktop statue or lamp to veterans interested in purchasing a keepsake to commemorate the war. (*Courtesy of the National Archives*)

an accompanying *Spirit of the American Navy* statue that was less popular, but seven still stand today alongside the doughboy statue in town squares throughout the south and Midwest.

Remembering the Dead

Every Legion post bore the name of a fallen soldier and each Armistice Day local posts reminded communities of the past war by organizing exhibits of war relics, providing drill demonstrations, and marching in parades. At 11 o'clock in the morning, legionnaires led their towns in observing 2 minutes of silence to remember the fallen and honor the cause of peace. The Legion also pressured local governments to rename streets and bridges after fallen comrades, placed commemorative plaques in court houses, and raised funds for hospitals, libraries, parks, playgrounds, schools, and meeting halls, which they named in honor of the community's war dead or the nation's war goals. These "living memorials" were meant to ensure that remembrance of the war remained part of the fabric of everyday life.

The U.S. government also commemorated the fallen soldiers of the war in a variety of ways. The War Department let families choose whether they wanted the government to bring the bodies of deceased soldiers back to the United States for burial at home or re-inter them in one of the official national cemeteries established overseas. Over 40,000 families, or nearly 70 percent, chose to repatriate their fallen relative and the government bore the cost of transporting the body to a cemetery selected by the family. These families withstood a vigorous campaign by the government urging them to leave their boys' bodies in France. Though concerned about the huge expenditure of funds required to transport these coffins home, the government worried mostly that depopulating France of American gravesites reduced the power of a collective gravesite to convey the scope of the nation's sacrifice. Consequently, the government tried to discourage families from scattering individual bodies throughout the United States where they would quickly be forgotten by all but their nearest and dearest. Only a minority of families acceded to the government's request that they let their sons lay in official military cemeteries overseas.

With so few bodies left overseas, the government decided to group them into eight national cemeteries where ample spacing between graves helped bolster the physical presence of American war dead on foreign soil. No regimental or personal monuments were allowed in the cemeteries, and each man regardless of rank received a regulation cross or Star of David to mark his grave. Each cemetery also housed a small chapel. In the early 1930s, in recognition of the sacrifice that individual families had made, the government funded a series of pilgrimages for mothers and widows to visit their sons' graves. The Gold Star Mothers (so-named for the gold starred flag that families with war dead hung in their windows) and widows headed to France at the height of the Great Depression from 1931 to 1933 to visit the battlefields and cemeteries and enjoy some sightseeing and receptions held in their honor. Often part of the working poor, many had never traveled outside the country before. The government, therefore, took care of all travel arrangements including passage on luxury liners with a nurse and an army officer in attendance to ensure their comfort, first class hotels, and lavish banquets hosted by the French or British governments. African American Gold Star Mothers traveled separately from white women, leading to protests from the NAACP and boycotts by a few women over the government's endorsement of segregation.

Not all families had a body to bury. The heavy use of artillery during the war ensured that a fair number of soldiers met their deaths by being blown to bits. After 1–3 years in the ground, other bodies were beyond recognition once they were found. Inclement weather usually erased any identifying information that the initial burying squad had scribbled on temporary wooden crosses. The Graves Registration Service worked diligently from dental records to identify as many bodies as possible. Despite these efforts, a sizeable number of men buried in American cemeteries remained "unknown soldiers." For relatives of the 4,500 American soldiers listed as missing in action, there was no grave to visit to mourn their loss. To honor these men and provide a place of remembrance for their families, the American government decided to follow the example set by England and France by laying one unidentified soldier to rest in Arlington National Cemetery. The Tomb of the Unknown Soldier stood as a symbolic final resting place for all the soldiers who went missing during the war.

Flag-draped coffin of the unknown soldier on horsedrawn caisson in front of the U.S. Capitol. (*Courtesy of the Library of Congress*)

In October 1921, as part of a solemn ceremony in Chalons-sur-Marne, Sergeant Edward Younger, a decorated wounded veteran, chose the casket that would travel to Washington, D.C. for interment in the Tomb of the Unknown Soldier. Captain A.E. Dewey described how French villagers from near and far gathered to lay flowers on the four caskets under consideration. As the mountain of flowers grew, each person "in that long steady line . . . bowed [his] head, offering a silent prayer, a prayer of sorrow and of thanksgiving, for the eternal rest of the souls of those Unknowns, far from home, who had given their lives in assisting France."[21] Many French visitors were young war widows, some of whom wept uncontrollably as they approached the flag-draped coffins. When the moment came to choose the unknown soldier, Younger walked around the coffins three times, carrying a single white rose to lay on the casket he selected. "Suddenly I stopped. It was as though something had pulled me. A voice seemed to say: 'This is a pal of yours.' I put the rose on the coffin in front of me and went back into the sunlight. I still remember the awed feeling I had, standing there alone."[22] When the selected casket arrived in Washington, D.C., the Unknown Soldier lay in state in the Capitol rotunda where more than 90,000 visitors filed past to pay homage. Congressman Hamilton Fish, Jr., a veteran who wrote the law that created the tomb, placed the first wreath upon the casket. On the morning of 11 November 1921, thousands of Americans lined the streets of Washington, D.C. to watch a slow-moving procession carry the casket from the Capitol to Arlington National Cemetery. The marchers included President Warren G. Harding and his cabinet, the entire Congress,

Supreme Court, state governors, Medal of Honor recipients, and numerous wartime officials. An ailing Woodrow Wilson also joined the procession in a horse-drawn carriage for a short time. Once the casket arrived at Arlington National Cemetery, Harding and dignitaries from several Allied nations, including Marshal Foch, decorated the Unknown Soldier with their highest military honors. Two inches of soil from the battlefields of France lined the crypt. After the Unknown Soldier was laid to rest, millions of Americans across the nation collectively observed 2 minutes of silence to honor the fallen warrior and pray for a peaceful future.

After the burial, the nation quickly returned to its normal affairs and the bad manners exhibited by some visitors to the cemetery outraged the American Legion. In 1926, the Legion convinced the government to post an armed guard at the Tomb of the Unknown Soldier to maintain the solemnity and sacredness of the site. Some careless visitors, the Legion complained, slighted the memory of the Unknown Soldier when they used the site as a bench or picnic table.

The government claimed that the body of the Unknown Soldier was selected without regard to race, religion, or rank. John Dos Passos, a veteran and renowned author, questioned this claim in one of the most famous passages he ever wrote, "The Body of an American," in his novel, *1919* (1932). "How did they pick Joe Doe? Make sure he ain't a dinge, boys. make sure he ain't a guinea or a kike, how can you tell a guy's a hundredpercent when all you've got's a gunnysack full of bones, bronze buttons stamped with the screaming eagle and a pair of roll puttees?," wrote Dos Passos.[23] As this passage indicates, remembering the war involved more than official ceremonies, monuments, and gravesites.

Interpreting the War through Literarature and Film

American writers, artists, poets, and playwrights also used the war to fuel an outpouring of creative works that interpreted the meaning of the war for postwar America. Many of these literary works cast the Great War as a giant sham that exploited the naiveté of youth. Intending to reveal the rotten core of Wilsonian idealism, fumbling army bureaucracy, wartime propaganda, and incompetent and uncaring officers, this literature of disillusionment recalled the war as a meaningless exercise in mass slaughter than revealed the worst in humankind. Works in this genre include novels by veteran writers such as John Dos Passos's *Three Soldiers* (1921), Laurence Stallings's and Maxwell Anderson's *What Price Glory* (1926), Stallings's *Plumes* (1924), William March's *Company K* (1933), and Ernest Hemingway's *A Farewell to Arms* (1929).

War novels that renounced any grand purpose for the fighting remained the most well-known literary reaction to the war. Another group of writers exposed the war's brutality without losing complete faith in humankind. Willa Cather's *One of Ours* (1922), Hervey Allan's *Toward the Flame* (1926), and John MacGavock Grider's *War Birds: Diary of an Unknown Aviator* (1926) offered unflagging views of combat, but did not abandon the possibility that heroism, loyalty, and patriotism survived its horrors in tact.

Postwar films made about the First World War often dealt gingerly with the reality of combat as filmmakers worried that too much pessimism might drive audiences away. Instead, Hollywood offered films that explored more traditional war themes such as heroism, glory, and the rite of passage into manhood. Popular interwar films often enveloped an antiwar theme with a triumphant tone that honored American soldiers for a well-fought war and persisted in seeing the war as a great, manly adventure. *The Dawn Patrol* (1930, and remade in 1938), for instance, explored the exploits of American pilots who faced a determined enemy in the sky and bumbling bureaucrats below. In between harrowing dogfights in their unreliable aircraft, the men found time for plenty of wine and high jinks. Laurence Stallings, who offered a bitter critique of a wounded veteran's difficult recovery in his novel *Plumes*, also bowed to these concerns within the film industry when he penned the hit film *The Big Parade* (a silent movie, 1925). Despite accurate and terrifying battle scenes, the heart of the film centered on the wartime adventures of its hero who finds love and friendship in France.

There were, however, some memorable films like *All Quiet on the Western Front* (1930), which presented an unflinching glimpse at the naïve romanticism that inspired a group of German schoolboys to enlist in 1914 and then traced their descent into death and disillusionment when they confronted the reality of fighting in the trenches. To some extent, these German youths represented all men who fought in the war, but such explicit criticism of a government's blind and inept leadership was a bit easier to make of enemy leaders than of one's own.

As the war clouds gathered once again in Europe, Hollywood refashioned some World War I stories to emphasize the importance of fulfilling one's duty as a citizen by taking up arms. *Sergeant York* (1941), a film about Sergeant Alvin York, focused primarily on the change of heart that York underwent when he abandoned his conscientious objector status and agreed to fight. The individual heroism that this modest man achieved on the battlefield for his feat of single-handedly silencing 35 German machine guns and capturing 132 prisoners provided an endorsement, rather than criticism, of patriotism and civic responsibility.

CONCLUSION

The end of the war came quickly for the United States, a bare six months after the army began active combat operations. As victory celebrations subsided along the Western Front and throughout the United States, soldiers turned to more immediate concerns such as leaving the army and resuming their civilian lives. Morale problems plagued the American army during the demobilization period. Troops resisted continued training, came into conflict with French civilians, and lobbied strenuously for their immediate return home. Once released back into civilian life, veterans received some help from the War Department and the American Legion in finding a job and securing veterans' benefits. For the most part, this aid was too limited to provide much help in making the transition from military to civilian society. As individual veterans strove to put the war years behind them, the American Legion worked diligently to keep the memory of the war in the forefront of the American imagination. A host of writers and filmmakers also tried to fashion some meaning for the war. Whether the war illustrated the futility of armed conflict or the heroic endeavors of brave and patriotic men remained a matter of dispute.

NOTES

1. *Pennsylvanian Voices of the Great War: Letters, Stories and Oral Histories of World War I*, ed. J. Stuart Richards (Jefferson, North Carolina: McFarland & Co., 2002), 178.

2. *Pennsylvanian Voices of the Great War*, 179.

3. Edward Coffman, *The War to End All Wars: The American Military Experience in World War I* (New York: Oxford University Press, 1968), 358.

4. Alfred E. Cornebise, *The Stars and Stripes: Doughboy Journalism in World War I* (Westport, Conn.: Greenwood Press, 1984), 133.

5. Jennifer D. Keene, *Doughboys, the Great War, and the Remaking of America* (Baltimore, MD.: Johns Hopkins University Press), 121.

6. Cornebise, *The Stars and Stripes*, 134.

7. Tyler Stovall, *Paris Noir: African Americans in the City of Light* (Boston: Houghton Mifflin, 1996), 23.

8. Cornebise, *The Stars and Stripes*, 156.

9. Mark Meigs, "Crash-Course Americanism: The A.E.F. University 1919," *History Today* (August 1994), 41.

10. Meirion and Susie Harries, *The Last Days of Innocence, America at War, 1917–1918.* (New York: Vintage Books, 1997), 438.

11. Mark Meigs, *Optimism at Armageddon: Voices of American Participants in the First World War* (New York: New York University Press, 1997), 163.

12. Keene, *Doughboys, the Great War, and the Remaking of America*, 164.

13. Meigs, *Optimism at Armageddon*, 211.

14. Meigs, *Optimism at Armageddon* 212.

15. Keene, *Doughboys, the Great War and the Remaking of America*, 174.

16. Thomas B. Littlewood, *Soldiers Back Home: The American Legion in Illinois, 1919–1939* (Carbondale, Il: Southern Illinois University Press, 2004), 121.

17. William Pencak, *For God and Country: The American Legion, 1919–1941* (Boston: Northeastern University Press, 1989), 83.

18. Dixon Wecter, *When Johnny Comes Marching Home* (Cambridge, Mass.: Houghton Mifflin, 1944), 523.

19. Mark Ellis, *Race, War and Surveillance: African Americans and the United States Government during World War I* (Bloomington, Indiana: Indiana University Press, 2001), 226.

20. W.E.B. Du Bois, "Returning Soldiers," *The Crisis* (May 1919): 13.

21. Robert B. Bruce, *A Fraternity of Arms: America and France in the Great War* (Lawrence, Ks.: University Press of Kansas, 2003), 291.

22. Bruce, *A Fraternity of Arms*, 292.

23. John Dos Passos, *1919* (Boston: Houghton Mifflin Co., 1946), 462.

GLOSSARY

Like many wars, World War I spawned its own vocabulary, but it is interesting to see how many terms that developed with this war came into common nonmilitary usage and are still widely used today, nearly 100 years later. Below are some of these words and phrases in addition to the terms that were specific to the Great War.

Ace: Popular name for fighter pilots, especially those who shot down enemy aircraft.

AEF: American Expeditionary Forces, the American military forces that served overseas.

Allies: The nations at war with Germany, including Great Britain, France, Russia, Italy and the United States.

Armistice: Negotiated suspension of hostilities that occurred on the Eastern and Western Front before peace negotiations. The final cease-fire with Germany began at 11:00 A.M. on 11 November 1918.

Barrage: Sustained artillery fire and shelling, often used before an attack across **No Man's Land**. Also called a bombardment.

Basket case: Term used to describe a fictional soldier who had lost both arms and both legs in combat. Now used to describe someone who is hopeless or in great difficulty.

Behind the lines: Phrase used by soldiers to describe rear-area duty away from the front lines.

Blockade: Use of naval forces to disrupt an enemy's trade.

Boche: A French word adopted by American soldiers to describe the German enemy, also called *Huns* by American troops.

Central Powers: The nations allied with Germany, including Austria-Hungary, Bulgaria and Turkey.

Conscription: Compulsory military service. Also known as Selective Service or the draft.

Convoy: The transport system adopted in 1917 by the Allies which used battleships to protect groups of merchant ships from German U-Boat attacks as they traversed the Atlantic.

Demobilization: Dismantling the wartime military forces.

Destroyer: Small ships used to protect convoys from German **U-boats**.

Dog-fights: Aerial combat between fighter pilots from opposing sides.

Doughboy: Nickname for American soldiers, also known as Yanks or Sammies.

Dud: A shell that failed to explode. Also used to characterize something or someone that is worthless or disappointing.

Dugout: An underground shelter in the trenches meant to protect soldiers during artillery shelling and gas attacks and from inclement weather.

Escadrille Lafayette: American pilots who flew with the French air service before the United States entered the war.

In the trenches: Phrase used by soldiers to describe front-line duty along the Western Front. Now used to describe a difficult job or task.

Meuse-Argonne Campaign: A forty-seven-day battle fought in the American sector of the Western Front between the Argonne Forest and the Meuse River which began on 26 September 1918 and lasted until the Armistice.

Mustard gas: A deadly gas employed in chemical warfare along the **Western Front**, named for its distinctive smell.

No Man's Land: A small strip of land between opposing trenches that neither side controlled. Now used to describe a disputed area or place of danger.

Over the top: Phrase used to describe leaving the trenches to mount an attack across **No Man's Land** on an enemy trench. Now used to describe excess.

Shellshocked: Unofficial term for a combat-related psychological breakdown that often lasted for years after the war, named for the artillery shelling thought to induce mental collapse. Now used to describe feeling overwhelmed.

Shrapnel: Fragments from an exploded shell.

Straggler: A soldier who deliberately moved slowly or lost contact with his advancing unit to avoid combat.

U-boat: A German submarine, from the German term *Unterseeboot*.

Western Front: The name given to the stretch of trenches that ran from the North Sea to Switzerland through Belgium and France.

BIBLIOGRAPHY

GENERAL WORLD WAR I HISTORIES AND REFERENCE WORKS

American Battle Monuments Commission. *American Armies and Battlefields in Europe: A History, Guide, and Reference Book*. Washington, D.C.: Center for Military History, 1992.

Gilbert, Martin. *The First World War: A Complete History*. New York: Henry Holt, 1994.

Keegan, John. *The First World War*. New York: Alfred A. Knopf, 1999.

Morrow Jr., John H. *The Great War: An Imperial History*. New York: Routledge, 2004.

Neiberg, Michael S. *Fighting the Great War: A Global History*. Cambridge, MA: Harvard University Press, 2005.

Stevenson, David. *Cataclysm: The First World War as Political Tragedy*. New York: Basic Books, 2004.

Strachan, Hew. *The First World War*. New York: Penguin, 2003.

Venzon, Anne C., ed. *The United States in the First World War: An Encyclopedia*. New York: Garland Publishing, 1995.

Winter, J. M. *The Experience of World War I*. New York: Oxford University Press, 1995.

AFRICAN AMERICANS IN WORLD WAR I

Badger, Reid. *A Life in Ragtime: A Biography of James Reese Europe*. New York: Oxford University Press, 1995.

Barbeau, Arthur, E. and Florette Henri. *The Unknown Soldiers: Black American Troops in World War I*. Philadelphia, PA: Temple University Press, 1974.

Cockfield, Jamie. "Eugene Bullard, America's First Black Military Aviator, Flew for France during World War I." *Military History* (February 1996): 74–78.

Ellis, Mark. *Race, War and Surveillance: African Americans and the United States Government during World War I*. Bloomington, IN: Indiana University Press, 2001.

Harris, Stephen L. *Harlem's Hell Fighters: The African American 369th Infantry in World War I*. Washington, D.C.: Brassey's, 2003.

Haynes, Robert V. *A Night of Violence: The Houston Riot of 1917*. Baton Rouge, LA: Louisiana State University Press, 1976.

Haywood, Harry. *Black Bolshevik: Autobiography of an Afro-American Communist*. Chicago: Liberator Press, 1978.

Keene, Jennifer D. "French and American Racial Stereotypes during the First World War." In *National Stereotypes in Perspective: Americans in France, Frenchmen in America*, edited by William L. Chew, 261–282. Atlanta, GA: Rodopi, 2001.

Keene, Jennifer D. "Protest and Disability: A New Look at African American Soldiers during the First World War." In *Warfare and Belligerence: Perspectives in First World War Studies*, edited by Pierre Purseigle, 215–41. Boston, MA: Brill, 2005.

Nalty, Bernard C. *Strength for the Fight A History of Black Americans in the Military*. New York: Free Press, 1986.

Roberts, Frank E. *The American Foreign Legion: Black Soldiers of the 93rd in World War I*. Annapolis, MD: Naval Institute Press, 2004.

Schneider, Mark Robert. *"We Return Fighting": The Civil Rights Movement in the Jazz Age*. Boston, MA: Northeastern University Press, 2002.

Stovall, Tyler. *Paris Noir: African Americans in the City of Light*. Boston: Houghton Mifflin, 1996.

Tuttle Jr., William M. *Race Riot: Chicago in the Red Summer of 1919*. New York: Atheneum, 1970.

AMERICAN ENTRY INTO THE WAR

Cooper Jr., John Milton. *The Warrior and the Priest: Woodrow Wilson and Theodore Roosevelt*. Cambridge, MA: Belknap Press of Harvard University Press, 1983.

Devlin, Patrick. *Too Proud to Fight: Woodrow Wilson's Neutrality*. New York: Oxford University Press, 1974.

Gregory, Ross. *The Origins of American Intervention in the First World War*. New York: Norton, 1971.

Hamilton, Richard F., and Holger H. Herwig, eds. *The Origins of World War I*. New York: Cambridge University Press, 2003.

May, Ernest R. *The World War and American Isolation, 1914–1917*. Cambridge, MA: Harvard University Press, 1959.

Simpson, Colin. *The Lusitania*. Boston, MA: Little Brown, 1972.

Tuchman, Barbara W. *The Zimmermann Telegram*. New York: Viking Press, 1958.

AMERICAN INTERVENTION IN MEXICO AND RUSSIA

Foglesong, David S. *America's Secret War against Bolshevism*: *U.S. Intervention in the Russian Civil War, 1917–1920* Chapel Hill, NC: University of North Carolina Press, 1995.

Graves, William S. *America's Siberian Adventure, 1918–1920*. New York: Peter Smith, 1931.

Kennan, George F. *Soviet-American Relations, 1917–1920*. Vol. 1, *Russia Leaves the War*. Princeton, NJ: Princeton University Press, 1956.

Levin, Norman Gordon. *Woodrow Wilson and World Politics: America's Response to War and Revolution*. New York: Oxford University Press, 1970.

AMERICAN MILITARY DURING WORLD WAR I

Braim, Paul F. *The Test of Battle: The American Expeditionary Forces in the Meuse-Argonne Campaign*. Newark, DE: University of Delaware Press, 1987.

Bruce, Robert B. *A Fraternity of Arms: America and France in the Great War*. Lawrence, KS: University Press of Kansas, 2003.

Coffman, Edward. *The War to End All Wars: The American Military Experience in World War I*. New York: Oxford University Press, 1968.

Eisenhower, John. *Yanks: The Epic Story of the American Army in World War I*. New York: Free Press, 2001.

Farwell, Byron. *Over There: The United States in the Great War, 1917–1918* New York: W.W. Norton, 1999.

Ferrell, Robert H. *Woodrow Wilson and World War I, 1917–1921*. New York: Harper and Row, 1985.

Feuer, A. B. *The U.S. Navy in World War I: Combat at Sea and in the Air*. Westport, CT: Praeger, 1999.

Fleming, Thomas. *The Illusion of Victory: America in World War I*. New York: Basic Books, 2003.

Freidel, Frank. *Over There: The Story of America's First Great Overseas Crusade*. Boston: Little, Brown, 1964.

Grotelueschen, Mark E. *Doctrine under trial: American Artillery Employment in World War I*. Westport, CT: Greenwood Press, 2001.

Hamburger, Kenneth E. *Learning Lessons in the American Expeditionary Forces*. Washington, D.C.: U.S. Army Center of Military History, 1997.

Harries, Meirion, and Susie Harries. *The Last Days of Innocence, America at War, 1917–1918*. New York: Vintage Books, 1997.

James, D. Clayton, and Anne Sharp Wells. *America and the Great War, 1914–1920*. Wheeling, IL: Harlan Davidson, 1998.

Keene, Jennifer D. *The United States and the First World War*. New York: Longman, 2000.

Kennedy, David M. *Over Here: The First World War and American Society*. New York: Oxford University Press, 1980.

Mead, Gary. *The Doughboys: America and the First World War*. New York: Overlook Press, 2000.

Millett, Allan R. "Cantigny, 28–31 May 1918." In *America's First Battles: 1776–1965*, edited by C. E. Heller and W. A. Stofft. Lawrence, KS: University Press of Kansas, 1986.

Millett, Allan R. "Over Where? The AEF and the American Strategy for Victory, 1917–1918." In *Against All Enemies: Interpretations of American Military History from Colonial Times to the Present*, edited by Kenneth J. Hagan and William R. Roberts. New York: Greenwood Press, 1986.

Millett, Allan R., and Peter Maslowski. *For the Common Defense: A Military History of the United States of America*. New York: Free Press, 1984.

Nenninger, Timothy K. "American Military Effectiveness during the First World War." In *Military Effectiveness*. Vol. 1, *The First World War*, edited by Allan R. Millett and Williamson Murray. Boston, MA: Allen & Unwin, 1988.

Schaffer, Ronald. *America in the Great War: The Rise of the War Welfare State*. New York: Oxford University Press, 1991.

Trask, David F. *The AEF and Coalition Warmaking, 1917–1918*. Lawrence, KS: University Press of Kansas, 1993.

Weigley, Russell F. *History of the United States Army*. New York: Macmillan, 1967.

Zieger, Robert H. *America's Great War: World War I and the American Experience*. Lanham, MD: Rowman & Littlefield, 2000.

AMERICAN SOLDIERS IN WORLD WAR I

Baldwin, Fred. "The Enlisted Man during World War I." Ph.D. diss., Princeton University Press, 1964.

Bristow, Nancy K. *Making Men Moral: Social Engineering during the Great War*. New York: New York University Press, 1996.

Chambers III, John Whiteclay. *To Raise An Army: The Draft Comes to Modern America*. New York: Free Press, 1987.

Cornebise, Alfred E. *The Stars and Stripes: Doughboy Journalism in World War I*. Westport, CT: Greenwood Press, 1984.

Ellis, John. *Eye-Deep in Hell: Trench Warfare in World War I*. Baltimore, MD.: Johns Hopkins University press, 1976.

Hoff, Thomas A. *U.S. Doughboy, 1916–1919*. Oxford: Osprey Publishing, 2005.

Keene, Jennifer D. *Doughboys: The Great War and the Remaking of America*. Baltimore, MD: Johns Hopkins University Press, 2001.

Keene, Jennifer D. "Intelligence and Morale in the Army of a Democracy: The Genesis of Military Psychology during the First World War." *Military Psychology* 6 (1994): 235–53.

Keene, Jennifer D. "Raising the American Expeditionary Forces: Early Decision Making in 1917." In *Battles Near and Far: A Century of Overseas Deployment*, edited by Peter Dennis and Jeffrey Grey, 48–70. Canberra, Australia: Army History Unit, Department of Defence, 2005.

Keene, Jennifer D. "Uneasy Alliances: French Military Intelligence and the American Army during the First World War." *Intelligence and National Security* 13 (1998): 18–36.

Keith, Jeanette. *Rich Man's War, Poor Man's Fight: Race, Class and Power in the Rural South during the First World War*. Chapel Hill, NC: University of North Carolina Press, 2004.

Kevles, David J. "Testing the Army's Intelligence: Psychologists and the Military in World War I." *Journal of American History* 55 (1968): 565–81.

Lee, David D. *Sergeant York: An American Hero*. Lexington, KY: University Press of Kentucky, 1985.

Meigs, Mark. *Optimism at Armageddon: Voices of American Participants in the First World War*. New York: New York University Press, 1997.

Schweitzer, Richard. *The Cross and the Trenches: Religious Faith and Doubt among British and American Great War Soldiers*. Westport, CT: Praeger, 2003.

Winterich, John T., ed. *Squads Write! A Selection of the Best Things in Prose, Verse & Cartoon from the Stars and Stripes*. New York: Harper & Brothers, 1931.

FICTION AND LITERARY CRITICISM

Cooperman, Stanley. *World War I and the American Novel*. Baltimore, MD: Johns Hopkins University, 1967.

Cummings, E. E. *The Enormous Room*. New York: Modern Library, 1934.

Dos Passos, John. *Three Soldiers*. Boston, MA: Houghton Mifflin, 1964.

Dos Passos, John. *USA*. New York: Library of America, 1996.

Haytock, Jennifer. *At Home: Domesticity and World War I in American Literature*. Columbus, OH: Ohio State University Press, 2003.

Hemingway, Ernest. *A Farewell to Arms*. New York: Scribner's, 1929.

March, William. *Company K*. Tuscaloosa, AL: University of Alabama Press, 1989.

Trout, Steven. *American Prose Writers of World War I: A Documentary Volume*. Detroit, MI: Thomson/Gale, 2005.

Trout, Steven. *Memorial Fictions: Willa Cather and the First World War*. Lincoln, NE: University of Nebraska, 2002.

FILMS, POSTERS, AND MUSIC

All Quiet on the Western Front (1930), dir. Lewis Milestone.

Big Parade (1925), dir. King Vidor.

The Dawn Patrol (1938), dir. Edmund Goulding.

A Farewell to Arms (1932), dir. Frank Borzage.

The Great War and the Shaping of the 20th Century (1996, documentary), dir. Carl Byker.

Hearts of the World (1918), dir. D. W. Griffith.

Hell's Angels (1930), dir. Howard Hughes.

James Reese Europe's 369th U.S. Infantry "Hellfighters" Band, The Complete Recordings, Memphis Archives, 1996.

Men of Bronze (1977, documentary), dir. William Miles.

Meyer, Susan E. *The James Montgomery Flagg Poster Book*. New York: Watson-Guptill Publications, 1975.

Niles, John J., ed. *Singing Soldiers*. New York: Scribner's, 1927.

Paret, Peter, Beth Irwin Lewis, and Paul Paret. *Persuasive Images: Posters of War and Revolution from the Hoover Institution Archives*. Princeton, NJ: Princeton University Press, 1992.

Paths of Glory (1957), dir. Stanley Kubrick.

Rawls, Walton. *Wake-Up, America! World War I and the American Poster*. New York: Abbeville Publishers, 1988.

Sergeant York (1941), dir. Howard Hawks.

Shoulder Arms (1918), dir. Charlie Chaplin.

Wings (1927), dir. William A. Wellman.

IMMIGRANT AND NATIVE AMERICAN SOLDIERS

Barsh, Russell Lawrence. "American Indians in the Great War." *Ethnohistory* 38 (1991): 276–303.

Britten, Thomas A. *American Indians in World War I: At Home and at war*. Albuquerque, NM: University of New Mexico, 1997.

Ford, Nancy Gentile. *Americans All! Foreign-born Soldiers in World War I*. College Station, TX: Texas A&M University Press, 2001.

Sterba, Christopher M. *Good Americans: Italian and Jewish Immigrants during the First World War*. New York: Oxford University Press, 2003.

LETTERS, DOCUMENTS, AND MEMOIRS

Aptheker, Herbert, ed. *A Documentary History of the Negro People in the United States, 1910–1932*. New York: Citadel Press, 1973.

Ayres, Leonard P. *The War with Germany: A Statistical Summary*. Washington, D.C.: Government Printing Office, 1919.

Brown Jr., Walt, ed. *An American for Lafayette: The Diaries of E.C.C. Genet, Lafayette Escadrille*. Charlottesville, VA: University Press of Virginia, 1981.

Dudley, William, ed. *World War I: Opposing Viewpoints*. San Diego, CA: Greenhaven Press, 1998.

Evans, Martin Marix, ed. *American Voices of World War I: Primary Source Documents, 1917–1920*. Chicago: Fitzroy Dearborn Publishers, 2001.

Fish, Hamilton. *Memoir of an American Patriot*. Washington, D.C.: Regnery Gateway, 1991.

Hallas, John H. *Doughboy War: The American Expeditionary Force in World War I*. Boulder, CO: Lynne Rienner Publishers, 2000.

Harbord, James G. *The American Army in France, 1917–1918*. Boston, MA: Little Brown, 1936.

Higonnet, Margaret R., ed. *Nurses at the Front: Writing the Wounds of the Great War*. Boston, MA: Northeastern University Press, 2001.

Hunton, Addie W., and Kathryn M. Johnson. *Two Colored Women with the American Expeditionary Forces*. New York: G.K. Hall, 1997.

Langer, William L. *Gas and Flame in World War I*. New York: Knopf, 1965.

Lawrence, Joseph. *Fighting Soldier: The AEF in 1918*. Edited by Robert H. Ferrell. Boulder, CO: Colorado Associated University Press, 1985.

Link, Arthur S., ed. *The Papers of Woodrow Wilson*. 69 vols. Princeton, NJ: Princeton University Press, 1966–1994.

Mackin, Elton E. *Suddenly We Didn't Want to Die: Memoirs of a World War I Marine*. Novato, CA: Presidio, 1993.

Marshall III, R. Jackson. *Memories of World War I: North Carolina Doughboys on the Western Front*. Raleigh, NC: Division of Archives and History, North Carolina Department of Cultural Resources, 1998.

Office of the Provost Marshal General. *Second Report of the Provost Marshal General to the Secretary of War on the Operations of the Selective Service System to December 20, 1918*. Washington, D.C.: Government Printing Office, 1919.

Pershing, John J. *My Experiences in the World War*. 2 vols. New York: Frederick A. Stokes, 1931.

Richards, J. Stuart, ed. *Pennsylvanian Voices of the Great War: Letters, Stories and Oral Histories of World War I*. Jefferson, NC: McFarland, 2002.

Rickenbacker, Edward V. *Fighting the Flying Circus*. Edited by W. David Lewis. Chicago, IL: Lakeside Press, 1997.

Trask, David F., ed. *World War I at Home: Readings on American Life, 1914–1920*. New York: Wiley, 1970.

United States Army in the World War, 1917–1919. 17 vols. Washington, D.C.: Center for Military History, 1998.

York, Alvin Cullum. *Sergeant York: His Own Life Story and War Diary*, edited by Thomas John Skeyhill. Garden City, NY: Doubleday, Doran and Company, Inc., 1928.

PARIS PEACE CONFERENCE

Cooper, John Milton. *Breaking the Heart of the World: Woodrow Wilson and the Fight for the League of Nations*. New York: Cambridge University Press, 2001.

Knock, Thomas J. *To End All Wars: Woodrow Wilson and the Quest for a New World Order*. New York: Oxford University Press, 1992.

Macmillan, Margaret. *Paris 1919: Six Months That Changed the World*. New York: Random House, 2001.

Widenor, William C. *Henry Cabot Lodge and the Search for an American Foreign Policy*. Berkeley, CA: University of California Press, 1980.

Widenor, William C. "The United States and the Versailles Peace Settlement." In *Modern American Diplomacy*, edited by J. M. Carroll and G. C. Herring. Wilmington, DE: Scholarly Resources, 1996.

VETERANS

Bennett, Michael J. *When Dreams Came True: The GI Bill and the Making of Modern America*. Washington, D.C.: Brassey's, 1996.

Bernstein, Irving. "The Bonus Army." In *The Underside of American History*. Vol. 2, edited by T. R. Frazier and J. M. Blum. New York: Harcourt Brace Jovanovich, 1974.

Daniels, Roger. *The Bonus March: An Episode of the Great Depression*. Westport, CT: Greenwood Press, 1971.

Lisio, Donald J. *The President and Protest: Hoover, Conspiracy, and the Bonus Riot*. Columbia, MO: University of Missouri Press, 1974.

Littlewood, Thomas B. *Soldiers Back Home: The American Legion in Illinois, 1919–1939*. Carbondale, IL: Southern Illinois University Press, 2004.

Pencak, William. *For God and Country: The American Legion, 1919–1941*. Boston, MA: Northeastern University Press, 1989.

Piehler, G. Kurt. *Remembering War the American Way*. Washington, D.C.: Smithsonian Institution Press, 1995.

Severo, Richard, and Lewis Milford. *The Wages of War: When America's Soldiers Came Home—From Valley Forge to Vietnam*. New York: Simon and Schuster, 1989.

Sledge, Michael. *Soldier Dead: How We Recover, Identify, Bury and Honor Our Military Fallen*. New York: Columbia University Press, 2004.

Wecter, Dixon. *When Johnny Comes Marching Home*. Cambridge, MA: Houghton Mifflin, 1944.

WAR WOUNDS AND ILLNESS

Barry, John M. *The Great Influenza: The Epic Story of the Deadliest Plague in History.* New York: Penguin Books, 2005.

Byerly, Carol R. *Fever of War: The Influenza Epidemic in the U.S. Army during World War I.* New York: New York University Press, 2005.

Crosby Jr., Alfred W. *Epidemic and Peace, 1918.* Westport, CT: Greenwood Press, 1976.

Fenton, Norman. *Shellshock and Its Aftermath.* St. Louis, MO: Mosby, 1926.

Shephard, Ben. *A War of Nerves: Soldiers and Psychiatrists in the Twentieth Century.* Cambridge, MA: Harvard University Press, 2001.

WOMEN

Gavin, Lettie. *American Women in World War I: They Also Served.* Niwot, CO: University Press of Colorado, 1997.

Greenwald, Maurine Weiner. *Women, War, and Work: The Impact of World War I on Women Workers in the United States.* Westport, CT: Greenwood Press, 1980.

Holm, Jeanne, Maj. Gen., USAF (Ret.). *Women in the Military: An Unfinished Revolution.* Rev. ed. Novato, CA: Presidio Press, 1992.

Schneider, Dorothy, and Carl J. Schneider. *Into the Breach: American Women Overseas in World War I.* New York: Viking, 1991.

Zeiger, Susan. *In Uncle Sam's Service: Women Workers with the American Expeditionary Force, 1917–1919.* Philadelphia, PA: University of Pennsylvania Press, 2004.

WEBSITES

First World War.Com. "Propaganda Posters—United States of America." http://www.firstworldwar.com/posters/usa42.htm.

The Great War Society. "Doughboy Center, The Story of the American Expeditionary Forces," http://www.worldwar1.com/dbc/dbc2.htm.

The Great War Society. Trenches on the Web. http://www.worldwar1.com/.

The Great War Society. Trenches on the Web. "Lieutenant James Reese Europe: Songs Brought Back from the Battlefield." http://www.worldwar1.com/sfjre.htm.

Johnston, Tom. "Life At Camp Funston: Reflections of Army Sergeant Charles L. Johnston." http://members.cox.net/~tjohnston7/ww1hist/.

Public Broadcasting Service. "The Great War and the Shaping of the Twentieth Century." http://www.pbs.org/greatwar/maps/index.html.

U.S. Library of Congress. American Memory. "American Leaders Speak. Recordings from World War I and the 1920 Election." http://memory.loc.gov/ammem/nfhtml/nfhome.html.

U.S. Library of Congress. American Memory. "Newspaper Pictorials: World War I Rotogravures." http://memory.loc.gov/ammem/collections/rotogravures/rotoprop.html.

U.S. National Archives and Record Administration. "Teaching with Documents: The Zimmermann Telegram." Telegram reproduced at http://www.archives.gov/education/lessons/zimmermann/.

World War I Military History List. Brigham Young University Library. "The World War I Document Archive." http://www.lib.byu.edu/~rdh/wwi/.

INDEX

CPSIA information can be obtained
at www.ICGtesting.com
Printed in the USA
LVOW13s0322040217
523200LV00001B/1/P